OPTIMISM IN POLITICS

OPTIMISM IN POLITICS

REFLECTIONS ON
CONTEMPORARY HISTORY

WALTER LAQUEUR

LONDON AND NEW YORK

First published 2014 by Transaction Publishers

2 Park Square, Milton Park, Abingdon, Oxfordshire OX14 4RN
711 Third Avenue, New York, NY 10017

Routledge is an imprint of the Taylor & Francis Group, an informa business

First issued in paperback 2017

Copyright © 2014 Taylor & Francis

All rights reserved. No part of this book may be reprinted or reproduced or utilised in any form or by any electronic, mechanical, or other means, now known or hereafter invented, including photocopying and recording, or in any information storage or retrieval system, without permission in writing from the publishers.

Notice:
Product or corporate names may be trademarks or registered trademarks, and are used only for identification and explanation without intent to infringe.

Library of Congress Catalog Number: 2013021571

Library of Congress Cataloging-in-Publication Data

Laqueur, Walter, 1921-
  Optimism in politics : reflections on contemporary history / Walter Laqueur.
 pages cm.
  Includes index.
  ISBN 978-1-4128-5266-1
  1. Political science—Philosophy. 2. Optimism—Political aspects. 3. Political science—History. I. Title.
  JA71.L264 2014
  320.01—dc23
                                                          2013021571

ISBN 13: 978-1-4128-5266-1 (hbk)
ISBN 13: 978-1-138-51281-8 (pbk)

For Susi with much love and gratitude

Contents

Acknowledgments	ix
Introduction	xi
Part 1: Optimism in Politics	1
Optimism in Politics	3
The Marxism Renaissance	13
Reflections on the Next Revolution	23
On Youth Movements (1970)	27
Young Germany	45
Part 2: Europe	51
Preface	53
European Futures	59
Night Thoughts on Europe	69
Europe United: An Essay in Counterfactual History (April 1, 2012)	79
Part 3: Middle East: The Arab Spring	93
Preface	95
The Arab Spring	97

Arab Autumn   101

Revolution in the Middle East?   105

Cassandra in Cairo   109

An Interview   121

Part 4: Israel and Jewish Affairs   125

The New Million   127

The Kibbutz at 100   135

Recollections of Jerusalem   141

Bloodlands—The Snyder Version   147

George Mosse: Berlin to Madison   153

Guttentag: Breslau to Cochabamba   159

The Kaiser's Spy, Jihad, and the Jewish Nazis   167

Part 5: Departure and Arrival   179

Preface   181

1938   185

Homecoming (1963)   213

Caucasian Diary   233

Index   245

Acknowledgments

Some essays in this volume are expanded versions of articles that appeared earlier on, others were reprinted unchanged. "Optimism in Politics" was first published in *World Affairs* (2013) as well as in *Commentaire* (2013); "Youth Revolt" in *Democracy Digest* "Terrorism—the Ticking Clock" in *Standpoint* (2011); "Night Thoughts on Europe" in *National Interest* (2011); "Youth Movement" appeared first in *Commentary* (1970); "European Futures" was published in *the New Republic* and a special issue of *Lavanguardia* Dossier on Europe (2011).

"Cassandra in Cairo" and the other comments on the Arab Spring appeared in *Lavanguardia, Die Welt,* and several other European newspapers. It also appeared in *Democracy Digest* and the website of the *New Republic*. "Kibbutz at 100" and "The New Million" appeared in *Jewish Review of Books*, winter 2012 and summer 2013 respectively; "Holocaust: the Snyder Version" in *Europaeische Rundschau* (2012). "Recollections of Jerusalem" is based on a public lecture in Princeton (2010); "George Mosse" is the preface to *George L. Mosse: Confronting History* (University of Wisconsin Press 2000) "Guttentag: Breslau to Cochabamba—Rare Idealist" was published in the *Times Literary Supplement* (December 2012); "Young Germany"—Times Literary Supplement (April 2013); "Homecoming" and "1938" appeared first in *Out of the Ruins of Europe* (New York 1971). "The Marxism Renaissance" was published in *National Interest* (2013). The other essays were not published previously.

Introduction

Some essays in this volume deal with current affairs, some with events that took place more than seventy years ago, and some with the future. The author happens to be the only common denominator. Events that occurred a long time ago shaped, by necessity, his views as historian and political commentator; how could it have been otherwise? Not every historical period is of equal interest; there is a poem by Gottfried Keller, the great nineteenth-century Swiss writer, to the effect that a day can be equal to a century, but also vice versa (*und ein Jahrhundert—nichts*). The period between the two World Wars is, today, of greater interest than that in the 1950s and 1960s—certainly in Europe, perhaps also in America. It was certainly a more dramatic and less "normal" time.

There is a connection between writing history and commenting on current affairs, but it is not remotely as close and simple as often thought. The idea that the historian is somehow better qualified than others to interpret the present let alone predict the future is certainly mistaken, and it is not borne out by the evidence. Some great historians have been good and reliable political commentators, and others have been miserable failures. There are, of course, "lessons of history," but since each historical situation is different, they cannot be applied like a recipe when cooking a dish (and even recipes for cooking cannot be slavishly applied because the quality of the raw materials and even the water may differ).

My first newspaper article—in a weekly—appeared in 1942 when the war was not going well and it dealt with what is now called soft power, propaganda in war time. My first book appeared five years later. It was a short paper back. At a time when paperbacks were rare and it dealt with oil in the Middle East, which, at the time, was not yet a very important subject. The literature existed of a handful of books and one or two periodicals. Looking back, I am not particularly proud of these limbering- up exercises, as there was nothing very original or profound about them.

I had followed international politics even earlier—I remember listening on the radio to the results of the German elections of 1930 in which the Nazis emerged as the second strongest party, which is to say that my first recollections were of a depressing character. However, befitting my age, my interest in sport was more intense. Unlike France (*L'Equipe*), Germany had no daily sports newspaper, but only weeklies, which appeared on Monday mornings. Why should I remember that a man whose name was quite similar to mine was running the hundred meters in my home town in 10.5? Given technical improvements such as the surface of race tracks, the running shoes (called spikes at the time) not to mention the intake of scientific foods and drugs (legal and illegal), I doubt whether contemporary achievements in the field are significantly better (with the notable exception of long distance running) than those at the time of my boyhood.

Looking back, I suspect my subsequent depression would have been deeper had I been younger and had my writing career began twenty or thirty years later. I also remember, from early on, annoyance with mistaken interpretations of current events—the prevailing opinions among the political class, academics, and commentators. True, academics according to my recollections were far more reluctant at the time to venture their views in public. My German literature teacher was an exception, which in some ways I found refreshing. I owe him a solid grounding in German right-wing and nationalist belles-lettres. Specific Nazi-inspired literature was relatively little there, and I did not suffer from discrimination as far as he was concerned.

Gaining an insight with regard to Nazi doctrine and watching Nazi practice, even at an early age, served as a useful antidote against naivete and wishful thinking in politics in later years. True, not every dictator was a Hitler and not every dictatorship as extreme as Nazi rule, but my years in Germany after 1933 had been a warning and an education.

Friends have suggested—perhaps, I had chosen the wrong profession in later years with a fixation on politics. Wasn't it too depressing, negative, and boring? I remember a questionnaire some years ago; if not at the present time, which period would I have preferred for living? I replied—Paris in the last quarter of the nineteenth century. It was a far more optimistic period than the present time, culturally more creative, more interesting, and eventually also more optimistic. My interest would certainly not have focused primarily on politics. I once asked a very educated elderly gentleman of my acquaintance from whom I had learned a great deal why he started reading the sports section of the daily newspaper before all others. His answer was that in the sport section human achievements are reported, and elsewhere, domestic or foreign policy, so it is mostly a story of setbacks, failures, and even disasters. When I graduated from school, the teachers advised me in writing to choose a career as a sports teacher or physician, since my inclinations and talents were obviously in this general direction.

However, having been born at that time, having missed Paris and the salon of the Impressionists, politics pursued me and history, after all, is yesterday's politics. I was greatly interested in cultural, much less in diplomatic history. I have further to confess: My taste in literature, music, and painting has been conservative unlike my political orientation, I have seldom enjoyed avant-garde works, and I had a certain weakness for popular (lowbrow) culture—especially if its products have lasted over a hundred years. Kitsch or not, there must have been something to it if so many were still interested in it and liked it. My parents musical taste was infinitely more highbrow than mine.

A personal experience: Low brow (or lower middle brow) music certainly gave me an uplift on some occasions in my life when I badly needed it. I describe, in one of the essays ("1938"), a night in a hospital in my hometown when my spirits were very low and all seemed lost with a war around the corner (the Munich crisis of that year) and me being caught in a trap: I had missed the last chance to leave my country. That night, I was listening with headphones in my hospital bed to a song from an operetta entitled *Landstreicher*—(the tramps) by Carl Michael Ziehrer. The song was *Sei gepriesen* (praise to you cozy night). The operetta was first performed in Vienna in 1899 and is now virtually forgotten, but this specific song is still a favorite of many lyrical tenors. It certainly gave me an uplift and got me out of my misery—it was obviously the melody not the text.

On another occasion in an hour of depression (and also real danger), I was listening to a song that miraculously lifted my spirits and got me out of despair. It was *Ich hab kein Geld, bin vogelfrei* (I am poor and an outlaw but refuse to give in). This was from the *Bettelstudent* (Beggar Student), first performed also in Vienna in 1883. The background was political in part—the action takes place in the early eighteenth century; the reckless young students want to save Poland from a sad fate. My favorite version is the one by the late Jussi Bjoerling, star of the

Metropolitan Opera singing in Swedish. The *Beggar Student* has been made into a movie not less than four times, and the Landstreicher only once. Bjoerling's bravado performance keeping the high C seemingly forever did not save Poland, but it saved me from accepting defeat at a turning point in my life and gave me fresh courage. How lowbrow, but how helpful. I do not think Mahler's *Kindertotenlieder* (songs of children about death) based on poems by the nineteenth-century German writer Friedrich Rueckert) would have had a similar effect. It is said that military marches and songs of this kind are to serious music what military justice is to genuine justice, but the witticism seems to me a little facile for each genre has its own uses and purpose, and if a piece of music has stood the test of time well over a hundred years, it is foolish to dismiss it as of no value and consequence. I am much less sure about the future prospects of contemporary popular music, but this is another story.

To repeat once again, I often wonder whether the fact that I spent some of the formative years of my youth under a particularly nasty and brutal dictatorship has not been of considerable help in sharpening political understanding. It certainly provided a strong antidote against delusions of various kinds. True, it also involved certain dangers such as an inclination toward cynicism and too often expecting the worst—becoming something of a political hypochondriac. My experience also generated occasionally a feeling of superiority (even infallibility), which I had to control by looking at some of my early writing, especially on the Middle East; not feeling strongly on religion and nationalism, I underrated, at the time, their great impact as far as the future was concerned. I tried to combat these pitfalls (and pessimism in general) as well as I could. An old French proverb says that the worst does not always happen.

I have often pondered the importance of political comment, and it is my impression that its impact is often exaggerated. Events in the real world, be it defeats and setbacks or victories and progress, have a far greater influence than arguments and comments, however persuasive. Premature warnings have seldom a major effect; to be mistaken in the right company is more effective than being right at a time when the message is as yet considered undesirable. There is the famous example of Sartre and Raymond Aron. Sartre was almost always wrong in politics and Aron almost always right, but Sartre had a mass following (when he died, 50,000 accompanied him on his last journey through the streets of Paris). The fact that Aron had been right was only reluctantly accepted toward the end of his life. For very long, there was a widespread belief that it was better to be mistaken with Sartre than right with Aron. This syndrome prevails even today.

The preoccupation with current and very recent affairs brought a great deal of frustration and frequently reminded me of Oxenstierna's well-known advice to his son about the absence of wisdom in this field. The question why otherwise intelligent people were reluctant and sometimes altogether unwilling to accept the obvious has preoccupied me for a long time, even though frequently I failed satisfactory answers. Not much insight and knowledge was needed in the 1930s to understand Hitler meant war, but there was great resistance against accepting the obvious. Later during the Cold War (to give another example), according to a widely prevailing consensus, in the academic world, both sides were more or less equally to blame. The other side was developing a different model of development and political institutions that we might not like but were perfectly workable and legitimate. Of course, they had committed mistakes, but one could learn quite a bit from them. Western Sovietology on the whole overrated both economic achievements and political durability of the Soviet Union.

To give yet another example—the consequences of the Six Days War. Unlike the post Zionist historians, I do not believe that this war could have been prevented, but it should have been clear that the continuing occupation of Arab territories was a major misfortune that would greatly harm Israel. It would lead to a binational state that would probably fail. There were of course reasons, strategic as well as political, for not surrendering these regions—a quid pro quo was wanted, a peaceful settlement. However, there was no such willingness on the other side and most occupied territories should have been surrendered in any case for a number of decisive reasons, demographic and others. It was not understood that in order to survive in a hostile surrounding, military power is an absolute necessity but so is a wise policy willing to make concessions, one sided if need be.

These are a few examples quoted more or less at random and one could bring many more from the recent past. The expectations of most of the politicians, the media, and even the experts as far as the Arab spring is concerned were far too sanguine and they were bound to lead to deep disenchantment. They failed to see that here were no democratic foundations on which the young rebels of January 2011 could build and that given the poverty of most of the countries concerned and the lack of natural resources, there were only very poor chances for solving the multiple social crises facing them. How could jobs be found for the young generation? The socialist and nationalist ideologies had failed in the Middle East, was it not inevitable that religious fundamentalism would have the support of a majority at least for a generation or two?

However, why single out the Arab spring as an example of wishful thinking? With equal justice, one could refer to the dreams about the achievements and prospects of a united Europe, which had so much support even a decade ago. It should have been clear that Europe lacked self confidence, that there was no European patriotism, that in the circumstances Europe could not possibly be considered a superpower in any meaningful sense, and that on the contrary its standing in the world was steadily declining. The demographic changes were ignored; Europe needed immigrants in view of the falling birthrate in order to sustain its standard of living and the welfare state. On the other hand, the integration of the immigrants, especially from the Muslim world, was far from successful.

A European currency was introduced but the political reforms necessary for the success of this venture were not carried out: The nation state was unwilling to give up any significant prerogative. This inevitably led to the crisis of 2008—first in Ireland, and later in the south European countries. One could equally refer to the exaggerated hopes attached to developments in Putin's Russia, a regime believed to move steadily in the direction of democracy and a free society.

However, how to get out of this crisis, which was primarily political (or perhaps spiritual) rather than financial and economic? The prime minister of Luxembourg—a little country not affected very severely by the crisis said: We all know how to get out of the present crisis but we do not know how to be re-elected thereafter. Cassandra, that famous figure in Greek mythology, was never popular and anyway Apollo had put a curse on her. Her prophecies and warnings would never be believed. What Europe needed was not Cassandra or a phalanx of Cassandras but a way out of lethargy, an infusion of political will. How to generate such will? Historically, such a powerful impetus has often come at a time (and as a result) of a deep crisis, a crisis of survival, for unless facing such a threat, there would be no sense of urgency. Unless there was a clear and present danger, why undertake great efforts and accept more often than not the need for great sacrifices? For great sacrifices were needed to overcome the crisis and to make a new beginning. So far, the European crisis did not have an effect of this kind; the decline of Europe is gradual and slow, not dramatic and alarming. It was not sufficiently severe to have a shock effect; perhaps, the feeling prevailed that with a little luck, countries and societies would be able to muddle through. Perhaps they will, but probably at a very low level, hardly a lodestar to the rest of mankind.

Why was there so much misjudgment interpreting recent crises? Ideological blinkers and wishful thinking may provide part of the answer but far from all. This is a vexing subject, which will be discussed in some greater detail further on. But I do not pretend having found wholly convincing explanations.

The Next Revolution?

Among the social and political groups shaping domestic and international politics, none has been paid less attention than the young generation. It is almost half a century that this age cohort played an important role in current politics, but its activities in the late 1960s were limited on the whole to university campuses, and it aimed by and large at a cultural rather than a political revolution. Since then, with the declining birth rate in the developed countries, the specific weight of the young generation has declined. At the same time, there has been a youth bulge in Africa and countries such as Pakistan. Gunnar Heinsohn has stressed in his work the connection between the youth bulge and social and political unrest, but the absence of a youth bulge in a continent such as Europe could also generate frustration and lead to social unrest. Youth militancy in some Islamic countries was an exception. If more attention was paid to them it had mainly to do with terrorist attacks—not considered a specific youth problem. The conclusions of various studies were contradictory. The German Shell study, which has been going on for almost fifty years, claimed that despite the economic crisis German youth felt confident about the future. American studies about generation X and Y—"Generation Me" (also known as Echo boomers and half a dozen other designations) were less optimistic.

The relative lack of interest in the views, values, and traits of the young generation in the US and the UK may be connected with the fact that specific youth movements have always been rare and even suspect in America and Britain; Italy and Russia (to provide an example) had their Young Italy and Young Russia, respectively, and Germany its *Jugendbewegung* (youth movement), which became politicized over the years. Bill Pollock, a British ambassador then at the beginning of his career put it well at a conference in the 1920s: He was not impressed by the self-conscious idealism and romanticism of the German youth movement. A youth movement in England would have the flavor of being for the doubtfully young and a patriotic movement for the doubtfully patriotic. The same applied mutatis mutandis to the United States, where the appeal of romanticism was always quite limited.

The Boy Scouts in Britain were essentially apolitical, even antipolitical and in any case were led by adults. In our time, there have been few studies of the young generation, very few names come to mind, and perhaps the long-term Shell study, mentioned earlier on, something akin to a very detailed public opinion poll.

However, there are certain indications that this could change in the years to come. While the birth rate has been falling (off late also in the United States) and the number of young people decreasing, youth unemployment has been rising almost everywhere, in some countries to unprecedented levels. Until fairly recently, young people assumed that they would live better than the generation of their parents, but this is no longer the case, they may have it worse. There has been much talk about the debt crisis, but its future social consequences have only rarely been discussed. The fact that people live longer and expect financial and other support after their retirement means a growing burden on a shrinking young generation. This is the so called "dependency ratio" meaning the number of people either too young or too old to be part of the work force and thus being dependent. These demographic trends have obvious economic and social consequences: In the past, three or four young people could take care of an elderly person; in society, the number of the young has halved. The dependency ratio has aggravated, particularly in Europe and Japan, but it will be affecting almost all countries including the United States.

There was, throughout much of history, an unwritten social contract between the young and old implying that while parents would bring up their offspring, the children would be responsible individually and as a group for the wellbeing of the preceding generation. It is no longer certain that such a contract can be taken for granted; there is growing social ferment and in view of demographic trends unlikely to change any time soon, a radicalization of the young seems increasingly likely.

Youth Movements, New Social Forces, New Social Media

This essay was written at a time of great ferment and tension on American campuses—and to a lesser extent in Europe—notably France and Germany. It tries to show that youth revolt, especially among the educated classes, is not a phenomenon of the twentieth century but appeared in a variety of manifestations in many ages and countries. More important than what happens at the present time on European and American campuses are expressions of youth revolt in the Middle East—the Arab street and the *shabab*. Shabab refers not to the Somali terrorist group of that name but to young males in general, usually between ten and twenty-five years of age who are in the forefront of urban unrest. The *shabab* are not only the vanguard but contribute also the foot soldiers of these demonstrations.

This too is not a recent phenomenon, and it has been the case for at least two generations. It was not widely noticed in the West, but television is now showing it to many who were not aware of it in the past. The leading role of young males is not surprising—family fathers and elderly people seldom mount the barricades; this is true as much for Paris in 1830 and 1848 as for Cairo at the present time. The image of the *shabab* has been negative on the whole. Loud, aggressive, and inchoate, the movement had neither clear direction nor much staying power. It was easy to mobilize such crowds, but they tended to melt and disappear quickly. Perhaps, it is changing now, but it is too early to say.

In recent years, there have been interesting changes in the composition of these crowds. This too has frequently escaped the attention of many observers. The expression *classes dangereuses* (George Rude, Louis Chevalier) in the Paris of the first half of the nineteenth century referred mainly to the new working class, while the militants of the banlieues of Paris in recent years were mainly young people from North and Central Africa. The crowds in the big cities of the Arab world in the earlier decades of our time consisted of the flotsam and jetsam of the population, and frequently recent arrivals from backward rural regions. The demonstrations in the Arab street, more recently, have been joined by educated (or semi educated) members of this generation, often unemployed or half employed or frustrated by having to accept jobs well below their qualifications. Most of them are quite poor, compelled to live with their parents, for they lack money to get married and establish a home of their own. It is, to a large extent, a social phenomenon, the reaction of the frustrated. Politically, the orientation of the crowd is confused, and it is directed against those in power and can lead, with equal ease, to the left (quite seldom) or more often to the right or nowhere in particular. The Muslim Brotherhood and other fundamentalist groups can mobilize, if need be, even a greater number of people than the usual crowd, but they have done so in the past only if their immediate political interests have been at stake.

The revolutionary crowd in nineteenth-century Europe (the crowd in the novels of Victor Hugo, for instance) was on the whole quite different in composition, character, and direction. The activists of the Arab street today include largely "ultras"—members of the fan clubs of leading football teams such as the Cairo Al Ahly (Ultra Ahlawy "together forever" being their slogan), Zamalek, as well as Port Said and Ismailia or the Alexandria "Devils." Their political outlook, if any, is by no means coherent or monolithic—they are usually very patriotic, hate "Zionists," and dislike foreigners in general, but quite a few belong to the Muslim Brotherhood. The Brotherhood strongly dislikes the preoccupation with football, which distracts young people from their religious duties (such as the five daily prayers), and it is unhappy because it cannot control this important segment of the crowd. The same applies to the Shi'ite orthodoxy in Iran. But they also know that given the popularity of football they would seriously undermine their own influence if they were to turn radically against the devotees of soccer. All they have succeeded in so far was keeping out women from the game, even as spectators.

Another important political component of the Arab street is hip hop as performed, for instance, by Shadia Mansour, the queen of Egyptian rap, and other rap artists as well as groups such as MTM or the Alexandria band "revolution."Owing to a rapidly growing number of independent TV stations, they reach a wide public. There was (and is) censorship but also an underground rap scene. Their message is patriotic ("we are all Gaza"), even though many of the leading performers are not even of Arab or Muslim origin (Italian, Belgian, British—some are of Copt, Christian, or even Jewish origin). They also deal with topics such as poverty, drugs, and high cost of living. Some are secular and favor peace, while others, apparently the majority, advocate the cause of Hizbullah and Hamas (such as Mohamed Kamel Mostafa). As in the case of football, the fundamentalist leadership is quite hostile, but in view of the popularity of the rappers, they prefer to refrain from a frontal attack on the whole genre. While football generates interest and involvement on the part of virtually all social classes, hip hop and rap primarily attract the young generation of middle-class origin.

Initially, soon after the coming of the Arab spring, the political impact of rap and hip hop and the "social media" was greatly overrated by Western observers. It was thought to be an irresistible new weapon to mobilize the masses against the reactionary forces, but this was exaggerating the power of the new media and also misjudging the ideological contents of this movement, which was certainly directed against the status quo but vague and confused as far as its political aims were concerned. It is a phenomenon largely unexplored so far.

Part 1
Optimism in Politics

Optimism in Politics

A controversy is coming under way: How much optimism do we need in politics?

Psychological factors have played a decisive role in the assessment of political trends and their prediction, yet until recently, they have been rarely investigated. The neuroscientists refer to optimism and pessimism bias. According to their findings, most people tend to err in their thinking by embracing an optimism bias rather than pessimism (or realism). As Tali Sharot in her recent *Optimism Bias* puts it: "A growing body of scientific evidence points to the conclusion that optimism may be hardwired to the human brain." Neuroscience has taken over from the sociology of knowledge.

However, another school of cognitive scientists, on the contrary, see the main danger in being too much influenced by negative conclusions when faced by ambiguous social and political situations. In other words, "a negative bias can construct a more hostile worldview than if a person's focus tends to lands of friendly faces." What we need is something like a vaccine against negativity—I quote from the current special issue of the *American Scientist* devoted entirely to the optimism/negativism syndrome.

All this is very interesting, but a little caution is called for. Sometimes, it appears that prefixing the term "neuro" to a noun helps in our time to explain almost everything creating the appearance of a more or less scientific character. But, how scientific is it really? The science of optimism is of recent date, and only relatively few people have been interviewed over a few years and these were, on the whole, prosperous and optimistic years. Those interviewed were mainly students from Britain, the Netherlands, and Western Australia, not it would appear those living in Russia, China, India, Africa or believers in Islam, in other words the great majority of mankind. Such a limited approach, not infrequent among Western social scientists, may be difficult to overcome, but it is bound to lead to strange and dubious conclusions. The assertion that optimism is not eroded as a result of violent conflicts, high unemployment, and other threats and failures is not borne out by other public opinion polls, which reached different conclusions. Whether it is Pew or Gallup or Eurobarometer, they all reached the same conclusion that over the last five years belief in the future and their own personal future has markedly gone down. The number of suicides in Europe since the outbreak of the crisis in 2008 has certainly increased. There has been a palpable depression among the young generation.

There are, of course, great differences in the attitudes of generational cohorts and social groups and between nations. It is dangerous and often misleading to speculate about "national character," but quite obviously, young people are, on the whole, more optimistic than old people; some nations and some historical periods were or are more optimistic (or pessimistic) than others. Britain has been traditionally more optimistic than Germany, even though there was no realistic reason for such a difference in mood; it may have to do more with selective recollections of recent history than any other circumstance.

In our time, economic thinking (especially after 2009) has been manifestly more pessimistic than political, perhaps because in the economy immediate material interests were involved, which demanded caution and the readiness to accept risks was notably smaller. But there might be other considerations involved as well.

The thinking about the European situation (and Europe's future) was overoptimistic in the majority of cases, which undoubtedly had often to do with economic factors such as the status of the Euro. However, according to much of the evidence, it was not only the sovereign debt and the euro and the ups and (more often) downs of the stock markets that mattered in this context.

Economic facts hardly explain the massive optimistic bias with regard to the "Arab spring." At a time of global depression, the Egyptian economy registered an annual increase of 6–7 percent.

The Arab Spring or Bliss was It to be Alive

Western reactions to the Arab spring seem to justify the conclusions of the optimism bias theorists. The expectations were so high and almost unanimous reminding one of Wordsworth at the time of the French Revolution.

Bliss was it to be alive in that dawn
But to be young was very heaven

Or as a contemporary put it in early 1848: This revolution ("the spring of nations") was the greatest event in the annals of mankind since the days of Jesus Christ (Eugene Pelletan). By and large, the Left in Europe and the world was optimistic, and the Right (and a fortiori the reactionaries) were pessimists in accordance with their world view and the imperfections of human nature.

However, the distance between Left and Right is by no means as great as often believed. Many of the leading lights of the Enlightenment were not particularly optimistic. Voltaire poked fun at the optimists: In an answer to the question what is optimism?, he made Candide explain—it is the mania that says that all is well when one is actually in hell. Candide had not always believed this; his tutor had been the famous Dr. Pangloss whose unshaken belief that despite all disasters, everything was to the best in this best of all worlds had not weakened.

He taught the metaphysico-theologo-cosmolonigology demonstrating that things cannot be otherwise than they are. The nose is formed for spectacles, and therefore we wear spectacles. The legs are visibly designed for stockings, and therefore we wear stockings. Dr. Pangloss was eventually hanged by the inquisition, but his firm beliefs were not shaken to the last moment.

The socialists of a later generation such as Proudhon and Fourier were no less pessimistic than their political opponents. When the Arab spring broke out in the winter of 2010/11, it was welcomed by a tremendous amount of enthusiasm. There was jubilation not only among the foreign correspondents, who had arrived from many parts of the world with the first news about the deposition of the hated authoritarian rulers in Tunis, Egypt, and other parts of the Arab world, but enormous enthusiasm had also been generated among the masses of the young revolutionaries congregating day after day in places such as Midan al-Tahrir in Cairo. The air was intoxicating, as one of them wrote; the lion hearted Egyptians were risking their lives to overthrow the corrupt and cruel dictatorships, it was an uprising such as the world had not witnessed in living memory; it was people power at its best and it was a shining example for the whole world. These rebels had been inspired by America's example of freedom as they told the foreign correspondents. It was a great shame that American and other Western governments blinded and paralyzed by unreasonable fear of Islamism and the Muslim Brotherhood had not given full support to these fighters for freedom. In reality, there was nothing to fear—the foreign correspondents had talked to many women and Copts and they too supported the forces of democracy.

What followed is known. There were democratic elections in which the Muslim Brotherhood and the Salafis got an overwhelming majority. A new constitution according to the rules of Islamic Shari'ah was prepared. It was not what the freedom fighters had hoped for.

The retreat from the erstwhile optimism took place in several stages. At first, it was argued that revolutions do not proceed in a straight line; progress is followed by temporary retreats. The revolutionaries had been joined by backward elements who had to be educated (or eliminated). As it appeared that the lion hearted young men and women from Tahrir Square had been outnumbered or sidelined or simply disappeared, some of the earlier well wishers conceded that the revolutionaries had suffered a defeat. But there was no reason for despair because the bad old regime could not possibly be restored. The Muslim Brotherhood, which was now the leading force, was in the final analysis a great step forward in comparison with the old regime—a pragmatic, popular force trying to combine Islam with the modern world such as Turkey had done in recent years. It ought to be supported by the United States.

A comparison with 1848 was invoked at this stage, even by historians usually aware of the unique character of each such movement and suspicious of comparisons. In both cases, there was bitter disappointment after the initial enthusiasm. Eventually, the ideas of 1848 prevailed, but in the case of Germany, it took a hundred years, two world wars, and Adolf Hitler.

There were plausible reasons for the optimism prevailing in the Western media during the early months (and in some cases well beyond) concerning the prospects of the Arab spring. For a long time, only negative news had been reported from this part of the world—about stagnation, corruption, oppression, fanaticism, social unrest, civil war, assassinations, internal conflict of various kinds—how refreshing, how encouraging to witness a spontaneous mass movement toward freedom and progress. There had been nothing like it for a long time in any part of the world, and it seemed all the more remarkable, since it happened not in the form of a violent upheaval such as a military coup—the usual form of political change in this and other parts of the world.

In the circumstances, it seemed churlish to sound a note of doubt and to play Cassandra at the time of universal rejoicing. Forebodings arose for a number of reasons such as the absence of democratic traditions in most of these countries that could serve as a model for the rising democratic forces and with whom they could connect. The sources of the revolution (if a revolution it was) were social as much as political—poverty, unemployment especially among the young generation and so on. Given the lack of resources and the essential poverty of countries such as Egypt, Syria, or Yemen, how would the new elites solve these problems more efficiently than the old ones? The reports transmitted were exclusively about the happenings on Midan al-Tahrir, the center of the uprising. But Egypt is a country of more than eighty million people, and it seems that the foreign reporters had not been to poverty stricken places like Mahalla al Kubra, Kubra al-Cheima, or Manshiet Nasser (Garbage City), and other slums, let alone to the countryside where most Egyptians lived.

In brief, had we been given a realistic account of the mood of the country? Would the uprising lead to more freedom? What would be the fate of women, of ethnic and religious minorities, and of the secular? As Hussein Agha and Robert Malley wisely put it in the *New York Review of Books*:

> *Was the last century an aberrant deviation from the Arab world's inherent Islamic trajectory? Is today's Islamist rebirth a fleeting, anomalous throwback to a long-outmoded past? Which is the detour, which the natural path?*

However, they were asking this pertinent question only with a delay of two years—earlier on, they had been sanguine about the prospects and such doubts had not occurred.

In this troubled and confused picture of early 2011, there were certain rays of hope such as Tunisia where the Jasmine Revolution had started and Libya. These were smaller, less populated countries, where the social problems could probably more easily be solved—Libya was oil rich and in Tunisia, the secular forces were strong. There was reason for optimism—or so it seemed.

Since then, almost two years have passed and there is no need to go over the ground again as far as recent events in Libya are concerned. Optimism has not entirely disappeared. Gordon Gray, a former US ambassador to Tunis, speaking at the Middle East center in autumn 2012 was very optimistic concerning the country's transition toward a democratic system. Writing for *Bloomberg*, similar views were expressed by Noah Feldman, a Harvard Law professor, proficient in Arabic and not devoid of Middle East experience (he had been involved in preparing the new Iraqi Constitution). As he saw it, there had been violent conflict in the streets of Tunis, arrests, and a bit of tear gas, but otherwise the situation was normal, the press was free, and the Islamic democrats in the government could be trusted. He did not comment on the limitations on the rights of women in the new constitution.

The same syndrome could be observed with regard to Egypt: The *New York Times* columnist who had been among the first to welcome the progressives on Midan al-Tahrir was still enthusiastic two years later. However, the enthusiasm no longer concerned the progressive forces but the "mutually beneficial relationship" that had developed between the American embassy in Cairo, the Muslim Brotherhood, and even the Salafis, which was a radical and very positive departure in policy.

Such encouraging views were not shared by secular Egyptians and Tunisians. Perhaps, as a result of living in these countries, they were too deeply involved and excited and therefore were unable to see and understand the broader picture. However, perhaps because of being so closely involved and facing the realities of daily life, they felt more accurately in which direction the winds of change were blowing.

Panglossianism in Our Time

The reception of the Arab spring has been adduced as a recent example of Panglossianism and of the optimism bias but other examples could have been quoted. One could have referred to the misjudgments of the Soviet Union in the 1970s and '80s or the false optimism with regard to Europe and the European Union until quite recently. Among Western experts, it was widely believed in the Brezhnev era (which later became known as the *zastoi*, the years of stagnation) that the Soviet system was gradually developing into a welfare state "providing to its citizen massive economic security." It was said to be a perfectly viable system, the predictions by some Westerners of a coming breakdown or revolution in the country, the imminent revolt of the nationalities and the Soviet internal empire were nonsense: "The country will not in the next decade face a systemic crisis endangering its existence."

Less than ten years later, the Soviet Union no longer existed.

Such optimistic predictions were the rule rather the exception, and they were made at a time when inside the Soviet Union there was a marked turn from relative optimism to a pronounced pessimism not only among the general public but also among members of the party and the establishment up to the very top.

In the 1990s, the great and virtually systematic overestimation of the achievements of the European Union became a matter of course. True, the momentum had become a little weaker and there were some dissenting voices. However, by and large, there was immense optimism regarding Europe's emergence as a new superpower. This was most pronounced at the very top—the declarations of the European presidents and prime ministers at their meetings from Lisbon to Maastricht and beyond make now sad reading. There was nothing wrong with their ambitions and visions, but the basic assumption was far fetched that this could be achieved without a far closer political union for which there was neither desire nor readiness. These day dreams were accompanied by a confident literature predicting that the twenty-first century would be Europe's, which would serve as a shining example to the rest of the world morally and in virtually every other respect.

It may not be in good taste to disinter these visions of yesteryear, but it is a necessity to do so from time to time in the interest of mental and political hygiene. The observations of the optimism bias theorists had been astute in these cases. They well fitted the prevailing mental attitudes—but not for very long.

Happy Days are Here Again: Crises as Great Federators

And yet, with all this, a strong case can be made in favor of optimism—even excessive optimism, at a time of crisis. As a nineteenth-century cynic noted, a crisis is the period between two other crises. History is a sequel of crises, but most of them have not been fatal. Voltaire's pessimism (and that of many of his contemporaries) was shaped by the great earthquake of Lisbon (1755). But there has been no similar natural disaster in Europe since then.

Crises have their undoubted use—important decisions in the life of nations, especially if they were painful, are usually made as a result of a crisis, for in normal conditions, there seems to be no urgency to opt for change. Jean Monnet, the father of the European Union, rightly noted that crises are the great federators.

Tali Sharot, who was quoted earlier on with regard to the optimism bias, rightly notes that overly positive assumptions can lead to disastrous miscalculations—in our private life as well as in politics. But on the other hand, Schopenhauer, the great German apostle of pessimism cannot be recommended as a guide for our troubled times either. He was more interested in the plague of noise and the welfare of animals than in human beings. He was proud of having abstained from commenting on politics.

One of the dangers of false optimism is that it easily turns into dejection once the illusions have faded. Opinion polls in late 2012 reported a massive disenchantment in the West with the Arab spring. This could have been prevented had the reports and comments during the early months been more realistic. A similar disappointment took place (not for the first time) following developments in Putin's Russia, which, all things considered, was a step forward compared with Stalin's and Brezhnev's Russia and what more could have been reasonably expected given the mental makeup of the rulers of the country and the mood of the majority? And was not an authoritarian regime in need of an opponent to justify its very existence?

Pessimism at a time of crisis is a natural reaction, but it hardly helps to get out of the misery. If as the neuroscientists tell us optimism and hope are hardwired to the brain, there seems to be a similar connection with regard to the turn to escapism when things are bad. *Happy days are here again, the skies above are clear again* was composed in a short time before the Wall Street crash of 1929. But it was only thereafter that *"let's sing a song of cheer again"* became the great hit song of the period, and owing to Roosevelt who made it his campaign song in 1932, it even became a political event.

Escapism was the universal reaction in popular culture all over. In German-speaking countries, *The Congress Dances* (set during the Vienna Peace Congress of 1815) and *The Great Waltz* were the outstanding movies of the period—escape into the past and into remote countries was the rule—as the clouds of war increasingly threatened, millions enjoyed Tino Rossi singing about the great charms of the Isle of Capri. The great success on the stage was the *White Horse Inn* shown first in Berlin in summer of 1930 and soon after with equal tremendous success in London, Paris, and New York.

There was on the other hand the official optimism being part of the state ideology in Stalinist Russia and Nazi Germany. It seemed not at all so far fetched at the time but struck an emotional chord; it was what people (especially young people) wanted to be told.

There are no obstacles on our road . . . we achieve in a year the work of a century—happiness we take as of right (Anatole d'Aktil's March of the Enthusiasts). On the Kalinin line of the Moscow underground, there is, to this day, a metro station named Chaussee Entusiastov—Enthusiasts

Highway, even though the age of the enthusiasts in the Soviet Union belongs now to a distant past.

Hope Springs Eternal but Mr. Pope Carried Two Pistols

Optimism unless carried beyond obvious limits of reason and reality is a better guide to action in bad times than despair, lethargy, and what psychiatrists many years ago defined as *aboulia* (absence of will). But how to generate will? Schopenhauer, in one of his asides, noted that it is possible to wish—but not to wish to wish (wollen wollen). How to generate hope, will power, and dynamism?

It took Germany a mere fourteen years to rise again as a major power after the defeat in World War One, and Russia, about the same time, after the breakdown of the Soviet Union. These are not perhaps the most encouraging examples; fervent nationalism was the main element involved in both cases and a high price had to be paid or will eventually be paid. Modern medicine has produced a whole array of drugs acting as antidepressants and feel-good drugs. But there is no pharmacological answer as yet for collective depression.

However, there have been cases of spontaneous recovery, even if one cannot account for "objective reasons" that caused it. The history of France in the second half of the nineteenth century serves as an example. If oil and gas played a crucial role in the recovery of Russia in the age of Putin, France had no such good luck. There had been a great deal of depression even under the rule of Napoleon III, and after the defeat by Prussia in 1870/71, the feeling that the country was finished became fairly general, decadence was the prevailing fashion not only among the poets. The number of books was legion belonging to the *Finis Galliae* category. Some of them believed that a recovery though improbable was not impossible, but the majority thought the process was irrevocable: France was finished. A great many reasons were adduced: Demographic and economic trends (few children were born), and the French economy had been overtaken by Germany and Britain, military weakness, alcoholism, prostitution, defeatism, cultural exhaustion, and of course, a general mood of hopelessness.

This reached its apex in the last decades of the century and then suddenly; at first, imperceptibly the mood radically changed. Alcoholism and prostitution continued to be a social problem, there were some foreign political setbacks (Tangier and Fashoda) and not many more children were born. But astute observers noted a profound change in the public mood. It manifested itself in many ways: The upbeat repercussions of the Paris world exhibition (1900), the construction of the Eiffel tower built in a few months by a mere 300 workers (1889), the "banquet years," and *la belle époque*. Louis Bleriot in 1909 was the first to fly over the English channel pocketing 1,000 pound sterling prize money. Young people were more interested in sports than in prostitution, nationalism and religion became of more interest; there was a new, even exaggerated self-confidence. No one could explain why all this was happening—perhaps it was simply the emergence of a new generation bored by the pessimism and defeatism of their elders.

The case of France was by no means unique. It tends to show that decline is not irreversible, and that as in the case of the Arab world, a reversal of the present mood is not impossible, even though it is unlikely to happen in the near future. The present fundamentalist wave will probably have to run its full course and only after it will have shown its inability to provide answers to the social and economic challenges of this world as distinct from the next.

It tends to show that as in the case of Europe, the decline may not continue to the bitter end and that a modest reversal is possible, though quite probably only in response to a deeper crisis than the present. In the meantime, Western assessment and Western policy have to be based on the "as if"—the assumption that a change for the better is usually possible and should be hoped for.

It should not, however, be based on the assumption that the great change for the better had already taken place. Hope springs eternal is one of the most frequent quotations in English poetry. However, the man who wrote these lines (Alexander Pope) was a prudent person. He had many enemies and we have it on the authority of his sister that he never went on a walk unless accompanied by a great fierce looking dog, and he also carried two loaded pistols.

The Marxism Renaissance

Some knowledge of some of Marx's writings was taken for granted in my generation. This was not true with regard to the generation of the parents, let alone grandparents, but in our time, one-third of the world was reigned by systems that were (or claimed to be) guided by Marxism; how to make sense of current events unless one knew something about the ideology that was the lodestar of these countries? Such knowledge, let it be said at once, did not extend to Das Kapital; outside a small circle of specialists, I knew no one who had ever read it to the end. But it was the norm at least to pretend that one had started reading it.

This is no longer the case today: knowledge of Marx has become rare, I believe, among present generations, even though most would agree that Marx, admire him or not, was one of the most influential thinkers (if not the single most important one) of the nineteenth century. For this reason, if for no other, the publication of new Marx biographies should be welcomed. If time or inclination is lacking to read Marx, one should at least read about him.

It is reported that following the recent economic crisis, a renaissance of the greatest critic of capitalism is taking place. But it is a strange renaissance. To begin with some anecdotal evidence: our little apartment in London is located almost literally a stone throw from Marx's grave in Highgate. In the olden days, on an afternoon stroll, rain or shine, I was inevitably asked at least once for directions to the grave by visitors often from abroad which included students from Germany, middle-aged Americans, on one occasion by monks from some Far Eastern country. During the last two decades, the stream of those wishing to pay homage has dwindled, almost vanished. The visiting hours have been cut, but there has been no great outcry.

As for the circulation of Marx's works, an investigation, however cursory, shows that there has been a rise in recent years (1,500 copies of Das Kapital were sold in Germany in a year), but not an overwhelming one. They sell not notably more than other political theory classics, less than Milton Friedman's *Capitalism and Freedom*, considerably less than certain cult books such as Ayn Rand's *Atlas Shrugged and Fountainhead*. One exception is the *Communist Manifesto*, a long essay of 60–80 pages, depending on the language one happens to read.

Nuriel Roubini, the well-known commentator, also known as Dr. Doom has written that Marx was at least partly right arguing that a number of circumstances could lead capitalism to self destruct. This might be so, but Schumpeter had made the same argument many years ago. Roubini added that Marx's belief that socialism would be more effective has proved wrong. There is an inevitable story of the anonymous Wall street banker (names are unfortunately not given) who said that Marx was absolutely right with his analysis of capitalism. But I suspect that the banker is not among the readers of Marx either.

There have been, in recent years, many Marxism conferences and countless workshops from Chicago and Boston to Berlin; the London Marx "festival" (as it was called by the conveners) lasted five days. The invitation reads: "Crisis and austerity have exposed the insanity of our global system. Billions have been given to the banks while billions across the planet face hunger and poverty. Capitalism means austerity for the 99% and rule by the markets."

"Revolution is in the air" was one of the main slogans of the London festival. But is it really true? France got a socialist government, but it is already in trouble. Britain may follow, but would it fare any better? It seems only natural, at the time of crisis, that more often than not public opinion should turn against the party in power. Given the severity of the crisis and the slowness of the recovery, the rediscovery of Marxism is not surprising. Indeed, the fact that political reaction has been so mild is more astonishing.

The reasons are no secret. They can be given in a few words, China, the Soviet Union, and the former Communist countries including Albania and Cambodia under Pol Pot.

Professor Terry Eagleton, in a recent book, argues that this is a lazy argument. True, if Lenin had not left Zurich in 1917 and Switzerland had tried Bolshevism, it might have worked better than in Russia. But Switzerland did not try it.

Francis Wheen, author of a recent Marx biography, argues that it is preposterous to blame philosophers for any and every mutilation of their ideas ("the tree is known by its fruits"). It would indeed be wrong to blame Marx for Stalin or Pol Pot just as Nietzsche cannot be made responsible for Adolf Hitler or Adolf Eichmann. But for better or worse,

Marx provided an outline, even if somewhat vague for a postcapitalist world; perhaps, it was a tragedy that it was tried in places least likely to succeed. However, this is what happened; probably, it could not have come to power anywhere else.

Thus, the author of the draft of the future society is remembered by those who lived to witness it and this is why Moscow authorities have seriously considered to remove the last remaining statue of Marx in the Russian capital (opposite the Bolshoi theatre). In explanation it was argued that Marx after all never visited the city. This I find shabby; Marx was never in Maputu, the capital of Mozambique (formerly Lorenzo Marques), but there is Avenida Marx there, and for those locals who have not heard of him, it says "intellectual" on the street signs. Interest for Marx and Marxism is least today in the very countries in which his teachings were once invoked on every occasion and even school children had to study him.

The Marx renaissance is concentrated, on the whole, on the United States and Germany. The German city Karl Marx Stadt has again adopted Chemnitz, its old name. However, the local savings bank in Chemnitz has issued a credit card with Marx counterfeit (the "Marx card"), which proved to be a successful publicity stunt. Alexander Kluge, a leading West German movie producer, has given us a ten-hour "poetic documentary" (his words) of Das Kapital; the idea occurred earlier on to the great Eisenstein who tried to persuade James Joyce to collaborate in the project, but nothing came of it. Kluge's ten-hour documentary (available on DVD) is entitled "Ideological News from Ancient Times," and it takes the Eisenstein project as its starting point.

Projects of this kind should make one a little wary of the character and seriousness of the Marx renaissance. I fully sympathize with the misgivings of Jonathan Sperber, author of the most recent Marx biography, as he warns against the initiatives to make Marx's ideas "more relevant to our time" by adding or reinterpreting them in the light of structuralism, poststructuralism, postmodernism, existentialism, or elements of any other intellectual movement of the last 150 years. Attempts have been made to integrate Marxism and postcolonialism, but it is a heroic effort in view of what Marx wrote about Britain's progressive role in the development of India.

Who were and are the leading figures in the age of the Marx renaissance? Terry Eagleton who wrote, *Why Marx Was Right*, is a staunch fighter against Islamophobia and a leading theoretician in the field of literary theory. Others are students of religion, philosophy, psychoanalysis, postcolonialism, commensality (eating together), identity politics, gender relations, the environment, and so on—all no doubt important subjects but not the ones closest to Marx's heart and mind. Étienne Balibar is among them, who wrote on Spinoza, Alain Badiou's field of specialization is truth and logic, Slavoj Žižek writes and talks on psychoanalysis, film theory, and dozens of other subjects, Jacques Rancière made his name studying education. A distinguished New York professor offers a course "Close Reading of Das Kapital"; he is a professor of geography and anthropology. And who is notably absent? Economists and experts on finance—the subjects to which Marx devoted most of his life and which are at the bottom of the present crisis. (Historians are also missing.) No one argues that only economists and Marxism experts should participate in these debates, but their almost total absence makes one think.

It is difficult for an outsider to assess what creative impulses Marx contributed to "feminist notes on the validity of affects" (Rosemary Hennessy, Rice university—a paper given at the Berlin Marxism conference) or to the field of subaltern studies or other fashionable subjects.

If, as I suspect, the Marxist renaissance has little to do with the teachings of the historical Marx with which the poststructuralists, the postmodernists, and the experts in gender relations seem to be only vaguely familiar, how then to explain the renaissance, however modest—even if restricted to university campuses in a number of countries rather than the industrial working class? It seems that "Marx" has become something like a shortcut or a symbol indicating a predilection for radical change in a great variety of fields loosely named "cultural studies." It has little or nothing to do with the ideas of the author of the *Grundrisse: Foundations of the Critique of Political Economy* and other such works.

For an answer to these questions, one has to go back in time. Marx was a genius, but he was not the most reliable of prophets. Marx provided impulses of great importance to the study of the economy and of society, even if academic economists and sociologists largely ignored him at the time. Without historical materialism, the importance of the class struggle in history would not have been recognized to the same extent. His impact on twentieth-century politics was enormous. However, even before the nineteenth century ended, some of those closest to him realized that history was not moving in the direction he had predicted. Eduard Bernstein was not a genius, not a major theoretician, but a person of integrity and considerable common sense. A native of Berlin, he lived many years in London, was a friend of the family and together with Eleanor Marx, one of the daughters, edited much of the unpublished papers and correspondence of the master after his death.

Writing in 1898, his original intention was not to refute Marxism but simply bring it up to date in the light of events. Bernstein realized that pauperization, the process of increasing misery of the proletariat did not take place, nor the concentration of capital in a few hands, eventually causing the collapse of capitalism. Marx could not have foreseen the welfare state. True, there were recurrent crises in the capitalist system, but they were not those that Marx had assumed. In later years, it became clear that the workers of the world did not unite, that the industrial working class was not growing but shrinking, following technological progress, and that the composition of the working class changed—in Europe, it came to exist to a considerable degree of immigrants for whom religion was more important than class consciousness. The native working class frequently gravitated to the right—sometimes to the far right as in France. False consciousness or not, this is what happened and as Lenin taught us—facts are a stubborn thing.

A revolution occurred in some countries, not in the most developed capitalist countries, but in some of the most backward. The new societies in these countries were quite different from those Marx had imagined. Crises were shaking capitalism in the developed countries, but these were not the crises Marx had anticipated.

In these circumstances, the attraction for Marxism rested not on the scientific character of its teaching, which had been the ambition of the founders, but on the Utopian and the romantic idea of revolution. Marx had been contemptuous of the Utopian socialists of his time and his doctrine did contain scientific elements. But these were not the decisive elements—far more important was the general discontent among intellectuals with the status quo and the wish to do away with the social and cultural imperfections of the prevailing system and above all to introduce new cultural values and norms.

A trend that favored radicalization was the growing polarization of income and property both in the West and the formerly Communist countries. However, this was a relatively recent trend that intensified during the 1980s; it led to the growing critique of and opposition to the current system. But it did not lead necessarily to Marxism, for opposition to capitalism had come from many political quarters left, right, and center. What was the character of the future society to be and how was it to be built? Nowadays, even the most orthodox of Marxists do not suggest the Paris commune of 1871, nor a dictatorship of the proletariat as a model to be emulated.

One of the obvious manifestations of the Marx renaissance is the number of new biographies published in recent years—one could think of four in English alone. In the decades after World War Two, interest in Marx had been limited, even though Communist and Social Democratic parties had been strong at the time. The basic facts about Marx's life were of course known: his years as a student and involvement with the young Hegelians, his activity as a left-wing democrat and his discovery of socialism, the years in Paris and Brussels, and eventually his life in London studying capitalism, pondering the class struggle and historical materialism. Information and documents shedding light on the life and work of Marx however marginal, were collected in major institutes in Moscow, Amsterdam, and London. The Moscow Institute IMEL (Marx-Engels-Lenin) was the largest and best equipped of them, but it was closed in 1993; its holdings seem to be stored in some other museum, but I am told that they are not accessible at the present time. The Amsterdam Institute founded in 1935 still exists and so does the London Marx House/Memorial Library located in Clerkenwell Green in London's East end, once called Little Italy and center of much radical politics (including the Irish Fenians), but now largely Black and Muslim.

For many years, Franz Mehring's *Karl Marx: The Story of His Life*, first published in 1918 (still in print today), was the leading text in the field. Mehring was a "bourgeois" journalist who found his way to the socialist movement in midlife only. It is a decent work, very respectful of the master but not entirely uncritical. Orthodox Marxists never forgave Mehring that up to a point he defended Ferdinand Lassalle and Mikhail Bakunin against the often intemperate attacks by Marx. Lassalle of German-Jewish origin was the founder of the first German socialist party and a very talented even charismatic leader but highly unstable, given occasionally to harebrained schemes and actions. As a theoretician, he was not remotely in Marx's league, but he was in Germany and Marx was not and therefore more popular and better known among workers. (I have to admit to a certain weakness for the man, having lived as a child and young adult very close to the place where he spent his early years. Our address was, in fact, Lassalle Square until the Nazis renamed it.) Lassalle died young in a duel concerning the good name of a young lady of aristocratic origin. Marx who had been in close contact with him later referred to him as that Jewish nigger and used other such gracing epithets.

Mary Gabriel, author of another excellent biography of the Marx family, decided not to share this information (Marx about Lassalle) with her readers because it might create a mistaken impression; such language was after all common at the time. True enough, Lassalle was not exactly a proud Jew either; in a letter to his fiancé, he wrote that he hated them. However, in the end, such sanitation seems misplaced and judgment should be left to readers. Marx, to borrow a phrase coined by Freud was "badly baptized," instead of dissociating himself quietly and more or less elegantly from his tribe was self-conscious about his Jewish heritage, which seems to have bothered him.

As for Bakunin, the famous Russian anarchist, he too had been at one stage close to Marx, but later on, there was a fall out partly against a background of genuine political differences (Bakunin had moved toward anarchism), but also in part conditioned by Marx's deep and unshakable Russophobia. Marx was a great believer in conspiracy theories—for many years, he was deeply convinced that Lord Palmerston, the British Prime Minister, was a secret Russian agent. On the other hand, Marx trusted the spies that Prussian and German governments had planted in his inner circle. A great judge of his fellow human beings he was not.

The Mehring biography is no longer adequate for our age. It was bound to be incomplete because Marx's early writings became accessible to a wider public only in 1932, and the same is true for much of his correspondence. Nor was it known outside a very small circle that Marx had fathered a boy with Helen Demuth, the faithful domestic in the Marx London household. Marx's illegitimate son was the only member of the family to live and witness the victory of socialism (as it was then called) in Russia.

All these biographies should be recommended for their competence and reliability; the authors had certainly done their homework. There is general agreement that David McLellan's (1973, 1983) *Karl Marx* is the standard work. It was written in the 1970s before the breakdown of the Soviet Union and is now in its fourth edition. The other books put their stress each in somewhat different way. Jonathan Sperber (2013) is an expert on nineteenth-century Germany, and there is much in his book about Marx's adolescence in Germany, especially in his native Trier about which relatively little was and remains known. He also deals in greater detail than the other authors with Marx's relations with other German revolutionaries in exile and Marx's political activism, for instance, as one of the pillars of the First International. Sperber wants to see Marx above all as a nineteenth-century figure rather than through the lenses of more recent history. However, Marx's historical importance is of course mainly that of the man who gave Lenin his ideas, not the polemicist who wrote a book attacking Herr Vogt whom no one remembers today. Sperber is justified in turning against the attempts to update Marx, frequently ranging from the ridiculous to the absurd. But he goes too far dismissing as useless the preoccupation with Marxism which he calls Marxology. His private life and his interventions in the politics of his time, interesting as they are, are not why he is remembered today. The reader of his book would look in vain for the two most important works on Marxism (Lichtheim and Kolakowski), which are not even mentioned in the bibliography.

Francis Wheen's (2000) book is well-written and was well-received with stress on Marx's English years rather than his earlier life, and he deals, for instance, in greater detail than other authors with Marx's exchanges with Darwin. Wheen also takes issue with other biographers, but the bones of contention are not really fundamental.

Ms. Gabriel's (2011) *Love and Capital*, while also well-researched, is more preoccupied with the former than the latter. She deals primarily with Marx's wife and his children—four of the children predeceased him. Marx's relations with his children seem to have been very good, the daughters adored him. Mrs. Marx's (-von Westfalen) fate was not an enviable one; for most of the time, they lived in dire poverty. The husband was not of much help in this respect, and her aristocratic background and upbringing had not prepared her for a life in such miserable conditions. ("I am reluctant to go home facing the constant whining and complaining," Marx wrote on more than one occasion.) The only earlier serious and sympathetic study of her life was written by her nephew once removed, the Prussian nobleman Lutz Graf Schwerin von Krosigk who, while not being a member of the Nazi party served as Hitler's minister of finance from 1933 to the very end. He was given a ten-year sentence at Nuremberg but released from prison much earlier.

Thus, there is no lack of serious and reliable Marx biographies and also of his closest friend Friedrich Engels. However, his works have not been published in full to this day; a book of substantial length would be needed to relate the full story of the various false starts to publish his works over many years. The most recent initiative based on the

Amsterdam Institute originally envisaged 164 volumes, but this was cut back to 114 of which about half are now available. In contrast to earlier incomplete editions, they are free of censorship and partisan explanations.

What fresh impetus can reasonably be expected from the often invoked contemporary Marx renaissance? Expectations should not be too sanguine: Marx's preoccupation was with the inner contradictions of capitalism and the political future of the industrial working class. The renaissance was triggered off by the crisis in the developed countries, which began in 2008. Marx's interest focused on Britain and to a lesser extent on other European countries, which were at the time the capitalist vanguard. An analysis of capitalism today would have to focus not on England, but above of all on China, the most successful such country, some other Asian countries, and perhaps also Russia.

We listed the topics of main interest to those involved in the Marx renaissance to which one could add alienation, reification, and a few other literary and philosophical topics. However, the crisis in capitalism in Europe and America is a debt crisis and has to do with stimulus versus austerity to get the economy balanced and moving again; it is not Marx versus Böhm Bawerk, the protagonist of the Vienna school of GrenzNutzen (marginal utility theory), but it is now Keynes versus Hayek and Milton Friedman. In this situation, the state and regulations are bound to play a greater role than in the past. A great deal of ill will has accumulated vis-a-vis the financial system because of the greed displayed by some of its leading movers and shakers but above all because of their incompetence. However, no one so far, neither individuals nor political parties have suggested the wholesale nationalization of key branches of the economy, the means of production and of the banks—and this was, after all, what Marxism was all about.

The challenge facing Europe and also America is that of a new economic world order emerging and that Europe (no longer the rich and the main exploiter) will have to think and work hard to save the welfare state (and at least some of the entitlements in America). How to find a niche that will enable them to keep their standard of living or at least to prevent too rapid a decline?

If the various "rethinking Marx" conferences will be able to contribute to finding answers to these grave problems one ought to be deeply grateful to them. How to get out of the recession, how to become again competitive? But a look at the agenda of the most recent such meeting (at the University of Washington) makes one doubt whether they are on the right track. The papers to be discussed read as follows:

> *Reconsidering impossible totalities. Deployments of the Sublime.*
>
> *A few thoughts on the Academic Poet as Hobo Tourist*
>
> *Alienation and Community. Reading Hip hop at the intersection of culture.* Other papers deal with *Urban alterity (otherness), Annals of sexual states,* and *Stranger intimacy* .

To engage for a moment in counterfactual history: what would be the reaction of Karl Marx in his London apartment faced with such discussions at a gathering dedicated to rethinking his ideas? Would he be impressed, amused, speechless? Perhaps, it would remind him of the Carnival celebrations each February in his native Trier, wine, funny masks and customs, and all kind of pranks to be followed by a five- or six-day hangover.

References

Gabriel, Mary. 2011. *Love and Capital. Karl and Jenny Marx and the Birth of a Revolution*. New York: Little Brown, 707 pp.

McLellan, David. 2006. *Karl Marx, A Biography*, 4th ed. New York, 487 pp.

Sperber, Jonathan. 2013. *Karl Marx, A Nineteenth Century Life*. New York: Liveright, 640 pp.

Wheen, Francis. 2000. *Karl Marx. A Life*. New York: W. W. Norton, 431 pp.

Reflections on the Next Revolution

The current preoccupation with the Euro and the future of a united Europe, the fears of a global recession, and the possible consequences of the conflicts in the Arab world and Iran have largely overshadowed the emergence of another global crisis: The revolt of the young generation, which could have equally wide repercussions. It is a crisis that manifests itself in many ways, above all perhaps social and economic such as alarmingly growing unemployment. It has appeared in different ways in different countries—violent demonstrations and riots not only in European capitals such as in London in 2011, but also in Middle Eastern capitals such as Cairo. Elsewhere, it has generated new political parties (the Pirates). The only common denominator has been the surprise with which it was greeted—no one had expected these events.

The political significance of this issue is just beginning to be understood in America. Columns in the media are entitled "The screwed generation" and "Young Americans are getting the shaft." They note that a generational war is coming, that much more money is spent on the elderly than the young, that a college education has become far more expensive during the last few decades, that the job market for the young has deteriorated, and that as many as a hundred million Americans live in households that are earning less than their parents did at a similar age.

However, it is as yet far from becoming clear that this is by no means a specific American problem but a global trend, that it will not change for the better in the near future, and that it may have far reaching and disturbing political and social consequences. On the contrary, there has been a great deal of misplaced optimism shown, for instance, in the comments on the Arab spring and other false dawns or the high expectations attached to the emergence of the network generation, the social media, the virtual spaces, etc. Far greater attention has been paid to Mr. Zuckerberg than to the fate of the other members of his generation.

Youth and politics: Traditionally, youth has been a factor of hope. As the philosopher Martin Buber put it in a speech in 1913—youth is the eternal chance mankind possesses. The older generations are usually much less willing to care, they lack passion, idealism, and enthusiasm. They see above all difficulties and dangers and they stress the risks of change in politics, probably even more than in other human endeavors. They think of a hundred reasons why change for the better is dangerous or impossible.

Young people, on the other hand, have always been in the forefront of the struggle for freedom and against tyranny. They were always the pioneers of revolutions. When the French Revolution broke, Robespierre was thirty-three, Saint Just, the fiercest of them, was twenty-two, and Danton, considered an old man, was just thirty. At the time of the Russian Revolution of 1917, all the main actors were under forty—with the exception of Lenin who was in his forties and was therefore called *starik*—the old man.

However, the second part of Buber's statement when he talked about youth as the great agent of change and progress is usually forgotten—or omitted. He said, "What a pity that this chance is usually wasted."

The young generation has not only been in the forefront of the fight for freedom and progress, but it was also among the avant garde of all radical movements, some admirable, others much less so.

If youth is the season of hope, it is also the age of credulity and fanaticism. Mussolini was not yet forty at the time of the March on Rome, and those close to him were even much younger—Achille Starace, the secretary of the Fascist Party, was thirty-three, Dino Grandi, who was to become foreign minister, was twenty-seven, and Ciano just nineteen. The hymn of Fascism and later of Fascist Italy was *Giovinezza primavera di bellezza* (Youth, Youth spring of beauty . . .). Hitler was in his forties when he came to power, his deputy Rudolf Hess was thirty-nine; Hitler's closest followers were all very young when they became ministers—Goebbels was thirty-six, Himmler, head of the Schutzstaffel (SS) and the dreaded internal terror machine, was thirty-three, his deputy Heydrich was twenty-nine, and Eichmann, the Jewish expert and engineer of the holocaust, a mere twenty-seven.

Radicalization: Youth unemployment in Europe, the Middle East, and other parts of the globe is almost certainly leading to political radicalization. It has soared by 50 percent since the outbreak of the financial crisis of 2008 and reached almost 50 percent in South European countries such as Spain, more than 60 percent in Greece. The overall rate in the twenty-seven countries belonging to the Eurozone is 22 percent (2012), less in Germany but 23.9 percent in France. According to an authoritative survey issued by the International Labor Office (ILO), youth unemployment in North Africa amounts to 28 percent and 27 percent in the Middle East. However, even these alarming figures could be too optimistic because many young people have been forced into part-time and/or unskilled work, while many others have given up looking for a job after years of fruitless search. Many continue to study merely because they have not been able to find jobs commensurate with their education and training. Even in East Asia, the most dynamic economic region at the present time, the figures for youth unemployment are three times higher than those for adults.

This trend has come as a surprise even to the experts because it coincides with worldwide decline in the birth rate. To some extent, the global economic crisis of 2008 explains this rise in unemployment, but there are also other reasons to be studied and discussed in detail.

Left or Right?

That youth unemployment will have political consequences seems fairly certain, even though it cannot be predicted whether the extreme left or the far right will benefit more. The *indignados* movement in Spain was one of the precursors of political protest, and the "occupy" movement was and is to a large extent a phenomenon generated by youth unemployment. In various European countries, first in Sweden and recently more prominently in Germany, the Pirates have established themselves as a political force represented in regional parliaments. Their gains have come partly as the result of losses by the "Green" (ecological parties which appeared first on the European political scene twenty to thirty years ago). The Green parties have aged and their main concern has not been with social issues such as employment. However, it is more than doubtful whether the Pirates (who have appeared so far only in countries such as Scandinavia and Germany in which youth unemployment is not a major problem) will have much of a political future because their concern has been mainly with issues such as copyright, "direct democracy," and "participation" and not with the creation of places of work. Some leading German *Pirates* have come on record with statements close to the extreme right, but this reflected the political innocence of individuals rather than a party line and most of them have since been removed.

In the Middle East, it was mistakenly believed that the anti-establishment uprisings of early 2011 (the Arab spring—spearheaded largely by young men and women) would lead to democratization of politics and bring more freedom to societies. But as subsequent developments have shown, the traditional conservative forces were far stronger, the left and progressives were split in various directions, and the economic situation far from improving deteriorated as a result of the political unrest in these countries.

More likely than not, this extremist (perhaps even revolutionary) potential will be absorbed by new groups and leaders unlikely to be democratic in character. For they share the conviction that the system—parliamentary democracy—is failing.

So far, political radicalization has not been a notable success—this goes for the various "Occupy" initiatives, the Arab spring, and similar such movements. The reasons are manifold: they lacked a clear program, were internally divided, had no effective leadership, and their appeal suffered from the appearance of various sectarian demands in their ranks. However, the factors that gave birth to these protest movements have not disappeared and for this reason they are bound to reappear on the scene. Western (and not only Western) societies were based in the past on a consensus, an unwritten social compact or bond between young and old, which is now in danger of disintegration.

On Youth Movements (1970)

I can well imagine that on Saturday nights across the country, at hundreds of faculty parties where a year and a half ago, the main subject of discussion was the war in Vietnam, and thousands of professors and their wives now passionately debate the pros and cons of the student movement, the tactics of the Students for the Democratic Society (SDS), and the significance of the generational conflict. I myself have attended several such gatherings and have been struck not so much by the intensity with which the actions of the students are either approved of or condemned by their elders as by the baffled consensus among those elders that the movement is both unprecedented and totally inexplicable in terms of what the university has historically represented. When I am asked, as I invariably am, for the European view on these matters, I rarely manage more than a few words, to the effect that the American situation is unique and that anyway history never repeats itself—which needless to say, is of no great help to anyone. And yet, I believe there is something to be learned from the European experience, even if the lesson is an ambiguous one. Not the least thing to be learned is that the Western university has, by no means, always represented that tranquil meeting ground, so fondly misremembered now by American professors, of those who would gladly learn with those who would gladly teach.

Quite the contrary. Organized youth revolt has, for a long time, been an integral part of the European history. This is on one hand. On the other hand, the idea of the university as a quiet place, devoted to the pursuit of learning and unaffected by the turbulence of the outside world, is of a comparatively recent date. The medieval university certainly was no such place. As Nathan Schachner has pointed out, it was a place characterized more by bloody affrays, pitched battles, mayhem, rape, and homicide: "Indeed by the frequency of riots one may trace the rise of the University to power and privilege." In his monumental study, *Universities of Europe in the Middle Ages*, Hastings Rashdall relates the violence of the medieval university to the violence of medieval times in general, when the slitting of a throat was not regarded even by the church as the worst of mortal sins.

Thus, a Master of Arts at the University of Prague who had cut the throat of a Friar Bishop was merely expelled, while in the case of other offenders, punishment involved the confiscation of scholastic effects and garments. The police were openly ridiculed by students, and the universities did nothing to exact discipline from their own scholars. In dealing with the subject of students' morals, Rashdall is constrained to write in Latin. According to Charles Thurot's *History of Paris University in the Middle Ages*, masters frolicked with their pupils and even took part in their disorders. The university was a great concourse of men and boys freed from all parental restrictions; morality, as Schachner notes, was a private affair, as were the comings and goings of the students. Nor was the trouble localized; the same complaints were to be heard from Oxford to Vienna and Salamanca.

As for the professor, his position in the medieval university was not what it became in later days. He was, first of all, paid by the students. A professor at Bologna needed his students' permission if he wanted to leave town even for a single day; he had to pay a fine if he arrived late in class or if he ended his lecture before the chiming of the church bells; should his lectures not meet with favor, there was a good chance that he would be interrupted, hissed, or even stoned. Supported by the King and Church, medieval students enjoyed almost unlimited freedom. It was an unwritten rule, for instance, that they were always in the right in their clashes with the town's people. Of course, from time to time, the citizenry would get even by killing a few students; the Oxford town-and-gown riots of 1354 were one such response, if a major one, to student provocation—provocation that took the form, in the words of a contemporary chronicler, of "atrociously wounding and slaying many, carrying off women, ravishing virgins, committing robberies and many other enormities hateful to God." To be sure, the real troublemakers were a minority, some of them not even students but young vagabonds enjoying the immunities of the scholar, drifting from master to master and from university to university. For every scholar involved in felonious offenses, there were dozens whose story is unknown.

"They studied conscientiously, attended lectures and disputations worked hard, ate frugally, drank their modest stoup of wine, and had no time for the delights of tavern and brothel.

The annals of the virtuous, like the annals of a happy people, are short and barren" (Schachner). Nevertheless, it is a fact that only in later ages did the university begin to impose stricter discipline on its students.

If student violence in the Middle Ages can be ascribed mainly to the high spirits of youth, by the eighteenth century, a new figure had appeared on the scene: the student as freedom fighter. Die Räuber ("The Robbers"), the play that made Schiller famous, tells the story of a group of students who, disgusted by society and its inequities, take to the mountains to lead partisan warfare against the oppressors. Sturm und Drang, the first real literary movement of youth revolt, combined opposition to social conventions with a style of life that is familiar enough today: wild language, long hair, and strange attire. Within a few decades after its inception, the romantics had made this movement fashionable, if not respectable, all over Europe. Suddenly, there was Young Germany, Young Italy, Young Hungary, and Young Russia—all up in arms against the tyranny of convention, tradition, and outworn beliefs.

One of the very few places untouched by the cult of youth at that time was America, itself a young country, unencumbered by the dead weight of tradition: Amerika, Goethe apostrophized, du hast es besser. . . .

Some youth groups in the modern period have done much good, while others have caused a great deal of harm. It has been the custom in writing about them to divide them into the progressive and the reactionary, the wholesome and the decadent, so that, for example, the revolutionary Russian student movement of the nineteenth century, the Italian Risorgimento, and the Chinese May 29 movement fall in one camp, and the Fascist youth movements fall in the other.

However, this scheme is at best an oversimplification, since almost all movements of youthful revolt have contained in themselves both elements at once. The historical role a movement finally played depended, in each case, on political conditions in the society at large, the gravity of the problems the movement faced, the degree of its cultural development, and the quality of the guidance it received from its mentors.

The dual character of youth movements is illustrated. In the 1920s, when Piscator, who provided many new impulses and ideas to the contemporary theater, staged Schiller's *Die Räuber* in Berlin, he had Spiegelberg, one of the leaders of the gang and incidentally a Jew, appear in the mask of Trotsky. The dual character of the movement was brought out with particular clarity by the example of the early German student circles, the Burschenschaften. In his recent book, Lewis Feuer characterizes the members of these circles as "historicists, terrorists, totalitarians and anti-Semites," all of which is perfectly true. However, they were also genuine patriots who dreamed of German unity and set out to combat the tyranny and oppression of the Holy Alliance. Most of them, in addition, were democrats of sorts and their movement was regarded by the liberals of the day as one of great promise. Their story is briefly told.

The leader of the group was Karl Follen, a lecturer at Jena, of whom a contemporary wrote that "no one could be compared with him for purity and chastity of manners and morals. He seemed to concentrate all his energies upon one great aim—the revolution." In 1818, a certain Karl Sand, an idealistic and highly unstable student of theology who had come under Follen's influence, assassinated a minor playwright by the name of August Kotzebue who was suspected of being a Russian agent. Sand genuinely expected that this action, undertaken in the service of a holy cause, would trigger off a revolution. But the choice of victim was haphazard and the consequences regrettable: the government seized the opportunity to suppress the Burschenschaft as well as the whole democratic movement. Follen escaped to America, where he became a professor of German literature and preacher at Harvard (he later drowned at sea in a shipwreck). It took almost thirty years for the movement he had led to recover from the blow dealt to it by the authorities.

The idealism, spirit of sacrifice, devotion to one's people, and revolutionary fervor that marked the Burschenschaft have been an inherent part of all youth movements over the last hundred years. It is a mistake to assume that the Fascist youth movements were an exception to this rule and that their members were mainly sadistic, blindly destructive young thugs. To be sure, they preached the doctrine of violence, but as Mussolini said, "there is a violence that liberates, and there is a violence that enslaves; there is moral violence and stupid, immoral violence." The ideological forerunners of Italian Fascism, men like Corradini and Federzoni, were second to none in their condemnation of capitalism and imperialism and in their defense of the rights of the "proletarian nations." Early Fascist programs demanded a republic, the abolition of all titles, the redistribution of private income, and the confiscation of unproductive capital. They also placed great stress on youth.

Giovanni Gentile, the philosopher of Fascism, considered the sole aim of the new movement to be the "spiritual liberation of the young Italians." The very anthem of the Fascist regime was an appeal to the young generation: *Giovinezza, Giovinezza, primavera di bellezza.*

Similarly, in Germany, where the student movement after the First World War was strongly nationalist, the Nazi student association emerged as the leading force in the German universities (and in Austria) in 1930, well before Hitler had become the leader of the strongest German party. With 40,000 registered members out of a total of 132,000 students, the Nazis easily took control of the chief organization of German students several years before the party's seizure of national power. The declared aim of the Nazi student association was to destroy liberalism and international capitalism; point two on its program was to "purge the university of the influence of private capital"; point nine called on students to join the ranks of the workers. Mussolini's thesis about the difference between revolutionary and reactionary violence, between violence practiced by the oppressed and by the oppressors has a certain resemblance with ideas expressed in the 1960s and 1970s by Marcuse and others.

"Student power" made its first appearance at the Goettingen Studententag in 1920. Later on, it was linked to the demand that the university be made political, a real "People's University," and that all the academic cobwebs and so-called "objective sciences" be cleaned out. Even before Hitler came to power, leading German professors attacked the "idea of false tolerance" of the humanist university. Invoking Fichte, Hegel, and Schleiermacher, they held that liberal democracy was the main enemy of the true scientific spirit and demanded that henceforth, only one political philosophy be taught. The Nazis, needless to say, were still more radical: academic life, they said, had largely become an end in itself; located outside the sphere of real life, the university educated two types of students—the only expert and the only philosopher. These two types produced a great many books and much clever and refined table talk, but neither they nor the universities that sustained them were in a position to give clear answers to the burning questions of the day.

Criticisms like these were common at the time all over Europe. An observer of the French scene wrote in 1931 that the main characteristic of the young generation was its total rejection of the existing order: "almost no one defends the present state of affairs." One of the most interesting French youth groups was L'Ordre Nouveau, whose manifesto, written by Dandieu and Robert Aron, had the title, *La Révolution Nécessaire*. Ordre Nouveau stood for the liberation of man from capitalist tyranny and materialistic slavery; Bolshevism, Fascism, and National Socialism, it declared, had assumed the leadership of the young generation and for that reason would prevail everywhere. The young in France were deeply affected—to quote yet another contemporary witness—by a "tremendous wave of revolutionary enthusiasm, of holy frenzy and disgust." When several prominent young socialists seceded from the Serious Fraud Investigation Office (SFIO) in opposition to the rule of the old gang and established a movement of their own, this too was welcomed as one more manifestation of the rebellion of the young generation.

All these people were deeply troubled by the existing state of affairs and no doubt well meaning in their intentions; together with Jean Luchaire, who was the leader of Ordre Nouveau, some of them ended up as Nazi collaborators during the Second World War. The tactics adopted by these youth groups vis-à-vis the universities were the tactics of agitation. Even before the First World War, members of the Action Française had made it a custom to systematically disrupt the lectures of professors at the Sorbonne who had provoked their ire for political reasons. Nazi students perfected the system, forcing universities to dismiss Jewish professors, and even one Christian pacifist, well before 1933. However, the question must be asked again: was this rowdyism or an action undertaken in the genuine conviction that one's country was in grave danger and that the professors were enemies of the people who had to be removed? Among the Fascist youth movements in the late 1920s, one of the most sinister was the Rumanian terrorist band, the Archangel Michael, which later became the Iron Guard. Yet even the members of this group were not devoid of sincerity and idealism; Eugen Weber recently wrote of their leader:

From a mendacious people, he demanded honesty; in a lazy country, he demanded work; in an easy-going society, he demanded self discipline and persistence; from an exuberant and windy folk, he demanded brevity and self-control.

Whoever describes a youth movement as idealistic only states the obvious. Youth movements have never been out for personal gain; what motivates them is different from what motivates an association for the protection of the interests of small shopkeepers. The Fascist experience has shown that the immense potential that inheres in every youth movement can be exploited in the most disastrous way, but the potential itself must be seen as neutral.

Almost everything that is great has been done by youth, wrote Benjamin Disraeli, himself at one time a fighter in the ranks of generational revolt. Professor Feuer would counter: many disasters in modern European politics have been caused by students and youth movements. The exploits of the Burschenschaften, he argues, set back the cause of German freedom thirty years. Russian student terrorism in the 1880s put an end to progress toward constitutionalism in that country. However, for the terror and stress of the First World War (inaugurated by a bomb thrown by yet another student hero, Gavrilo Princip), Russia would have evolved in a liberal capitalist direction, and European civilization would not have been maimed by Fascism and a Second World War. According to Professor Feuer, the qualities needed to bring about peaceful social and political change are not those usually found in youth movements, and he accuses students of almost always acting irrationally in pursuing their objectives. Unfortunately, however, peaceful change is not always possible in history, nor are patience and prudence invariably the best counsel.

Take the Munich students who revolted against Hitler in 1943 and the student rebels who were recently sentenced in the Soviet Union. Had they acted entirely rationally, they might well have convinced themselves that as a consequence of long-term political and social processes, the dictatorship would disappear anyway or at least be mitigated in its ferocity. Why therefore endanger their lives? To their eternal credit, such rational considerations did not enter the students' minds. The impetuosity, the impatience, and sometimes the madness of youth movements have been a liberating force in the struggle against tyranny and dictatorship. Tyranny cannot be overthrown unless at least some people are willing to sacrifice their lives, and those willing to do so usually do not come from the ranks of the senior citizens. It is only when youth movements have launched a total attack against democratic regimes and societies—in Germany, France, and Italy in the 1920s and in other countries later on—that they have come to play, by necessity, a reactionary and destructive role.

Most of the basic beliefs and even the outward fashions of the present world youth movements can be traced back to the period in Europe just before and after the First World War. The German Neue Schar of 1920 were the original hippies. Long-haired, sandaled, and unwashed, they castigated urban civilization, read Hermann Hesse and Indian philosophy, practiced free love, and distributed in their meetings thousands of asters and chrysanthemums. They danced, sang to the music of the guitar, and attended lectures on the "Revolution of the Soul." The modern happening was born in 1910 in Trieste, Parma, Milan, and other Italian cities where the Futurists arranged public meetings to recite their poems, read their manifestoes, and exhibited their ultra-modern paintings. No one over thirty, they demanded, should in future be active in politics. The public participated actively in these gatherings, shouting, joking, and showering the performers with rotten eggs. In other places, things were not so harmless. "Motiveless terror" formed part of the program of a group of young Russian anarchists, the *Bezmotivniki*, in their general struggle against society. The *Bezmotivniki* threatened to burn down whole cities, and their news sheets featured diagrams for the production of home-made bombs. Drug-consumption as a social phenomenon, touted as a way of gaining a new experience and a heightened sensibility, can be traced back to eighteenth-century France and Britain. The idea of a specific youth culture was first developed in 1913–14 by the German educator Gustav Wyneken and a young man named Walter Benjamin, who later attained literary fame. In 1915, Friedrich Bauermeister, an otherwise unknown member of the youth movement, developed the idea of the "class struggle of youth." Bauermeister regarded the working class and the socialist movement (including Marx and Engels) as "eudaimonistic"; the socialists, he admitted, stood for a just order and higher living standards, but he feared that once their goals were achieved they would part ways with the youth movement. Bauermeister questioned whether even the social revolution could create a better type of man or release human beings from their "bourgeois and proletarian distortions."

The ideas of this circle were developed in a little magazine called *Der Anfang* in 1913–14. Youth, the argument ran (in anticipation of Professor Kenneth Keniston), was *milieulos*, not yet integrated into society. Unencumbered by the ties of family or professional careers, young people were freer than other elements of society. As for their lack of experience, for which they were constantly criticized by their elders, this, far from being a drawback, was in fact a great advantage. Walter Benjamin called experience the "mask of the adult." For what did the adult wish above all to prove?

That he, too, had once been young, had disbelieved his parents, and had harbored revolutionary thoughts. Life, however, had taught the adult that his parents had been right after all, and now he in turn smiled with condescending superiority and said to the younger generation: this will be your fate too.

For the historian of ideas, the back issues of the periodicals of the youth movement, turned yellow with age, make fascinating reading. The great favorites of 1918 were Hermann Hesse, Spengler's Decline of the West, Zen Buddhism and Siddhartha, Tagore's gospel of spiritual unity (Love not Power), and Lenin. It is indeed uncanny how despite all the historical differences, the German movement pre-empted so many of the issues agitating the American movement of today, as well as its literary fashions.

Some youth movements in the last hundred years have been unpolitical in character. Most, however, have had definite political aims. Of this latter group, some have belonged to the extreme Left, while others have gravitated to the extreme Right; some have sought absolute freedom in anarchy, while others have found fulfillment in subordinating themselves to a leader. To find a common denominator seems, therefore, very nearly hopeless. However, the contradictions are often more apparent than real, not only because many of those who originally opted for the extreme Left later moved to the Right, or vice versa, or because the extremes sometimes found common ground as in the National Bolshevik movement, which gained some prominence in various countries in the 1920s. Whether a certain movement became political or apolitical, whether it opted for the Left or the Right, depended on the historical context: it hardly needs to be explained in detail why youth movements were preponderantly right wing after the First World War, while more recently, most have tended toward the Left. But beyond the particular political orientation, there are underlying motives that have remained remarkably consistent throughout.

Youth movements have always been extreme, emotional, and enthusiastic; they have never been moderate or rational (again, no major excursion into the psychology of youth is needed to explain this). Underlying their beliefs has always been a common anticapitalist, anti-bourgeois denominator, a conviction that the established order is corrupt to the bones and beyond redemption by parliamentary means of reform. The ideologies of democracy and liberalism have always been seen as an irretrievable part of the whole rotten system; all politicians, of course, are crooks. Equally common to all youth groups is a profound pessimism about the future of present-day culture and an assumption that traditional enlightened concepts like tolerance are out of date.

The older generation has landed the world in a mess, and a radical new beginning, a revolution, is needed. Youth movements have never been willing to accept the lessons of the past; each generation is always regarded as the first (and the last) in history, and the young have always found admiring adults to confirm them in their beliefs.

This leads us to the wider issue of Kulturpessimismus.

The idea that the world is in decline—an idea that is about as old as the world itself—had an impact on modern youth movements through the mediating influence of neo-romanticism. The themes of decadence and impending doom can be traced like a bright thread through the nineteenth century from Alfred de Musset ("Je suis venu trop tard dans un monde trop vieux"), to Carlyle, Ruskin, and Arnold with their strictures against the universal preoccupation with material gain. Kulturpessimismus enjoyed such widespread fashion that one can scarcely find a single self-respecting nineteenth-century author who did not complain about the disjunction between mankind and the world, between idea and reality, or about the spiritual bankruptcy and moral consumption of his age. In Germany, as *mal du siècle* turned into *fin de siècle*, a whole phalanx of Cassandras raised their voices, denouncing mass culture, crass materialism, and the lack of a sense of purpose in modern life. Kulturpessimismus induced in some a sense of resignation and gave rise to decadent moods in the literature and arts; at the same time, however, it acted as a powerful stimulus to movements of regeneration. Whereas dissatisfaction led some to ennui and perversions (*La jeune France*, an all-out revolt against social conventions, was decadent and wholly apolitical in character), elsewhere and in other periods, boredom gave birth to activism.

Thus, on the eve of the First World War, a whole generation of young Europeans, having pronounced themselves culturally suffocated, welcomed the outbreak of hostilities as heralding a great purge, a liberation that would somehow put things right. The close connection between Kulturpessimismus and boredom deserves more study than it has received so far, as does the connection between boredom and prosperity. Max Eyth, the German popular writer, astutely diagnosed the illness of his age in the autobiography he wrote during the Wilhelminian era: "Es is uns seit einer Reihe von Jahren zu gut gegangen (We had it too good for a number of years)...."

One of the main problems facing the decadents was that of combining their hatred of modern civilization with their love of the refinements that civilization had made possible.

(This is still very much of a problem, although some of today's revolutionaries seem to have solved it on the personal if not on the ideological level.) The decadents also faced the dilemma of squaring their langueur-Verlaine:

Je suis l'Empire à la fin de la dècadence—with their fascination with violence and revolutionary action. The indiscriminate assassinations and bombings carried out by the French anarchists found many admirers among both the decadents and the right-wing futurists. "What matter the victims, provided the gesture is beautiful," Laurent Tailhade wrote.

D'Annunzio's career as a writer progressed from descriptions of courtesans in modish clothes, luminous landscapes, and villas by the sea, to the most lavish praise of the freshness and joy of war. Having begun by calling on youth to abolish all moral restrictions, he ended as the prophet of moral regeneration and the poet laureate of Fascism. The list could be lengthened: Maurice Barrès made his way from the decadent movement to the Action Française; Johannes R. Becher, who in the early 1920s was known in Germany as the mad expressionist poet who had killed his girlfriend, was to become in later life Minister of Culture in Walter Ulbricht's East Germany.

If the youth movements of the early twentieth century arose, then in a milieu in which the sense of decadence was wide spread, they represented at the same time an attempt to overcome it. Their leaders were moralists, forever complaining about the evils of corporate guilt. Like all moralists, they exaggerated those evils, speaking out of the anti-historical perspective, which is a hallmark of the moralist.

For the study of history teaches that other periods have, broadly speaking, not been much better than one's own.

This is why the moralist and the revolutionary regard history as a reactionary discipline, the story of big failures and small successes. The study of history is a breeding ground of skepticism; the less the moralist knows of it, the more effectively will he pursue his mission with an untroubled conscience. Thomas Mann, pleading in a famous speech to German students in the 1920s for "aristocratic skepticism in a world of frenetic fools," was sadly out of touch with the mood of an audience longing for firm belief and certain truths.

If my remarks have indicated a certain ambivalence of feeling toward youth movements in general, it is because I have been trying to distinguish between the various ideas that they have espoused—ideas that are certainly deserving of criticism—and what I take to be of even greater significance is the depth of emotional experience that they have provided their members. (I say this as one who shared that experience at one stage in his life). Although I originally intended this as a statement about youth movements of the past, I now read in Martin Duberman's review of Christopher Lasch's new book, *The Agony of the American Left*: "I think what is most impressive about the radical young people is not their politics or their social theories, but the cultural revolution they have inaugurated—the change in life style."

The politics and culture of youth movements have always been a reflection of the Zeitgeist, a hodgepodge, often, of mutually exclusive ideas.

A proto-Nazi wrote about the unending and fruitless discussions of German youth movements in the 1920: Look at their leaders and their intellectual leapfrogging from Dostoevsky to Chuang Tze, Count Keyserling, Spengler, Buddha, Jesus, Landauer, Lenin, and whichever literary Jew happens to be fashionable at the moment. Of their own substance they have little or nothing.

There was, let's face it, more than a grain of truth in this criticism; a list of the main formative intellectual influences on the American movement would look even more incongruous. However, what was essential about the German youth movement, at least in its first phase, was not its "intellectual leapfrogging" and confused politics but something else entirely. The movement represented a form of opposition to a civilization that had little to offer to the young generation, a protest against the lack of vitality, warmth, emotion, and ideals in German society. As Hoelderlin had put it a hundred red years earlier: "It can conceive of no people more dismembered. . . . You see workmen but no human beings, thinkers but no human beings, priests but no human beings, masters and servants, youth and staid people, but no human beings. . . ." It wanted to develop qualities of sincerity, decency, and open-mindedness to free its members from petty egoism and careerism, to oppose artificial conventions, snobbery, and affectation. Its basic character was formless and intangible and its authentic and deepest experience was difficult to describe and perhaps impossible to analyze: the experience of marching together, of participating in common struggles, and of forming lasting friendships. There was, of course, much romantic exaltation as well, but although it is easier to ridicule the extravagances of this state of mind than to do it justice, the temptation should be resisted. Experiences of such depth are very serious matters indeed.

The nonpolitical phase of the German youth movement ended, roughly speaking, with the First World War. Summarizing the early phase, I wrote several years ago that "if lack of interest in politics could provide an alibi from history, the youth movement would then leave the court without a stain on its character." In retrospect, this judgment seems a trifle misplaced; the truth is that the movement was simply not equipped to deal with politics. Being romantic and opposed to "arid intellectualism," its thought was confused and its outlook illiberal. Oriented toward a mythic past and an equally mythic future, it was darkly suspicious of the values of the enlightenment—an attitude that did not have much to commend it in a country where the enlightenment had not met with conspicuous success anyway—and it was easily swayed in different directions by philosophical charlatans and political demagogues preaching all kinds of eccentric doctrines.

All this appeared very clearly in the second political phase of the German youth movement after the First World War. By 1930, the youth movement was displaying an incontinent eagerness to rid Germany of democracy. Almost all its members shared the assumption that anything at all would be better than the detested old regime. Lacking experience and imagination, they clearly misjudged the major political forces of their time. One of their leaders wrote the following much later:

We had no real principles. We thought everything possible. The ideas of natural law, of the inalienable rights of man, were strange to us. As far as our ideas were concerned we were in mid-air, without a real basis for our artificial constructions.

It was, in brief, not an intellectual movement, and any attempt to evaluate it at the cultural and political level alone will not do it justice; it moved on a different plane. The movement arose in response to a certain malaise; it attempted, without success, to solve the conflicts facing it, and it was, in retrospect, a splendid failure. With all its imperfections, it did succeed in inspiring loyalties and a deep sense of commitment among its members.

I am not sure whether today's youth movements such as they are (or will be) can achieve even this much. "People who screw together, glue together," claims the Berkeley SDS, but if that were true, the Roman Empire would still be in existence. Some time ago, I happened to meet with members of a radical pacifist communal settlement in upstate New York. This settlement had had its origins in the early German youth movement; its members were believing Christians who took their cue from the New Testament: "Ye cannot serve God and Mammon" and "the love of money is the root of all evil." Setting out to realize the ideal of social justice in their own lives, they established two settlements in Germany, moved to England in 1934, then to Paraguay, and finally to New York State. Still convinced that their way of life is the best of all possible ways, the surviving members have recently been trying to find supporters and active followers. On their tours of college campuses, they are invariably met with tremendous enthusiasm and a great show of willingness to join. Then, a few days after each appearance, they send a bus around to take prospective candidates for a tour of the settlement. No one shows up. One could argue that it is unfair to compare the depth of commitment and the ardor of present-day revolutionaries with that shown by those who challenged less permissive societies in bygone days. Where the nineteenth-century revolutionary risked the gallows or a lifetime in Siberia, the rebel of the 1960s risks a warning from some disciplinary committee. In these adverse circumstances, a breed of devoted revolutionaries is unlikely to arise. That may be finally all to the good, but I for one confess to a certain nostalgia for the breed.

It has been said of youth movements: blessed is the land that has no need of them. For a long time, America was such a land. In the nineteenth and early twentieth centuries, it alone among the major Western countries did not experience a widespread movement of generational conflict. The reasons for this are not particularly obscure. For one thing, the burden of the past was not felt as heavily in America as it was in Europe. Less distance separated parents and children, and teachers and students; adventurous young men went West, and the country was forever expanding; society as a whole was far less rigid. Then in the twentieth century, when these factors had ceased to be quite so important, America was spared a movement of youth revolt by a series of economic and foreign political crises. For it is a rule of youth movements that, like Kulturpessimismus, they prosper only against a background of rising affluence. Another rule appears to be that they cannot strike deep roots in a country whose general mood is basically optimistic.

America in the 1960s was a prosperous society, but it was no longer optimistic: the American dream has been lost on the way to affluence. It was, thus, in a sense inevitable that when the worldwide wave of youth revolt broke earlier in that decade, American youth should assume a leading role. However, the American situation is a complicated one, not only because it is accompanied by such factors as a general breakdown of authority, a crisis in the universities, and a widespread sense of cultural malaise, but also because of the response it has elicited in the society at large. (I am not speaking here of the black student revolt, because this is not a generational conflict but part of a wider movement for full political and social emancipation, and the success or failure of this movement will depend ultimately on the blacks themselves.)

Youth movements have come and gone, but never before has one been taken so seriously. Never in the past has an older generation been so disconcerted by the onslaught of the young. Previous generations of adults, more certain of their traditions and values, less ridden by feelings of guilt, have shown little patience with their rebellious sons and daughters. The middle-aged, middle-class parents of today clearly do not feel themselves to be in any such position of certainty. The milieu in which the youth of America have grown up bears striking resemblance to a past period in the European history, as described by Max Nordau:

"There is a sound of rending in every tradition and it is as though the morrow would not link itself with today. Things as they are totter and plunge, and they are suffered to reel and fall because man is weary, and there is no faith that it is worth an effort to uphold them. Views that have hitherto governed minds are dead or driven hence like disenthroned kings. Meanwhile interregnum, in all its terrors prevails and there is confusion among the powers that be . . . what shall inspire us? So rings the question from the thousand voices of the people, and where a market-vendor sets up his booth and claims to give an answer, where a fool or a knave begins suddenly to prophesy in verse or phrase, in sound or color, or professes to practice his art otherwise than his predecessors and competitors, there gathers a great concourse around him to seek in what he has wrought, as in Oracles of the Pythia, some meaning to be divined and interpreted. . . . It is only a very small minority who honestly find pleasure in the new tendencies, and announce them with genuine conviction as that which is sound, a sure guide for the future, a pledge of pleasure and of moral benefit. But this minority has the gift of covering the whole visible surface of society, as a little oil extends over a large area of the surface of the sea. It consists chiefly of rich educated people, or of fanatics. The former give the ton to all the snobs, the fools, and the blockheads; the latter make an impression upon the weak and dependent, and it intimidates the nervous. . . ."

Nordau's *Degeneration* is an exaggerated, polemical tract, but some of what he wrote about the malady of his age was pertinent. He realized correctly that ideas, books, and works of art exercise a powerful, suggestive influence far beyond the small circle of the avant-garde:

"It is from these productions that an age derives its ideals of morality and beauty. If they are absurd and anti-social, they exert a disturbing and corrupting influence on the views of a whole generation." The moral and esthetic ideals of today's avant-garde theater and cinema have certainly had their effect—as have the works of Jean Genet and Frantz Fanon.

The deliberate gibberish of some recent movies and novels finds its reflection in the involuntary gibberish of certain strands of youth politics; it has its parallel in certain aspects of the wider cultural revolution; the theater of the absurd is not unconnected with the politics of the absurd. Indeed, the crisis of rationality has had a powerful impact. Affirmation replaces analysis and argumentation; *fin de siècle* revolutionaries arrange happenings and call it a revolution, or discuss salon-Maoism before enthusiastic audiences and call it radical commitment.

Afraid to appear unfashionable or out of step with the avant-garde, those who ought to know better seem willing to take every idiocy seriously, trying to "understand" if not to accept.

The American youth movement, *Corruptio optimi pessima*, with its immense idealistic potential, has gone badly, perhaps irrevocably, off the rails. For this, a great responsibility falls on the shoulders of the gurus who have provided the ideological justification for the movement in its present phase—those intellectuals, their own bright dream having faded, who now strain to recapture their ideological virginity. There is perhaps some tragedy to be glimpsed in this endeavor of the old to keep pace with the young, but at the moment, one cannot permit oneself the luxury of a tragic sense. The doctors of the American youth movement are in fact part of its disease. They have helped to generate a great deal of passion, but aside from the most banal populism they have failed to produce a single new idea. Most of them stress their attachment to Marx. However, one needs to only read *The Eighteenth Brumaire* to find Marx's opinion on the value of Bohemianism in the revolutionary struggle, and his polemics against Bakunin leave little doubt as to his feelings with regard to the idea, first propagated one hundred years ago, of a coalition between lumpenproletariat and lumpenintelligentsia. Students should not be criticized for ignoring the lessons of the past and the dangers of chiliastic movements. They always do. The historical memory of a generation does not usually extend back very far, and the lessons of historical experience cannot be bequeathed by will or testament. However, their mentors do remember, and their betrayal of memory cannot be forgiven.

The American youth revolt was sparked off by Vietnam, by race conflict, and later on by the crisis of the university. At any point along the line, rational alternatives could have been formulated and presented. Instead, the movement preferred a total, unthinking rejection, and so became politically irrelevant. Yet, a revolution is in fact overdue in the universities. There is nothing more appalling than the sight of enormous aggregations of students religiously writing down pearls of wisdom that can be found more succinctly and profoundly put in dozens of books.

There is nothing more pathetic than to behold the proliferation of social-science nonsubjects in which the body of solid knowledge proffered stands usually in inverse ratio to the scientific pretensions upheld. Whole sections of the universities could be closed down for a year or two, and the result, far from being the disaster to civilization, which some appear to anticipate, would probably be beneficial. Unfortunately, this is about the last thing that is likely to happen, for it is precisely the nonsubjects, the fads, and the bogus sciences to which the "radicals" in their quest for social relevance are attracted as if by magnetic force. As for the consequences of all this, one thing can be predicted with certainty: those to be most directly affected by the new dispensation in the universities will emerge from the experience more confused and disappointed than ever, and more desperate, in need of certain truths, firm beliefs.

An American youth movement was bound to occur sooner or later; youth revolt is a natural phenomenon, which is part of the human condition. However, the particular direction the American movement would take was not at all foreordained, and it is, therefore, doubly sad that in its extreme form it has taken a destructive course, self-defeating in terms of its own aims.

It seems fairly certain at this point that the American movement will result in a giant hangover, for the more Utopian a movement's aims, the greater the disappointment which must inevitably ensue. The cultural and political idiocies perpetrated with impunity in this permissive age have clearly gone beyond the borders of what is acceptable for any society, however liberally it may be structured. No one knows whether the right-wing backlash, so long predicted, will in fact make its dreadful appearance; perhaps, we shall be spared this reaction. It is more likely that there will be a backlash from within the extremist movement itself, as ideas and ideologies undergo change and come into conflict with underlying attitudes. Insofar as those attitudes are intolerant and irrational, they will not quickly mellow, and for that reason, America is likely to experience a great deal more trouble with its enragés.

The American youth movement of the 1960s, infected by the decadence of the age, missed the opportunity to become a powerful agent of regeneration and genuine social and political change. However, decadence, contrary to popular belief, is not necessarily a fatal disease. It is a phase through which many generations pass at various stages of their development. The boredom that gives rise to decadence contains the seeds of its own destruction, for who, after a time, would not become bored with boredom?

2012

More than forty years have passed since the heyday of the events alluded to in this article. The rebels of the 1960s and '70s are now retired or will reach this stage in their life very soon. What is the legacy of the children of the sun and the age of Aquarius? To look for its traces, one has to turn to the cultural field rather than to politics. But cultural tastes too have changed contemporary youth, music differs substantially from that of the bygone age and students today have only a vague idea of what a hippie was or a beatnik, and their psychedelic interests are limited. True, present day youngsters favor peace over war as much as the flower children of yesteryears. As these lines are written, marijuana has become legal in the District of Columbia but their political interests are much less pronounced. Given a difficult situation and unemployment (and a high and rising cost of a college education), priorities have changed.

Young Germany

Barbara Stambolis (ed.), Jugendbewegt Gepraegt. Essays zu Autobiographischen Texten von Werner Heisenberg, Robert Jungk und Vielen Anderen. V&R Unipress. Goettingen, 2013. 819pp Eur. 59.99.

During the siege of Mafeking in the Second Boer War in early 1900, the "Mafeking Cadet Corps" was established and this, as every Boy Scout and former Boy Scout knows, was the origin of a movement that eventually spread all over the globe and still has millions of members. In the same year, a Berlin student named Karl Fischer became the head of a group of ramblers at a high school in the Berlin suburb of Steglitz. This was the beginning of a movement named *Wandervogel*. Though confined to German speaking countries, it has entered the annals of history as a phenomenon of considerable interest that helped to shape the character of two generations.

Both Boy Scouts and Wandervogel were addicted to rambling, camping, woodcraft, and generally speaking, the desire to escape big city life and be closer to nature. There were essential differences: Baden-Powell, the founder of the Boy Scouts, was the youngest colonel in the British army at the time, but he was still forty-three years of age at the time of Mafeking, whereas Karl Fischer was a mere nineteen. The Boy Scouts wanted to give young people from all social classes what was often missing in family life and schools, an education toward self reliance and good citizenship. The Wandervogel and its successor groups were an elite movement of young people who wanted to be among contemporaries, not supervised and led by adults. It was patriotic with quite often an admixture of religion. The Boy Scouts favored brass bands, and the Germans believed in folk songs and dances (shawms, guitars, recorders, and drums came in only later on).

Rambling had been an important feature of German romanticism, almost a way of life; it appears as a prominent motive in Schubert's songs, in the pictures of Caspar David Friedrich, in folksongs that were rediscovered at this time, and in countless novels. However, it was also an act of defiance against the restrictions of city life and the stifling climate of Wilhelmian society.

The Wandervogel (and its post-World War One descendants, the *Buende*) were more ambitious and gradually they became more rebellious, whereas, the Boy Scouts were very much pragmatic. The symbol of the Wandervogel in its early days was the blue flower symbolizing the romantic longings so movingly given expression by Novalis and Eichendorff a century earlier on. It expressed a longing for a different, better world, for more friendship, and love in a society very much devoid of it. It stood for inner truthfulness (part of the famous Hohe Meissner formula of 1913 [about which more below]) and a cultural renaissance. It demanded radical reforms in society and life in general, including for some even the attitude to food and drink. It was at this time that the first "reform" (organic food) shops came into being. Lieutenant General Baden-Powell and his followers had no such far-reaching reform aims.

There were some girls and young women among those who came to the Hohe Meissner in 1913, but they were inconspicuous, except perhaps at the time of dancing, which was part of the program; not one of the many speeches made at the occasion was held by a female member of the Wandervogel, which was essentially a male creation for males. This trend became even more pronounced during the second postwar phase of the German youth movement. After 1918, the various Buende (as the components of the movement were now called) became even more elitist; their ideal was no longer the romantic dreamer but the medieval knight belonging to an order. They were not exactly a monastic order, nor were they jousting on horses, but like their medieval models, they believed in the code of chivalry and practiced heraldry with an emphasis on flags and various regalia. And just as there had not been female knights, there were hardly any female members of the Buende, except in the confessional groups that developed on the sidelines of the churches and the Jewish community.

Such separation of the sexes was, by no means, a specific German feature. To give another example—prior to the Stockholm Olympic games (1912), women did not participate in Olympic sports, and even at Stockholm, they were a small minority. (There were, to be precise, forty-seven women out of a total of 2,400 participants.) Opposition to female participation at the time came mainly from America rather than Germany. Schools too were not coeducational then, but in the case of the youth movement, the separation of sexes gave rise to speculation about the sexual orientation of the members of the movement. The theories concerning a homosexual motivation seem to have been exaggerated; it certainly existed but probably no more than outside the movement. The separation was part of the Zeitgeist and the assumption that at a certain age boys and girls seem to be more comfortable in the presence of their own sex than in mixed groups.

The present volume appears a hundred years after the meeting at the Hohe Meissner mountain, east of the city of Kassel. For the first and last time, a few thousand members of the various sections of the German youth movement gathered on this occasion. Among those who met were many who became famous in various fields in later years—politicians, poets, scientists, more than a few theologians as well as educators. Walter Benjamin was there but also the physicist Werner Heisenberg of the "uncertainty principle" fame. A future minister of culture of the Prussian government made an appearance but also a future minister of culture of the Communist DDR.

In brief, it was an interesting meeting; what became of the participants and their movement in later years? The present volume includes fairly detailed biographies of about seventy members (including two women) of the Wandervogel and its successor movements—among them Willy Brandt and Johannes Rau, a future President of Germany. At the same time, the book tries to find common denominators—did they have much in common, did their experiences as boys and girls (and later as students) in the youth movement influence their views and shape their character in later life? For a variety of reasons, this interesting question does not lend itself to indisputable conclusions. An honest answer would be as clear as one of the Sibylline oracles: *Vivit et non vivit*, it lived on but it did not.

The German youth movement was (or in any case believed to be) apolitical—some of its members moved to the Left including the Communists, more gravitated to the Right and even National Socialism. The Nazis in their turn despised the youth movement because of their utopian, neo-romantic aspirations and their desire to keep out of party politics. And it is true that the majority, even those who became Nazi fellow travelers in later years, were never deeply involved in politics. Perhaps, their years in the youth movement had persuaded them that according to an old German saying politics had a detrimental impact on character. It would not help creating a new, more sincere, more selfless new generation. There were shared memories and on occasion mutual help. But was the youth movement tradition more important than the old school tie?

Why—in contrast to the Boy Scouts—did the German youth movement change so much after 1918 and why did it virtually cease to exist after 1945? Probably, because the ambitions of the Scouts had been more modest and their expectations less far reaching. Furthermore, the impact of the First World War on a defeated country was much greater than in the Western countries. The certainties of the world of yesterday had vanished and radical solutions seemed far more plausible. This led to the downfall of the Weimar Republic and also the disappearance of the youth movement.

Before 1914, the focus had been on the individual; in later years, it was the collective that counted. But the collective too had not succeeded in what it had wanted to achieve. True, there are some groups in Germany even now that claim to continue the traditions of the youth movement. But they are hardly noticeable and seem not to attract a new elite. The environment too has changed what with fewer forests and other places to practice woodcraft. If the Greens in their early history were drawn toward nature, today's Pirates are far more attracted to hacking and computer games than the world of forests, bird song, flowers, and a full moon shining on enchanted old castles.

A project sponsored by the Shell company has investigated for many years the mood and desires of the young generation in Germany. It found far less dissatisfaction and a spirit of rebellion and more optimism in Germany than in other European countries. It is open to question how much of the contentment prevails after the economic crisis of recent years. Perhaps, it does not matter that much because as a result of demographic trends all over Europe, the number of young people has considerably decreased.

However, with all this, it seems premature to write off the spirit of rebellion among young Germans. Its origins may now be quite different: the Wandervogel and its successors did not greatly worry about jobs and money. In their diaries and even more in their songs, they expressed their disdain of materialism; if only possible, they would have abolished money or even thinking about it. They believed in a simple, frugal life, and took it for granted that eventually they would find more or less congenial work and a place in society. The young people of today will have to carry a heavy burden connected with various debts and obligations incurred by earlier generations. Having reached a certain age they worry, for instance, about the housing situation, whether they will be able to move out of the parental home and to a place of their own. It is this prosaic fear, not the blue flower and romantic dreams that could generate the next youth revolt.

Part 2
Europe

Preface

As the twenty-first century was rung in, the mood in Europe was one of optimism. True, the European economy did not progress with giant steps and the advance toward political unity was slow but the general trend was positive.

A common currency had been introduced as the result of the Maastricht treaty in 1991 and several other important resolutions had been adopted (the so-called pillar system) aiming at a closer policy structure of the European Union (EU). True, in the years that followed there were certain setbacks; the new European Constitution was turned down in a number of countries including France and the Netherlands but on the other hand new members joined the EU or were about to join. Originally, there had been six; by 2012, the number of members of the EU had grown to twenty-seven. Its gross national product was 17 trillion dollars in 2012. And in the same year it received the Nobel Peace Prize.

It seemed only natural that in these years of relative prosperity a whole literature should come into being predicting that Europe's future was brilliant. Not China but Europe was the second superpower, its political system, its way of life were superior to all others (especially the American); it was the model for the rest of the world, not a great military power but a civilian superpower—its attraction was such that all others wanted to be part of it. As a British commentator put it—the twenty-first century would be Europe's. This theme appeared in many variations in books on Europe published in the United States at the time.

These to repeat, were the relatively good years in Europe. Europe's achievements were somewhat exaggerated by its well wishers in the United States; there was on the whole more triumphalism in the United States than in Europe where some uneasiness prevailed concerning the economic base of the welfare state. Perhaps American liberal attitudes had more to do with the shortcomings of the United States for instance in the field of social services than with the objective situation in Europe. Be that as it may, the encomiums heaped on Europe were many and could hardly be more laudatory. This did not of course refer to the conservatives for whom the welfare state was a socialist abomination—a fate worse than death. These opponents failed to understand that the essential social services in Europe had been accepted by the right as well as the left. Neither Mrs. Thatcher nor the German Christian Democrats would dream to abolish them.

For American Europhiles, those refusing to accept these new realities were shortsighted reactionaries for only such people could be hostile to the progressive European model. They failed to see the brittle foundations of the movement toward the EU. They grossly overrated the extent of European solidarity. There were some dissenting skeptical voices such as a book by the late Tony Judt (originally a number of lectures) in which he wrote that it was unlikely that a truly united Europe would emerge in the foreseeable future because Europe had not proceeded beyond the nation state toward a truly supranational government. Judt rightly thought that it was unwise to believe that the frequent invocation of the "promise of Europe" could substitute for solving problems and crises. But Judt was put in his place by Harvard's Stanley Hoffman as a "Jeremiad too fond of gloom and doom." Paradoxically, Judt took such criticism to heart and a few years later as the European situation deteriorated he reached the conclusion that the twenty-first century may after all belong to Europe.

But then—sometimes suddenly, sometimes gradually—the mood changed—well before the economic setbacks beginning in 2008. It is not easy to decide what precisely caused it. True, the economic performance of various European countries deteriorated. If in the early years of the new century Germany had been considered Europe's problem child, the German situation improved following a number of painful but necessary reforms, whereas it deteriorated in Southern and Western Europe. However, the economic difficulties were probably not the decisive ones as far as the change of mood, the growing skepticism in Europe was concerned. Time and again in international affairs it became clear that Europe was not a superpower, that its influence was declining, that others did not want to emulate the European example, that there was no European foreign policy let alone defense policy. Europe was highly dependent on energy supplies from outside but there was no serious determination to lessen this dependence that also had obvious political implications.

As these manifestations of weakness became clear, Euro-optimism waned. Some of the erstwhile enthusiasts turned skeptics or even pessimists envisaging a bleak future for Europe unless far reaching changes would take place. Others preferred to turn their attention to events in other parts of the globe. Lastly, there were those, not many in number, who despite all appearances fervently believed that Europe was still powerful and would become even stronger and that the current crises were no more than temporary setbacks.

My own views with regard to the future of the continent gravitated toward skepticism or, to be precise, Eurorealism. The European crisis as I saw was multiple in character. It had to do with the weakness of the European economy, but demographic trends were also prominently involved (the aging of the continent, the shrinking of its population, and at the same time the frequent lack of success in integrating the new immigrants). To a large extent it seemed to be a case of aboulia—a term coined by French psychiatrists in the nineteenth century to describe cases of lethargy, an absence of will.

Above all, there was the inability or unwillingness of most Europeans to make up their minds whether to move toward a truly united Europe, which would have involved surrendering many sovereign rights, or whether to prefer a loose federation of nation states that would have kept the right to take all important decisions concerning the future of their countries. What most Europeans apparently wanted resembled more the Latin American model rather than Paneuropa. I doubted whether a bit of unification and a bit of separatism could work. The decision to have a common currency could not work in the long run unless there was supervision and control from the center.

The title of a book of mine published in 2006 (*The Last Days of Europe*) did not of course mean that Europe would disappear without a trace like Pompeii following the eruption of Mount Vesuvius. But I suspected that the Europe my generation had known was on the way out and that the visions of Europe as a superpower belonged to the realm of fantasy as far as the foreseeable future was concerned.

These fears were shared by some—their number had grown by 2011 when *After the Fall* appeared—but others dissented, believing in a more positive outcome of the present crisis. Events since have shown that the fears were not unjustified and not exaggerated.

How to explain the continued Euro-optimism among American observers at a time when there seemed to be few facts to justify it? This is a subject that may preoccupy us for a long time to come. It could well be that the euro will be saved and also the Eurozone, simply because any other outcome would be too costly, perhaps disastrous. But this would be no safeguard against a collapse during a future crisis. There could be no true economic union without a much larger extent of political union. The stream of refugees to Europe in recent decades, most of them not political refugees had created difficulties of various sorts; it could well be that as a result of the economic crisis the attraction of Europe as a target of immigrants from Asia and Africa would be substantially reduced. (But there was a great deal of internal migration from South to North, from the countries suffering most from the recession to those less affected by it.) At the same time it would become more difficult to attract immigrants needed to keep the European economies going and the welfare state funded as the result of the shrinking overall working population.

It could be that the present crisis might act as a "federator" compelling Europe to adopt reforms that in normal periods would have been unthinkable. This has happened time and again in history especially if the change needed was difficult and painful. But the recognition that Europe faced a crisis of survival had not yet been widely accepted and but for recognizing this, far reaching change was not to be expected. As these lines are written, the markets have calmed down a bit, no country has collapsed so far (as was feared at one time) and the feeling has been growing that Europe may not only survive but recover. But a recovery within what limits? Euro-enthusiasm certainly has not grown. According to the semi official Eurobarometer (May 2012), a majority of Europeans—52 percent—felt no attachment to Europe. This is a new record; there had always been some resistance against Brussels and all it stood for. But in the past it had not exceeded 30–40 percent. As these lines are written, it seems that while the Euro might be saved at least for the time being, the chances for closer European unity are less than brilliant. To overcome the resistance, a deeper and more threatening crisis might be needed.

A strong case can be made for optimism in politics. But for such a belief it is unlikely that Europe will get out of its present depression and regain the political will needed to move ahead. Europe immersed in whining and complaining will not be in a position to do so. But to move forward Euro-optimism must not distance itself too much from realities. It needs hope and a vision but a vision rooted in realities rather than wishful thinking.

Preface

Counterfactual History

My views with regard to this genre are mixed. Many of the imaginary alternatives could never have happened and in any case why deal with events that never took place? But the belief that what happened was bound to happen is deeply rooted and it is certainly not true.

Most of the disasters affecting Europe in the last century (and eventually the whole world) have their origin in the First World War. But the war of 1914–1918 was not inevitable. The arguments that the arms race between Germany and its enemies (and the naval race between Britain and Germany) made an armed conflict in the long run virtually inescapable are not persuasive. There was the traditional conflict between Germans and Slavs—but neither side was particularly eager to acquire new territories in Europe or new colonies. France wanted Alsace-Lorraine back, which had been lost to Germany following the defeat of 1870/1. But it is doubtful whether it would have gone to war for it and it would not have had the support of its allies. Would America have been drawn into European and world affairs but for World War One? But American intervention in Europe was only short lived at the time—as soon as the First World War was over it did what it could to detach itself. Isolationism was still going strong.

Without the First World War, there would have been neither Communism nor Fascism. True, the Tsarist regime was weak and Russia faced something akin to a revolutionary situation. But it still took three years of war, major defeats, and much suffering until the revolutions of 1917 occurred. It seems quite likely that the Tsarist regime would not have lasted, nor the German semi-authoritarian monarchy. There might have been a revolution in Russia but not one headed by the Bolsheviks. Political change in Russia and Germany might have taken decades and there is no saying what the outcome would have been—perhaps a constitutional monarchy, perhaps something else. The Austro-Hungarian multinational empire would probably not have lasted either. But there could have been a peaceful transition toward a commonwealth of nations, which after all shared many interests.

Without the first world war, the Second would have been highly unlikely. One could go further: Even if the Nazis would have come to power, another world war was not inevitable, if the bullet that killed Scheubner-Richter who walked next to Hitler at the famous protest march to the Feldherrnhalle in Munich in November 1923 would have hit the Fuehrer there would probably not have been a war. For neither the Nazi leadership nor the supreme military command with all their aggressive ambitions felt sufficiently confident and ready to engage in such an adventure. It has been the fashion for a long time to play down the importance of individuals in history but the case of Adolf Hitler points in a different direction. It seems that only Hitler's fanaticism, single-mindedness and megalomania made the Second World War a certainty. Mussolini on his own might have engaged in minor adventures such as the invasion of Ethiopia or Albania but hardly in anything more ambitious.

Would Japan have dared to attack in 1941, but for the fact that its enemies were (or would be) immersed in a war in Europe? It is unlikely that the European colonial powers would have been able to hold on for many more years to their possessions in Asia and Africa, but the process of decolonization would probably have taken place gradually, over a longer period.

On the other hand, it is extremely doubtful that but for the Second World War with all its horrors and devastation the movement toward a united Europe, such as it is, would have come under way. All of which tends to show that questions concerning the what might have happened are by no means altogether idle.

European Futures

What will Europe be like in fifteen, twenty, and thirty years from now? The question has been asked and answered many times. The predictions cannot possibly be entirely right, and this for a number of obvious reasons, for the situation in Europe depends also on events in other parts of the world—in America, Russia, and China, on the consequences of a war in the Middle East (if such a war should break out) as well as on other circumstances. It is an equation with too many factors.

Paradoxically, it is usually easier to predict long term than short-term trends in Europe. Why? Because in the short term almost anything might happen, whereas in the long term the possibilities are more limited. Not all the seemingly dramatic events of the next few years will have a lasting impact—the long-term consequences of a war in the Middle East might be less dramatic than we think, and the same refers, to give other examples to the outcome of elections in America or a power struggle in the Far East.

True, the economists have many sophisticated models for analysis and prediction. But as one of them recently put it—the ultimate causes of the slowdown in the economy are really psychological and sociological—difficult or even impossible to quantify.

All that can be reasonably done is to deal in broad outline with the most likely trends.

The emphasis in looking ahead should be on political trends. True, the economic factors, the debt crisis, and the other present difficulties are most urgent and have to be resolved one way or another. But inasmuch as the future of Europe and the unity of Europe are concerned it appears that Jean Monnet was right. He is the man who more than anyone else was responsible for the United Europe project during and after the Second World War. Many years after he said: If I had to start again, I would begin the movement towards a European federation with the emphasis on cultural rather than economic factors. When he mentioned "culture" he had of course something far broader in mind than poetry or painting.

In the early postwar years a Coal and Steel Union seemed the most likely basis for cooperation. There were obvious common interests. But as the movement toward a united Europe continued and became more ambitious it appeared that the economic factors could lead only to an economic union but not much beyond. Furthermore, as the fate of the Euro has shown, without greater political federation close economic cooperation could not work. But there was no agreement within and between the countries of Europe whether greater political federation was indeed desirable.

Jean Monnet, the French politician who always remained in the background was an economist and a businessman—his family owned an important cognac company in southwest France. But he was aware from the very beginning of the limits of economic cooperation.

In August 1943, in a speech to the French National Committee in London (France Libre, the de Gaulle movement), he said: There will be no peace in Europe if the states are reconstituted on the basis of national sovereignty. The countries of Europe are too small to guarantee their peoples the necessary prosperity and social development. The European states must constitute themselves into a federation.

These words were prophetic. True, there has been peace in Europe—except in its backyard, the Balkans. Not because Europeans had all become pacifists but because they had become too weak to conduct and endure an extended war. The European states took some steps toward a federation and made progress toward prosperity and social development. It could also be argued that it was not at all certain that Monnet's ideas to base a European federation initially on "culture" would have succeeded. Was there enough European solidarity, sufficient feeling of common values to lead the continent toward a United States of Europe? We all know about the strong centrifugal trends not only between the countries of Europe but also within them. Was the idea of a common foreign and defense policy at all realistic? Was it by accident that all previous federal movements in Europe had failed—most recently, Count Coudenhove-Kalergi's Paneuropa in the 1920s and 1930s? Many agreed with him but nothing came of it.

It was also Jean Monnet who said that the crises are the great federators in history. Important, far reaching decisions (especially painful ones) are taken only if the situation is very bad. If there was progress toward a European Union (EU) in the last century it came as the result of a major crisis—the Second World War. It persuaded Europeans that close economic cooperation was in everyone's best interest. But it was not sufficiently traumatic to go beyond this. The belief in national sovereignty proved stronger than the idea of a European federation. Hence the current crisis . . .

The causes of the economic crisis—the debt crisis, the Euro crisis are well known—it was mainly the attempt to make a great economic step forward without having first established the political preconditions. The various initiative to get out of the economic mess—whether by cutting and saving or by spending thus giving a major impetus to economic growth have been widely discussed. But our concern here is with the future of Europe—will it move toward closed unity or is the opposite likely to happen.

Most of the participants in the debate about the Euro and the Eurozone are economists or business people which in view of the gravity of the crisis is understandable. But the root of the problem is a wider one for even if the Euro will be saved and the Eurozone will survive for the time being, this will leave open the issue of federalism and European unity. Assuming that following massive intervention by the European Central Bank (ECB) under the leadership of Mario Draghi, the Euro and the Eurozone will survive the basic problems that will persist and the conflict between national sovereignty and the United States of Europe. If the European institutions will be greatly strengthened by reforming the Economic and Monetary Union and imposing budgetary discipline, this will make the Eurozone more competitive, it will stabilize banks, control state budgets, debts and deficits. All this is very important but it will not make for a stronger Europe which will still remain as a former Belgian foreign minister (Eyskens) put it "a political dwarf and a military worm." It may not even prevent another deep economic crisis in the not too distant future.

Such reforms may be essential for the survival of a common market but to make them lasting and to transform them into stepping stones to a European federation, something more far reaching akin to a revolution will be needed. For it will imply profound changes in mentality: A far greater readiness to surrender national sovereign rights—a near-total break with the past.

There are no indications that there is a readiness to do so at the present time.

All polls show that a majority, even a great majority, of the European public opposes the surrender of traditional institutions and rights of (in many cases) thousand years of history. It is not just a matter of euroscepticism—doubts concerning the efficiency of a Brussels bureaucracy—it is a matter of the basic foundations of national existence, of patriotism, national solidarity, and so on. It would be as some see it a matter of virtual surrender of most national values amounting to national suicide.

There have been situations in the history of nations in which such willingness existed, but they have been rare, usually this happened in conditions of utter despair. When France was about to be defeated in the Second World War, Winston Churchill proposed a virtual union of the two countries which was accepted by the British war cabinet. According to this document, France and Britain would no longer be two nations but one, the British and the French would have the same nationality. But the resolution was overtaken by events. France was defeated and surrendered. It was an example of an attempted union born out of despair.

Far reaching, radical decisions affecting the fate of nations are almost always taken facing a clear and present danger, for only in such situations is there a motive strong enough to opt for radical change.

But the crisis facing Europe at the present time is not yet of the same gravity; there seems to be no immediate danger of a collapse. It may well be extremely dangerous but it is a creeping crisis, the factor of immediacy is missing. A famous British literary figure (Dr. Johnson) once noted that nothing clears the mind of an individual as much as the certainty that he (or she) will be hanged within a day or two. But if the date of execution is not that close there is always the hope that something will occur to make the sad fate less certain and as a result the clearing of the mind will not take place.

It is difficult to think of events which may soon solve the problems of the debt-ridden countries. But it is also true that in history, bankrupt countries have not only survived but also recovered (most recently Argentine in 1999–2002) and similar hope persists today. There is a hope that the more affluent countries of Northern Europe, above all Germany will bail out the less fortunate Southern European countries, not perhaps because of strong feelings of solidarity but because a breakdown of the Eurozone would cause them much harm. And once the present crisis is overcome what with the upturn of the business cycle there will be fresh growth and all might turn out well. The United States after the end of the Second World War (and again toward the end of the last century) were heavily indebted but managed to flourish during the years after.

How realistic are such expectations? One does not know. But they are not unthinkable. In history, some attempts to create a common currency have failed, but a few have succeeded and it took the dollar 120 years to be finally accepted.

But if an economic recovery of sorts is not impossible, it leaves essential questions open. Will such a recovery take place within the entire present Eurozone—or a smaller one? Will it be possible without a far larger measure of federalism and surrender of sovereign rights and will there be sufficient popular support? Who will be the decision takers in a reformed United Europe?

A number of declarations demanding "more Europe" were made last September (2011). One was the annual report of Jose Manuel Barroso, head of the European commission, calling for a "new thinking for Europe" which had become necessary in view of the prevailing crisis of confidence. Globalization demands more European unity. More unity demands more integration. Barroso proposed a "decisive deal for Europe" safeguarding the irreversibility of the Euro. Barroso stressed sustainable growth, and the completion of the single market through a new Single Market Act. He wants to reduce Europe's energy dependence, etc. He stands for political progress in the direction of radical surrender of national sovereignty. Barroso also demanded more democracy mentioning it not less than eleven times in his speech. But what if there was not sufficient support for such surrender?

The same dilemma appeared in a statement by the foreign ministers of Germany and Poland ("A new vision of Europe") a few days later. They were summarizing the deliberations of a group of eleven foreign ministers about the future of Europe. For Europe to be a really strong actor and global leader, it needed a strong institutional setup, a streamlined and efficient system for the separation of powers. Also needed were a directly elected European Commission president who personally appointed the members of the European government—his cabinet—and a European Parliament with two chambers and with the powers to initiate legislation.

This vision amounts to a new EU. But it left open the all important questions of the division of power. There will be national governments and a European government, national and European laws, national armies but also a European army. Will the national or the European have the final, decisive say?

The intentions of the visionaries might be admirable, a great ideal. But is it what Europeans want? The prevailing mood of Europe has been thoroughly investigated—by Eurobarometer, Pew and other specialists engaging in public opinion polls for many years. The mood in Europe is pessimist at this time, considerably more so than in the United States even though America faces broadly speaking the same problems Europe does and the American debt is huge.

Europeans worry about unemployment, the future of their children, and rising prices. Sometimes these worries have little to do with realities—according to Pew 93 percent of Greeks are concerned about rising prices even though there is hardly any inflation in that country (the rate is little more than 2 percent); 62 percent of the Czechs worry about their public debt even though the ratio of their debt to the GDP (gross domestic product) is smaller than in most European countries.

But our concern is with political rather than economic issues. With few exceptions (Germany), Europeans doubt the competence of their leaders and have little trust in them; the faith in the leadership has been sinking. But they trust Brussels even less. Some of the results of the polls are seemingly a paradoxical. While there is a major concern about the national debt, there is not much support for policies to reduce it such as austerity measures. Among the countries in which faith in the leadership is very low are Poland and the Czech Republic, even though "objectively" these countries have not done particularly badly under their leadership.

Support for Angela Merkel, the German chancellor is considerably higher outside Germany (although inside Germany she is also doing quite well). Reports about growing European Germanophobia seem to be exaggerated. Resistance to further bail outs to countries in need is greater in Britain (62 percent) and France (56 percent) than in Germany (48 percent). The reports and comments widely broadcast in the media that the split in Europe is according to religious lines (Northern Protestants versus Southern Catholics seems equally exaggerated).

The economic crisis has not led so far to the dramatic rise of extremist parties of the left or the right and political upheaval. But this could change if the situation deteriorates. Anti-immigration parties have made some progress in some countries and populism has become more fashionable in some circles but this has not amounted so far to a decisive change in the political landscape.

More significant has been the erosion of support for the EU and its institutions over the last years. It was always below 50 percent in

Britain but it has substantially declined in most other countries—for instance, by twenty points in Spain and Italy during the last five years. Even in a country such as France, 63 percent now believe that European integration had a negative impact on the national economy.

This inevitably leads to the question whether membership in the EU is a good thing or bad in the view of Europeans. Britain was always divided on this issue but in recent years other countries have become equally divided; 54 percent reached a negative view in Spain, 48 percent in France, and in Eastern Europe too the initial European enthusiasm has waned.

Many of these polls took place before the crisis reached its height. Since then the negative trends have continued and even intensified. If there is so much doubt about a European federation even in their present loose form, how much enthusiasm is there for a much closer political unity? In view of the current European mood, the prospects for the realization of a new vision of Europe seem dismal.

But there are two considerations which make it less likely that there will be a total unraveling of the present day EU. While a collapse remains possible, it seems more likely that the European core will survive and that perhaps after an interval a new attempt will be made to proceed on the road to a United States of Europe. Firstly, the great cost of a disintegration of Europe in its present form and secondly, the well-known fact that moods tend to change.

No one knows for certain what the short-term consequences of the dissolution of the Eurozone would be. But it is certain that they will not be cheap. According to some estimates, the cost will be close to 20.000 Euros per household in the richer European countries, about half that sum in the poorer. There is sentimental pressure for a return to the Deutschmark, the franc, the peseta, and even the drachma. But the price will be high and the long-term consequences are uncertain.

More important yet are the imponderabilia, the factors that cannot be quantified and predicted. The present mood in Europe may be one of doubt, fear, and pessimism. But such moods have existed quite frequently and they have changed—sometimes for reasons that seem obvious in retrospect—and sometimes for reasons which are not clear at all. At the end of the Second World War, the prevailing mood in Europe—particularly in Germany was one of despair. Many thought that after the great devastation the continent would never rise again. Yet within ten years the famous miracle took place and everyone was optimistic again. The reasons were obvious. The material damage had been exaggerated and following a real effort all over Europe a spectacular recovery took place and major steps were taken toward closer cooperation.

France after the defeat by Germany in 1870/71 was in truly bad shape. Books appeared with the title *Finis Galliae*—the country was not only militarily defeated but also it was claimed to be corrupt to the core, decadent, doomed to go under. This negative, pessimistic mood lasted for about two decades and then for no obvious "objective" reasons the mood changed to optimism (the building of the Eiffel Tower as an example of the new mood), aggressive patriotism, a great, perhaps exaggerated, hope in the future of the country. No one knows why this sea change took place.

Could there be a similar recovery in the years to come in Europe?

Seen from a perspective of winter 2012/13, the prospects are not brilliant. An economic upturn (perhaps after a further deepening of the crisis) is possible. But a mental revolution, a profound change in basic attitudes, a breakthrough in the direction of a United States of Europe seems far less likely. Nationalism has proved so much stronger. And even if it should occur it would not necessarily mean the emergence of Europe as a superpower. It is unlikely but it is not impossible. What could generate it? To repeat once again: Most likely a deep existential crisis.

It is unlikely that Europe in the years to come will make significant progress toward political unification. It is equally unlikely that there will be a total breakdown, a return to the Europe before 1939. Too many have to lose too much if such came to happen.

Most likely, therefore is a prolonged period of muddling through—of trying to strengthen the center (Brussels) a little—but not too much—for instance, by greater oversight over the banking system thus creating greater stability on the continent. Muddling through could save the Euro temporarily, but it will not prevent future crises. No one can say with any certainty what will happen once the policy of muddling through comes to an end—it depends to a large extent from events in other parts of the world.

What can be predicted with a large degree of confidence is that the years to come will be difficult for all of Europe, not only the countries immediately threatened by various economic disasters, unemployment, and so on. Even the countries which seem to be at present in relatively good shape have to be concerned. Some have demanded that Germany should either take the lead in Europe—or leave it. But if it will take the lead, it will be accused of imperial ambitions and if it refuses to do so it will be charged with national egoism, lack of solidarity, and isolationism. Human memory is notoriously brief. Very often it is forgotten that seven years ago Germany was considered economically the sick man of Europe and its recovery is of very recent date.

The economic crisis has pushed into the background other basic dangers threatening the continent—the demographic challenges, a declining birthrate, immigration which is needed but is not integrated and often contributes little to the welfare of society. But these problems as well as many others will not go away—they are long-term dangers, whereas the debt crisis is clear and present.

Europe is not doomed, even if at the present time it may be difficult to predict what could generate its recovery. But one should never underrate the dangers facing other parts of the world. Europe will not be a superpower in the years to come, not even a "civilian superpower." But since most Europeans believe that power is no longer very important in the contemporary world, they have accepted this and it is causing no great unhappiness. May there be no rude awakening.

Night Thoughts on Europe

This is not the ideal time to write about the state of Europe and its prospects what with so many crises confronting it and the uncertain future of this and other continents. True, I learned long ago that a crisis is the period between two other crises, but the present crisis is considerably deeper and could be fateful.

My memories of Europe go back to a childhood in Weimar Germany, and growing up in the Nazi Third Reich. I left Germany shortly before the outbreak of the Second World War. I have returned after the war for many short visits and some long stays, I have been to most European countries and it has been one of my fields of study. My children went to school on both sides of the Atlantic. European culture has been the formative influence in my life, that of the past admittedly more than the present. Thus, I had the good fortune to benefit from a variety of global perspectives. When I look out of our windows in Washington DC, I can see the raccoons and squirrels on the trees of Rock Creek Park, when I look out of our apartment in Highgate, London, I see the squirrels of Waterlow Park, and in winter, when the leaves are down, the grave of Karl Marx.

Having seen Europe and the Europeans in good times and bad, the time may have come for a summing up. I tried to do so some five years ago in a book entitled *The Last Days of Europe*. This referred to the passing of an Europe I had known. The reception was skeptical in part, the views I expressed were unfashionable, the book certainly came too early. According to a wide consensus, the twenty-first century belonged to Europe, the civilian superpower which would be envied and emulated by all others.

Five years can be no more than a minute in history but it can also be a long, long time. When the book first appeared it was widely believed that, all things considered, Europe, and especially the European Union (EU), was not doing badly at all. Had it not progressed to a common currency? The reviewer in the *Economist*, my bible among the weeklies, blamed my book for "unduly apocalyptic conclusions." And now I see that a recent editorial about the future in the same journal is entitled "staring into the abyss."

But I had not stared into the abyss at the time and I am not now. I was merely considering the possibility of Europe turning into a museum or cultural theme park for well-to-do tourists from East Asia. Not a heroic or deeply tragic future, but not my idea of an abyss or apocalypse either. True, at the time I was dealing more with the long-term challenges facing Europe such as for instance, the demographic trends. More recently, as the result of the global recession and especially the European debt crisis, the immediate dangers have been in the foreground. This is only natural, for the collapse of banks, austerity budgets, rising unemployment are clear and present dangers affecting everyone, whereas long-term threats can be pushed aside. There is always a chance that they may not happen.

With all this I feel uneasy facing the apocalyptic utterances of yesterdays Euro-enthusiasts spreading panic, having turned into prophets of unmitigated doom. This for two reasons: It simply is not true that the present crisis is entirely the fault of Keynes and the Social Democrats. Keynes has been dead for a long time and no major European country but Spain has been ruled by Social Democrats for years. (This was written before the fall of the Zapatero government and the electoral victory of the Socialists in France.) But the financial markets have been going strong and, to put it mildly, not functioning too well. The postwar generations of European elites aimed to create more democratic societies. They wanted to reduce the extremes of wealth and poverty and provide essential social services. They had quite enough of unrest and war. For several decades, many European societies had more or less achieved these aims and had every reason to be proud of this. Europe was quiet and civilized, no sounds of war or civil war either.

When and why did things go wrong? At a certain period, the European idea began to lose steam. It was based on the assumption of permanent economic growth and it did not take into account the problem of aging European societies. Once growth stalled and people lived longer, the base of the scheme was eroded. It was a difficult problem but not a lethal one. The experience of some of the smaller European countries has shown that reforms are possible and that while benefits have to be reduced and abuses harshly be dealt with, a welfare state keeping its essential services can survive. Basic mistakes were made in other respects such as the accumulation of debts, the belief that an economic-financial union could be established in the absence of a political union.

But with all the importance of the economic crisis it is only part of our story and, for all one knows, not the decisive one. Underlying it was a lack of European identity and values, of national interests prevailing over a common European interest. It is a crisis of solidarity, of leadership and above all political will. It appeared that internal integration at home had largely failed as shown for instance by events in Britain in July 2011.

For years, European elites had been living in a state of denial. They wanted more democracy but were surprised and unprepared when it appeared that the erosion of authority was leading to anarchy. The elite, the media, and to a considerable extent public opinion had become oblivious to the darker aspects of domestic affairs, ignoring also the growing disparity in income and property and the effects of youth unemployment. With regard to foreign affairs they had come to believe (as Robert Cooper put it) in peaceful interdependence and modern cooperation. Power politics was a thing of the past. But the policy of the rest of the world was rooted in ideas of traditional spheres of influence and balance of power. In the meantime, the enthusiasm for Europe waned among a large segment of public opinion.

Such lethargy and false optimism and the subsequent collapse of illusions were bound to lead to dejection. Had Europe still a future? Would it still exist in a decade from now? Or would it revert to what it had been before—a mere geographical concept? One is reminded of Prince Metternich's famous letter in 1847 to the Austrian ambassador in Paris in which he said that Italy was a "useful geographical concept" but had no reality as a political concept.

True, at about the same time Carlo Alberto Amedeo, King of Sardinia, in an equally famous aside said *Italia fara da se* (Italy will take care of itself). One hundred and sixty years later and considering the present state of Italy, it is still not clear whether Metternich was right or the King of Sardinia. The present state and the future prospects of Europe resemble those of Italy at that time: Will Europe be able to take care of itself?

A year or two later, in 1849, the year of the "spring of nations," a peace congress took place in Paris. The main address given by Victor Hugo, the most famous author of the time, announced that:

> *A day will come when you, France—you, Russia—you, Italy—you, England—you, Germany—all of you, nations of the Continent, will, without losing your distinct qualities and your glorious individuality, be blended into a superior unity, and constitute an European fraternity.... A day will come when the bullets and bombshells will be replaced by votes, by the universal suffrage of nations, by the venerable arbitration of a great Sovereign Senate, which will be to Europe what the Parliament is to England, what the Diet is to Germany, what the Legislative Assembly is to France.*

One hundred and sixty years have passed since this noble vision was enounced; a European Parliament of sorts has come into being, but not exactly a European Brotherhood, and one suspects that Victor Hugo would still not be too happy with the present state of Europe.

Pondering the future of Europe, one is reminded of Raymond Aron's *In Defense of Decadent Europe* published in the 1950s and the debate it triggered off. Despite his native pessimism, Aron did not believe that decadent Europe would fall victim to the superior ideological attraction of Communism and the economic, military, and political power of the Soviet Union.

Present day challenges to Europe are different in character: Neither Islamism nor Chinese Neo-nationalism nor Russia's Putinism present serious ideological challenges.

China might be the object of envy as far as its economic progress is concerned and the phenomenal growth of its exports. But for good reason it does not export its ideology, even though the Chinese critique of European (and American) democracy should be taken seriously, meaning a system that seems to be unable to push through necessary, long overdue but unpopular measures to improve the economic situation. Furthermore, the Western awe of the rising superpowers all too often ignores the immense difficulties that will be facing the BRIC (Brazil, Russia, India, and China) countries in the years to come.

With all his sympathy for liberal Europe, Aron was aware of the process of decadence (or decline to use a more value free term) which set in with the First World War and accelerated with the Second. The reasons are known, the devastations of the two world wars, the great bloodletting, Fascism, and Communism. By the 1950s and 1960s, Europe had largely recovered in the material sense, it was better off than ever before. But it had not recovered its self confidence. True, there was much talk about common European values, but in truth consumerism and materialism (not of the philosophical variety) as a way of life were certainly more important factors.

And yet, students of history know all too well that the subject of decline in history has to be approached with caution and there have been many false prophecies. There have been incidents not only of survival but of recovery of countries and continents and civilizations that had been given up. When Western Rome fell, it was generally assumed that the eastern part of the Roman Empire was also doomed, but Byzantium survived for another thousand years. To refer again to the French nineteenth-century experience: After the defeat by the Prussians in 1870/1, the general view in France was that "Finis Galliae" had arrived, that in view of the shrinking population, general defeatism, the lack of patriotism, and self respect as well as social evils such as alcoholism and what was then called "eroticism," France was finished, never to rise again. And yet, within thirty years the situation radically changed, decadence became unfashionable, it was largely replaced by militarism and even chauvinism, the Eiffel tower was built, sport was discovered and became popular, and France was herself again. More recently, it took Germany a mere fifteen years after the defeat in the First World War to reemerge as the strongest and most feared country in Europe. It took Russia, helped by the oil and gas bonanza, even less time to reemerge as a major power after the breakdown of the Soviet Union. Turkey in the 1980s and 1990s was anything but an optimistic country. But then within a few years the mood changed from pessimism to self confidence, even *hubris*, the aspiration of attaining even superpower status. The change had to do with the rise of a new elite and this sufficed, at least temporarily, to inspire wide sections of the population—never mind the fact that the optimism rested on shaky foundations: the weak infrastructure in Turkey, the price of oil and gas in Russia.

Could there be a similar swing in the mood of Europe? The continent is not rich in raw materials but depends on expensive imports. There is no religious or nationalist revival in sight (as in Turkey) or the appearance of a new political religion to provide a fresh impetus. It would be unfair to conclude that the continent has become lazy, but it certainly has become inward looking, lethargic, lacking curiosity and enterprise. There is nothing wrong with the desire to enjoy life, but it is disconcerting if this is accompanied with a lack of interest in the future.

Sometimes in history, profound changes have come with the rise of a new generation, the eternal lucky chance of mankind in Buber's words. But young generations have also produced great mischief in Europe such as the victories of Fascism and Communism which, initially at least, were movements of the young generation.

If there will be a rejuvenation of Europe it will come to a considerable extent from young people with a non-European background. But with notable exceptions, Europe has not been able to attract the best of them and there is no need to recapitulate in detail the great problems that have arisen in the integration of so many of the new immigrants. In any case, the youth cohort will be shrinking in Europe in the decades to come. The continent is aging as the result of low fertility and rising life expectancy. This means not only increasing pressure on the European health services and pension schemes but also, quite likely, a decline in the standard of living. At the same time, paradoxically massive youth unemployment is likely to persist and the young will also have to shoulder the burden of the massive debts accumulated in the past. A far smaller cohort of young people will have to work for the well being of a far larger group of the old.

Hence, the dire predictions of the covenant between the generations were replaced by generational conflict. Youth revolts have not been infrequent in the nineteenth-century Europe but they were mainly political, not social in character. More recently, rebellions of the young have taken place in France, Britain, Spain, and Greece. Will national (or European) solidarity be strong enough to withstand these pressures of the coming years?

A shrinking and aging of the population has certain benefits. It makes war between nations less likely. There will be less unemployment and less congestion on the roads. But internal conflicts of interest will probably grow stronger. If so, what hope is there for a change for the better in Europe? There is a chance of a major crisis generating the feeling of urgency and of renewed energy to carry out the radical reforms which have so far not been tackled. Historical experiences show that only deep crises, major clear and present dangers, did have such an effect. It was the crisis after the Second World War in Europe which generated the idea of an EU.

But there is no guarantee for such an outcome. The crisis may come too late, the decay may have gone too far and it may result in mere handwringing and deepening of despair rather than generating the energy needed for a new beginning. It is certain that Europe faces an existential crisis of this kind; its outcome is uncertain.

Many Europeans complain about a lack of democracy and they fear, rightly perhaps, that a Europe dominated by Brussels will be even less democratic. Few complain about a lack of leadership even though this is certainly as much needed if not more. For Europe has been drifting and it is not even clear in what direction.

How much democracy could there be in the word of tomorrow? The system of the old Polish Parliament with its *liberum veto* when the negative vote of one sufficed to bring any initiative to a halt certainly will not work. The last Lisbon treaty (2009) brought some change in this respect but in practice it has not changed that much. Germany and France got together to streamline the EU and to make the decision process quicker and more efficient and also to impose stricter regulations and controls. But it did not help much and there has not been full agreement between the two. Other countries did not like the attempts to remodel the EU in the image of France and Germany, however badly they needed help. But they, of course, had no alternative either.

The Asian political philosophers and statesmen were probably right when they told the Europeans that their more authoritarian model of governance will be more suitable to confront the tasks of the years to come. Europe, as they see it, is a spent force, essentially a customs union which never seriously intended to become a global force. They find it strange that Europe seems not to be aware of its modest role in world affairs and has not come to terms with it. Whether there will be one Europe, or a *Europe des patries* (in de Gaulle's phrase) or no united Europe at all, it will hardly be more democratic than at present. It will be increasingly difficult in the struggle for survival to maintain the present level of democratic freedoms.

As these lines are written, the headlines in the newspapers (many of which possibly on the way out) announce "The end of the European super state" and "Only Germany can save the Euro." But there never was an European superstate, not even the blueprint for one. Germany might indeed save the Euro, but it is doubtful whether it will be able and willing to save the Eurozone again in the next crisis unless there are radical reforms for which there are few indications at present.

But is a united Europe really needed? True, there are common interests but could not Latin America serve as a model? The countries of Latin America live in peace with each other and cooperate to a certain extent, they have established a common market of sorts (Mercusur) providing free transit of goods and a customs union. Two hundred years ago, Simon Bolivar had more ambitious plans for unifying the continent but his vision collided with Latin American realities and it was not to happen even though these countries had much more in common than Europe, even, with the exception of Brazil, a common language. There have been off late some attempts to establish a closer political framework (UNASUR), but it seems doubtful whether substantial progress will be made.

However, the European situation is different in essential respects. Poor in raw materials and energy resources, it will find it difficult to maintain its standard of living and social achievements unless united. Unlike Latin America, its geopolitical location makes it far more exposed to political pressures from its energy suppliers. Unless there will be stronger economic governance there will be recurrent crises, the imbalances between the countries will increase and there will be a return to economic nationalism and protectionism. Unless there will be a common energy policy, Europe will find it difficult to compete in the world markets. Unless there will be a common defense policy, Europe will count for even less in world affairs.

There are a variety of scenarios as far as the future of Europe is concerned and only the very brave will predict which of these will be chosen or in which direction Europe will drift. The EU may break up wholly or in part—not immediately but in a few years. Just as integration usually takes longer than expected so does disintegration. The stronger economies may stick together renegotiating a new framework. Some historically minded Europeans have mentioned the Hanseatic League which existed from the thirteenth to the seventeenth century as a possible model for the years to come or in a period of transition. It mainly engaged in trade but also had its own legal system. It included many cities from Scotland and Norway to Novgorod in Russia and provided some mutual help and security. The tags on motor cars in the city of Hamburg (HH—Hansa Hamburg) are one of the reminders of that distant period.

The weaker countries, facing unacceptable borrowing costs will not be able to settle their debts and walk out or be excluded. They will face the future on their own or perhaps form a loose union in a second league—to borrow a concept from the world of European soccer. The richer countries will help the poorer to muddle through. They may succeed this time, but will it be sufficient to deal with the crisis after?

The minor countries will find it very costly to opt out of Europe, even more costly than staying in. For this reason, the unraveling of Europe, if it should come to this, may take longer than often assumed. Or some compromise might be found for the continued existence of the EU as a looser body: A big but not very happy family, constantly bickering and complaining that their national interests are not sufficiently taken into account, incapable to coordinate their domestic policies, let alone having a common foreign and defense policy but still agreeing on some issues. Such a union could survive for years, perhaps many years, but certainly not as a civilian and moral superpower, the great model for all mankind in the twenty-first century.

At present, a majority seems to be undecided what way to choose. They are reluctant to make a clean break with the EU but equally reluctant to move forward toward a superstate. Some feel that they may fare better facing the years to come alone; small it used to be said is beautiful. Small town life in the past had its great charms. Life as depicted in the pictures of Spitzweg, the German romantic painter, was certainly more pleasant than life among the satanic mills of England.

Perhaps the common ties and values and the mutual trust are not strong enough to serve as basis for a real union. Perhaps with each fending for itself they will do as well as with forces combined.

And if they will not do as well, this could be compensated by greater happiness. It is not certain that even a united Europe will have the vigor and political will to play a truly important role in world affairs. And there is always the chance that the coming storms will bypass a Europe taking a low profile. Keeping a low profile seems to come easier these days than generating political will and certainly appears to be less risky.

Unfortunately, there are no certainties in this unquiet world. Spengler was not always wrong; he was certainly correct when he noted that opting out of world affairs does not guarantee immunity from the effects of international politics. How then to ensure that Europe's withdrawal from the top league of great powers will be relatively painless, a soft landing rather than a crash? There are no magic solutions only commonsense behavior. Psychologically, such an adjustment to a reduced state in the world may not come easy to a continent which once ruled the world. Having been accustomed to being strong and influential it will be difficult to give up old habits. Ambitions will have to be reduced. Europeans will have to stop preaching to the world about human rights, freedom, and democracy as they want it. As the

Chinese foreign minister told his Singapore colleague: You are small and we are big and you should behave accordingly.

This then is one of the more likely European scenarios, it may come better and it may happen worse. Disasters that cannot be foreseen may befall Europe's rivals, the rising powers of today. But this would not necessarily be of great benefit to Europe, united or divided. Or miraculously, Europe may get a second wind for unfathomable reasons, becoming smarter and more energetic as some of the futurists predict—not enough to attain superpower status, but sufficient to remain a part of the world to be reckoned with.

In any case *Nil desperandum*, never say die, is still a better guide to survival than the violent changes in mood about the future of Europe which we have witnessed over the years resembling the hysterical convulsions on the stock markets.

Europe United: An Essay in Counterfactual History (April 1, 2012)

Missing the Target in Sarajevo

Visiting the military history museum in Vienna some time ago, I came across the pistol from which on that fatal morning in Sarajevo in 1914, the shots were fired which led to the outbreak of the First World War. Gavrilo Princip, the young terrorist tried to commit suicide minutes after but the poison he swallowed was not effective. What if his pistol had jammed? The idea that small things may have major consequences has been perpetuated in many forms and languages, in nursery rhymes ("For want of a nail") as well as in modern chaos theory. King Richard II in the battle of Bosworth Field (1485) was ready, we are told, to give a kingdom for a horse. Modern historians on the other hand have tended to belittle the importance of the horse. They would argue that what Richard III needed was a helicopter rather than a horse since the warriors were stuck in deep mud.

The miseries of contemporary Europe have their origins in the First World War. It has been argued that the tensions in Europe were so acute what with the armament race, traditional enmity between German and Slavs, economic rivalry, mutual suspicions, and many other factors that a war was virtually inevitable. If not over Sarajevo, it would have broken out following some other confrontation bound to occur sooner or later. But these arguments are not quite convincing; a war might have broken out but it was not foreordained.

What would twentieth-century history have been if this war had not happened? Not a single person appearing in the following account is fictitious. They might have acted not the way they did but differently in which case Hitler would have ended his days as a disgruntled official in the municipality of his native city of Linz and Stalin perhaps as governor of the prison in Tbilisi, Georgia.

Archduke Franz Ferdinand, Inspector General of the Austrian army, arrived in Sarajevo on June 27, 1914 to watch local maneuvers just outside the city. There had been some warnings to postpone the visit in view of rumors about possible attacks by hotheads among young Serbians, but such warnings were frequent and no attention was paid. And so at 10:00 in the morning of the twenty-eighth a motorcade of six cars began moving from the army camp to the city hall in the center of town. It was a sunny, warm morning but the trip did not go well, a bomb was thrown by one of the four young Serbian terrorists belonging to the Black Hand underground. It failed to hit the target. Somewhat shaken, the Archduke and Sofia, his wife, safely reached the town hall where they had to listen to a welcoming speech by the mayor—how happy everyone was to welcome the august guest and so on.

Next, the Archduke was to visit a museum and it was decided not to change plans—only the route the motorcade was going to take. But the young would-be assassins had been placed along Appel Quai as well as Franz Joseph Street and Lateiner bridge—all possible roads leading toward the museum. When nineteen-year-old Gavrilo Princip standing in front of the Moritz Schiller food store saw the cars approaching, he jumped on the jumping board of the third car and fired his pistol twice before members of the crowd and policemen seized him. He smiled triumphantly having fulfilled his mission. It took him a few minutes to realize that he had failed, choosing the wrong car for his attack. The bullets hit the Archduke's military secretary, a lieutenant colonel, and the lady in waiting of the Archduke's wife, and their injuries were not serious either.

The Sarajevo terrorist attack created a stir all over Europe but it was the summer season, politicians and diplomats were on their holiday, reluctant to be disturbed. Everyone knew that the Balkans was a hotbed of intrigues and sedition and also terrorist attacks, what with the Serbians and the Internal Macedonian Revolutionary Organization (IMRO) in the forefront of violent campaigns. Only a short while earlier there had been a serious international crisis—lasting a few hours until it became clear that the King of Greece had been attacked in the Athens zoological garden not by an Austrian (autrichien) as a French news agency had reported but by an ostrich (autriche).

The Sarajevo events were of course widely reported in the leading newspapers. Theodor Wolf, editor of the *Berliner Tageblatt*, wrote in an editorial covering half of the front page that the Balkans had been and remained a dangerous cockpit in world politics and there was the danger that with nationalist emotions running so high it would sooner or later trigger off a war much broader and destructive than the Balkan wars of 1912/13, unless the major powers would agree on firm and lasting arrangements removing the main bones of contention. He suggested an international conference on the lines of the Berlin Congress of 1878 which would however have to be carefully prepared. Wickham Steed, chief foreign correspondent of the *London Times* (who was to become editor-in-chief a few years later), expressed a similar point of view. Sharply condemning the terrorist attack he argued, however, that much of the blame had to be attributed to the Vienna government which was responsible for the tension prevailing, having been unwilling for six years to find a solution to the Bosnia/Herzegovina conflict. Steed who had served as a correspondent in Vienna for many years was well known for his Germanophobia; he also tended to attribute many of the world's present day evils to "international Jewry"; he had been given his first major journalistic assignment by Joseph Pulitzer. The very popular (and strongly pan-Slavist) Russian *Novoe Vremya* condemned terrorism wherever it occurred but also tended to blame aggressive pan-Germanism rampant in Austria/Hungary and suggested that it should be carefully checked whether Vienna and Berlin secret services were perhaps involved in the Sarajevo incident. Perhaps it had been an act of provocation which had gone wrong?

Franz Ferdinand and his wife returned to Vienna and a few weeks later, the Sarajevo incident was all but forgotten. Emperor Franz Josef consulted his physicians whether it was wise for him to go to Bad Ischl as he did every summer. In Berlin, the municipality was engaged in preparations for the Olympic Games which were to take place in that city in 1916. British high society gathered at Ascot for the races and in Cowes for the annual yachting races. In France, everyone was still preoccupied with the Caillaux affair; the wife of the finance minister had shot the editor of *Le Figaro* who had threatened to publish some indiscreet love letters. A few cognoscenti were reading the first volume of *Remembrance of Things Past* which had just been published privately, all Paris publishers having rejected Proust's manuscript. In Russia, there was serious unrest culminating in mass strikes in St. Petersburg which showed no sign of abating.

Europe was calm, calmer than for many decades. However, dramatic, even sinister events took place in Berlin the year after, even though few knew about them at the time. No newspaper dared to report them and the most reliable source to this day is a long cable by Sir Edward Goschen, the British Ambassador in Berlin to Sir Edward Grey, the Foreign Secretary. Some excerpts will be quoted in the following:

H. M. Ambassador in Berlin to Foreign Office (January 1915)

The first indication (Goschen wrote) that something was seriously wrong came two months ago when I was asked by the Emperor to meet him at the royal palace. (Goschen was of German origin, his father had been born in Leipzig. However, he went to Rugby as a boy and was an outstanding real tennis and cricket player which naturally compensated for his non-British ancestry). Great was my astonishment when I realized that the Emperor's favorite horse was fed in the same room in which the interview took place. The Emperor told me that the horse named Jackie was his best friend and closest adviser and that his grand mother (Queen Victoria) would have wholly approved of consulting Jackie. A few minutes later, the Emperor started barking whereupon two big Danish dogs which I had not noticed before replied in a similar vein. The Emperor told me that this meant the end of the interview but he hoped to see me soon again and I was free to bring my own horse and dogs if I wished to do so.

Two weeks later, I heard from an unimpeachable source that the Emperor had convened his family in the Grosse Orangerie of Charlottenburg Palace and announced that he had decided to convert to Judaism and that those of his family who would not follow his example would be publicly hanged. To say that this caused a shock among those present would be a grave understatement. Some of the Emperor's behavior had been strange for years but nothing had prepared those present for an exhibition of this kind. The Empress Queen Auguste Victoria consulted the Emperor's physicians, the family preacher, the supreme court, the chancellor, as well as the army commander-in-chief, all of whom were sworn to strictest secrecy. All refused to take responsibility for taking action arguing that neither the constitution nor past experience provided any guidance. In the end, a group of trusted physicians was convened including Prof. Emil Kraepelin, the leading psychiatrist of the day; he had coined the term schizophrenia. After long deliberations they reached the conclusion that H. M. was suffering from overwork and exhaustion but that the usual conservative treatment (rest and cold showers) would not be indicated. Their findings were submitted to the chancellor, Count Hohenlohe.

So far, the ambassador's report dated June 1915. The following month an unsigned communique was published which said that the royal family had to announce with great sadness that H. M. had suddenly fallen seriously ill owing to overwork, that one of the causes was early tuberculosis, that for a cure a very dry climate was needed and that H. M. had therefore departed with some of his entourage for the Kalahari desert in German South-West Africa where a special sanatorium had been established. Further, reports about his state of health were not expected very soon since the healing process would take considerable time.

In early 1916, several months before the Olympic games, a further announcement was made which said that unfortunately no significant improvement had taken place in the state of health of H. M. and affairs of state were to be handled for the duration by the Emperor's second son Eitel Friedrich, the first born and heir presumptive had been killed in an hunting expedition the year before. Eitel Friedrich, who was second in succession, had been given a military education at cadet training institutions and as a young man tended to be conservative in his political outlook. However, following a long stay with his relations, the British royal family, he had been strongly influenced by the British political system. He now thought that the Hohenzollern should refrain from taking a very active part in politics. This would be in the best interest of the country and also of monarchy, for the emperor and his court would not be involved in the conflicts that were an inescapable concomitant of domestic and foreign politics. The monarch would be above politics and hence more highly respected. The reforms introduced by Eitel Friedrich were warmly welcomed by most of the parties and the public except the archconservatives who claimed that Germany had not sufficiently matured for such liberal innovations which most probably would not fit the mood and the needs of the country in the foreseeable future.

The Berlin Olympic Games 1916

The quiet and happy years after 1914 are now remembered above all because of the economic prosperity and, of course, the great success of the Berlin Olympic games. Prepared with German efficiency, they attracted enormous attention and generated passions among millions all over the world including many not ordinarily interested in sports and records. If some forty countries had participated in the preceding games in Stockholm, the number of those represented in Berlin was almost double. In Stockholm, 2,359 men and a mere 48 women had taken part, whereas in Berlin there were 8,155 and 1,001, respectively. If the highlight in Stockholm had been the Greco Roman wrestling match between Klein and Askainen which lasted eight hours and forty minutes, and above all the men's 5.000 meters final, the dramatic race in which Hannes Kolehmainen from Finland overtook Jean Bouin, the Frenchmen, in the last few meters and won by a tenth of a second—the time, 14 minutes and 36.6 seconds, a new world record was electrically measured. There was a repeat performance of sorts in Berlin but this time the German Mueller-Ingolstadt overtook Kolehmainen with his last strides and won in a new record of 14.26.6 a time thought to be beyond human capacity. (As these lines are written the world record for the distance is 12.37.35 established by Bekele, Ethiopia in Hengelo, Netherlands in 2004. He would have finished some eight hundred meters ahead of the man from Ingolstadt.) Parts of the roof of the Grunewald stadium came down apparently as the result of the frenetic jubilation of hundreds of thousands. Almost a hundred people were injured but none seriously. The scene was watched by a young handicapped boy from the Rhineland who twenty years later was to become Germany's most famous and most popular radio (and later television) sports commentator. His name was Josef Goebbels and his inimitable style was copied by commentators all over the world. As in earlier games, the United States gained more gold medals than any other country but Germany came a very creditable second. Altogether, some thirty-six new world records were established.

Spengler's Bestseller

The general climate of opinion in these years was one of great optimism and belief in steady progress. A typical manifestation of the Zeitgeist was a book published in 1917/18, which became the bestseller of the decade. Its title was *Occident Triumphant (Der Siegeszug des Abendlands)*, its author a hitherto unknown writer hailing from Brunswick district, named Oswald Spengler.

Spengler whose original training had been that of a classicist but who had never taught at university level, was a man of great erudition and fervent convictions. He argued on the basis of an enormous mass of historical material, moving with equal ease in the ancient period, the Middle Ages, and modern history that as far as Europe and particular Germany were concerned the best years were as yet to come. He criticized in great detail the wave of cultural pessimism which had engulfed not only Germany but most of Europe during the first two decades of the new century. Spengler demonstrated that politically, economically, and above all culturally Europe had been in the forefront of progress, it had pioneered new ideas as well as new technologies since time immemorial and this was unlikely to change in the foreseeable future. He acknowledged American advances above all in the economic field but stressed that like Japan, America wholly depended on European science and technology. American universities and research institutes were lagging behind those in Europe. European military power was overwhelming.

Spengler predicted conflicts between Europe and America (above all between the United States and the United Kingdom), trade wars turning into military conflicts in the years to come because of economic rivalry. Asia had been a historical backwater for many centuries and was likely to remain one. Africa did not appear in Spengler's thinking at all. Spengler concluded his great work with a quotation from Seneca—*volentem fata ducunt, nolentem trahunt*—which freely translated meant that the course of history was predestined. The rest of the world should accept Europe's preeminent status, if not, it would be compelled to accept it anyway.

Trotsky, Parvus, Thomas Mann, and the Emergence of a New Russia

Events in Russia during the first half of the twentieth century were anything but peaceful; later on the violent storms subsided, there were calm seas, and a feeling of having anchored in a secure haven. Constant strikes and agrarian unrest as well as riots in Poland, the Caucasus, and Central Asia acted as a serious obstacle to the social and economic development of the country. Dissatisfaction with the indecisiveness of the Tsar was widespread, shared even by the upper ranks of the army and the Okhrana (the political police). This led eventually to the abdication of Nicholas II but the rule of the regents appointed to replace him brought at first no significant improvement. The Tsarist family was confined to a monastery headed by Rasputin, the well-known religious moralist. A few years later, the Tsarina ("Alix"—also a granddaughter of Queen Victoria) moved on to the German city of Darmstadt where she had grown up. She opened a travel agency which did not however flourish.

The Bolsheviks and other militants of the extreme left organized a few local uprisings but these were quickly suppressed; the country was clearly not prepared for a major violent revolution—an assessment even shared by Lenin who said in a speech in Zurich in January 1917, that his generation would probably not live to witness the inescapable revolution.

An interesting initiative was launched at that time which was to have far reaching consequences. The Russian revolutionary Alexander Parvus (born Israel Lazarevich Helphand in the village of Barazino in White Russia) convened a conference in Davos in 1918. He was close to the leaders of the Bolsheviks and the more moderate Mensheviks, had coined the term "permanent revolution" but was also a successful businessman who had helped to finance the activities of the Russian far left. The Bolsheviks had met twice before in Zimmerwald and Kienthal, two Swiss villages, this time the more fashionable Davos was chosen so as not to attract the attention of the Swiss police. (The annual Davos conferences are convened to the present day even though their character has been slightly changed.) His suggestion for a revolutionary strategy to be followed were simple; the prospects of a socialist revolution were nil at the present time, therefore different strategies were to be chosen—such as the establishment of major business enterprises to earn the capital needed for financing revolutionary action. He suggested in the first instance to concentrate on the Baku oilfields—given the growing importance of oil and gas in the twentieth-century economy. Lenin hesitated at first but subsequently agreed with Parvus. Yuli Martov leader of the Mensheviks opposed these "adventurist plans" which he said were wholly contrary to the Socialist ethos. Such petty bourgeois scruples (Lenin's terms) annoyed the Bolshevik leader no end; his polemic against Martov found expression in a book entitled "Reformist Scruples and the Strategy of the Proletariat." He reminded Martov that Friedrich Engels had after all been the owner of a cotton factory in Manchester (Ermen & Engels); without his help there would have been no Marxism. One evening in the foyer of the Davos Grand Hotel, Parvus entered a long conversation with a middle aged man seated at a single table who, it soon appeared, was a German writer of some renown. He had just taken his wife to one of the local sanatoria and wanted to stay near her for a few months. The German writer listened with great interest to Parvus' stories; he confessed that Russian literature (and the famous Russian soul) had always fascinated him, as did the disputes among Russian intellectuals: were they Scyths belonging to Asia, should they join the Pan-Mongolism movement or were they really part of Europe? Years later a friend drew Parvus' attention to a book entitled *The Magic Mountain* by a certain Thomas Mann and he soon realized that some of the monologues and dialogues of the leading personages such as Naphta and Settembrini were largely based on his conversations that September evening in the bar of the Davos Grand Hotel.

Thus in 1920, BP was founded (Bakinski Petroleum) not to be confused with BP (British Petroleum, the two subsequently merged). Under different names, this corporation acquired oilfields all over the Middle East and Southeast Asia and became one of the greatest international concern second only to Standard Oil. BP headed in the early years by Lenin and Trotsky greatly prospered and established close relations with Rockefeller and his American consortium. Lenin died in 1924 and Trotsky dropped out soon after. He wanted to devote himself to his literary work but facing a major writer's block moved for a few years to Vienna to undergo treatment by a physician in the Berggasse named Fried or Freud. After his return to Russia, he became editor of a leading Moscow newspaper, but he was also much in demand as a guest professor at American universities; he shared a course with Spengler in the Harvard government department. They were replaced by Stalin and Bukharin, but Stalin too did not last very long as his interests had shifted; he had become chairman of the Russian association for the abolition of capital punishment and this consumed much of his time.

BP flourished and so did, to everyone's surprise, the Russian economy. The stormy development of Russian industry and agriculture during the first half of the twentieth century is well known even if its causes are a matter of dispute to this day. Russia was a country rich in resources but very much underdeveloped in every respect. Witte and Vishnegradski, the Tsarist ministers of Finance had realized early on that agriculture would never provide a sufficient base for strong economic development and they promoted therefore industry, transport, and the building of a modern infrastructure. However, most of the initiative came from entrepreneurs (many of them Old Believers and Jews) with heavy foreign investment also involved. Between 1915 and 1930, the Russian GNP grew an average of 12 percent a year, the Ural machine industry expanded, challenging the Ruhr and overtaking the Midlands, coal mining in the Ukraine and oil production in the Caucasus grew by leaps and bounds. St. Petersburg a city of sky scrapers overtook London as the biggest town in Europe. Moscow at the time was a poor second behind Berlin, Paris, and Vienna.

The nationality question rather than the class struggle remained Russia's Achilles heel. While the ultra Nationalists were bitterly opposed to any concessions in this respect; some of them even suggested to transfer the capital to Tambov, a symbol of deepest Russia in contrast to the artificial creation of Peter's "window to Europe." They maintained that no such window was needed. However, wiser and more moderate counsels prevailed in Tsarskoe Selo where the regents were residing. Most of the non-Russian regions were given far reaching autonomy and some of them such as Poland and the Baltic countries even received their own governments. According to an inofficial schedule which was agreed upon, they had their representation in the central government. While the prime minister was always to be a Russian, one of his deputies would be an Ukrainian, the other a Muslim, the minister of finance an Armenian, the minister of war a Balt or a Baltic German, the Pole Jozef Pilsudski became minister of railway transport and religion, and so forth. Similar ingenious schemes were later adopted by Lebanon and several other countries.

Thus, within two decades Russia changed out of recognition. The number of strikes and terrorist actions declined to almost nil. Once the most backward European country, it turned into one of the most developed. An American journalist named Lincoln Steffens visited Russia in the 1930s; on his return, he published a book entitled "I Have Seen the Future and It Works" and another, John Reed, was the author of another bestseller "Twenty Years Which Changed the World."

How Britain Became Euro-Enthusiastic

Britain in the sunset of the Victorian age was a country in decline despite the fact that even the leading futurists of the day such as H. G. Wells were hardly aware of it. A later day bestseller was entitled *The Strange Death of Liberal England*. It referred to the Irish troubles, the growth of the Labor party challenging the Liberals, the struggle of the suffragettes, and some other trends. But not just the liberal party and liberal values were under attack, the causes of decline went considerably deeper. Since the fall of Napoleon, British political influence in Europe had been predominant, it was ruling the seas, it was the pioneering industrial and the leading trading nation. It had, needless to add, the greatest empire in history. But its predominant position was challenged on all fronts. It was outproduced by the United States and

Germany, almost everywhere in its colonies the spirit of opposition became rampant. The self-confidence of the ruling class seemed unbroken, but the forebodings among the experts such as the economists increasingly became stronger and more frequent: Was it not true that the empire had become a burden? Once upon a time the empire had been a great asset and the source of great wealth. But as time passed by did it not become an increasingly heavy burden? Far from adding to the wealth of the nation, the colonies caused expenses which the country could ill afford. British imperial strategy caused endless conflicts all over the world—the naval race with Germany, the confrontation with France over Africa (Fashoda), and with Russia in Central Asia.

And so the unthinkable came to happen, many of the younger British strategic thinkers reached the conclusion that Britain's future had to be in close cooperation with Europe. There was no more fervent British imperialist than Alfred Viscount Milner who had played a central role in South Africa as well as in Egypt and became Lloyd George's right-hand man when he was prime minister. Milner though partly of German extraction firmly believed in the superiority of the British race and its imperial mission. In his "credo" meant to be his spiritual testament he gave expression to his thoughts: "I am an imperialist not a little Englander" he wrote, "I am a British race patriot. Nothing of the empire should be given up because we cannot part with much of our best blood. . . ."

It was not known at the time that Milner left a second credo written two years later in which he stated, evidently with considerable reluctance, that while nothing had changed as far as his fundamental beliefs were concerned, it was also true that the fighting spirit and the self-confidence had gone out of the nation, it had become lazy and indolent. India could no longer be controlled by a hundred thousand Englishmen and once the crown jewel of the empire was gone, neither Egypt nor the other colonies and protectorates were needed. Given these dismal prospects how to ensure a soft landing and orderly retreat rather than a disaster?

How to ensure that England would still have a say in world politics? Britain alone was no longer strong enough, it had to enter a close alliance with its European rivals such as France and Germany.

Milner's second credo was communicated at the time only to his close circle of friends which included many budding politicians and the historian Arnold Toynbee but gradually it became part of what some called the British ideology shared by all the major statesmen and political parties. This turnabout must have been exceedingly painful not just for Milner but for the political establishment which accepted his reasoning. They had to overcome deeply rooted beliefs—the uniqueness of Britishness, the superiority of the British way of life, the dangers of becoming too closely involved with French, Germans let alone other Europeans with whom they had little if anything in common (and some of whom they abhorred). But dire necessity made this mental revolution imperative and it was this strategy which eventually led to the dramatic events in the 1940s described below.

By the turn of the century, France had almost wholly recovered from the trauma of the defeat by Prussia and its allies in 1870. It was no longer argued that *finis Galliae* had come, that the country was weak, decadent, and rapidly approaching an inglorious end. On the contrary, patriotism, even chauvinism, again became fashionable, manly virtues were praised, sport became popular, and the general mood changed from one of dejection and pessimism to sanguine optimism. But there was one issue which deeply rankled—that of Alsace-Lorraine which had been incorporated by Germany after the war of 1870/71. As Clemenceau put it: *Y penser toujours, n'en parler jamais* which directly translates as Never to speak, always to think of it.

But how could Alsace-Lorraine be recovered? France alone was not strong enough to confront Germany and Britain, and Russia had made it abundantly clear that they would not engage in a bloody European war to pursue French national interests. And so after Clemenceau's death a painful reorientation took place in French political thinking and some of his followers such as Eduard Herriot, mayor of Lyon, and head of the Radical party, the leading in the country, was looking for partners for a dialogue in Germany. These early discussions led nowhere—the most of their German interlocutors were willing to concede was a French-German codominion and this the French rejected.

Pan-Europa Triumphant

At about this time, Coudenhove-Kalergi's Pan-European movement was taking off. Richard Nikolaus Eijiro von Coudenhove-Kalergi (1894–1972) was of cosmopolitan background, his father an Austrian diplomat belonged to the Bohemian nobility, and the Kalergis were a wealthy Greek family from Crete. Coudenhove's mother was from a leading Japanese family. From about 1923, Coudenhove had been trying to promote his ideas aiming at European Union but without notable success. An aristocrat, he was talking to other counts and dukes and leading politicians (among them Masaryk, Sforza, Aristide Briand—in later years even Churchill and de Gaulle). He argued that a divided Europe stood no chance in a world in which other major powers were emerging. He had the support of leading intellectuals and artists of the day such as Paul Valéry and Claudel, Thomas Mann, Arthur Schnitzler, and Franz Werfel, as well as countless others. But neither Richard Strauss nor Rilke carried much weight in the chanceries of Europe. The leading politicians of the day, except perhaps a few of the French, did not take him very seriously. His outreach was narrow and the financial resources of the movement were exceedingly limited.

But then about 1930, some anonymous donors came to his help and advisers familiar with modern methods of mass communications helped to make this a movement of considerable influence. To this day, the identity of these financial and political supporters remains unknown. But there is reason to believe that Coudenhove's membership in an important Masonic lodge and his connection in these circles played an important role. Suddenly, Paneuropa became the talk of the day, almost a new religion. Of course, the old parochial arguments were still frequently heard—that the European Union was not really needed, that nationalism had much greater attraction, that vested national interests were much stronger, and so forth.

But Coudenhove and his young and energetic coworkers had now a considerable outreach. They could argue that only a European union would prevent a disastrous European war. Given the many national conflicts besetting Europe and of course the minority problems within the nation states which could only be resolved in the framework of an European Union, this then was the only road to peace and prosperity. And it was the only way that Europe could retain some of its influence in the world. Coudenhove was behind the efforts to solve the Alsace-Lorraine conflict, the South Tyrol problem, and other sources of unrest. Thus, after many years of futile discussions, agreement was reached—parts of Lorraine were to become French again and the residents of Alsace were to vote about the future of their region in the year 2000 whether to return to France or stay with Germany. A third solution probably preferred by a majority—existence as a independent unit would not be put to a vote because it seemed not feasible in present conditions. However, since both France and Germany would be part of the new European Union these arrangements would be no longer matters of vital importance.

The Pan-Europa project leading to a federal European Union was of course rejected by militant nationalists in many European countries. It was said to be an artificial construct, it had no emotional appeal like nationalism, people felt no loyalty toward the continent. All this was true, but this propaganda nevertheless failed to persuade let alone stir the masses, partly no doubt because the project was to proceed gradually over a period of a hundred years—from 1930 to 2030. On the other hand the immediate benefits were obvious—closer trade relations, the emergence of a common European market, freedom of movement within Europe, and many other mutually beneficial arrangements.

The transition period witnessed many difficulties and conflicts and at times it seemed that the European project was doomed. It were not only disputes on budgetary allocations—who would get what?—issues of leadership, of common currency and common language, it meant in many instances a farewell to traditions that were a thousand years old, there was great reluctance to have *Europa ueber alles* replace the old German anthem and *Allons enfants d'Europe* did not sound right either. *Europe of Hope and Glory* did not even rhyme. *Europe is not yet lost* (originally in Latin—the Polish anthem) sounded not exactly uplifting. But as we now know outside pressures as well as internal trends helped to make the European project a success and became what many consider the most important development in the twentieth century. And so, on the evening of January 30, 1933, millions of enthusiasts took part in the torch parades along Unter den Linden, the Champs Elysees, Moscow's Red Square, and London's Mall celebrating the first stage of this turning point in world history.

Part 3
Middle East: The Arab Spring

Preface

Once upon a time, the story of the Middle East was one of brilliant achievements. It was in the forefront of human civilization, and its cultural contributions were legendary, second to none. It was the golden age of al-Andalus, of the Abbasid Caliphate and the Ummayad in Spain, when Baghdad was known as *Madinat as-Salam* (the city of peace), the age of Ibn Khaldun's *Muqaddimah*, of Ibn Rushd and Ibn Sina, of the finest architecture, of leading in astronomy and mathematics as well as in philosophy and medicine. It excelled in the sciences and the arts flowered, the most advanced spirits in Europe such as Frederick II, Emperor of the Holy Roman Empire (he was called "stupor mundi" the wonder of the world), surrounded himself with Arab advisers and teachers, learned their language and went to Palestine to be part of what was then, in many respects, the most advanced culture. It was in the vanguard not only of knowledge but also of civilized behavior; when Christian Europe was often immersed in religious fanaticism, Muslim thinkers and some rulers pioneered a new humanist spirit preaching tolerance.

All this lasted for a few centuries, and it was followed by a dark age: the greater the erstwhile glory, the deeper and more abject and painful the fall. The history of the region since and especially during the last century has been mostly a narrative of stagnation, decline, fanaticism, and backwardness. That such a process took place is seldom denied, and why it occurred is still a matter of dispute.

For this reason, the dramatic events that took place in the region in 2011/12 generated so much excitement and great hopes for a better future. The following selection of current comments (there were many more) try to explain why from the very beginning, I found it difficult to join the chorus of jubilation.

The Arab Spring

Of all the headlines covering the Egyptian situation, I found only one with which I could fully agree—Jubilation Today, Future Uncertain. It is not tactful to play Cassandra in the middle of universal rejoicing, but I fear that the high expectations of today will lead to bitter disappointment.

This for the following reason. What happened in Egypt was not a revolution, certainly not so far. It brought about the deposition of a ruler who was a dictator but by no means the worst dictator in the Middle East. The worst dictators will not be attacked by Al Jazeera because they are (rightly) afraid of them. Mubarrak probably misappropriated state funds, but all that has been found so far is one house in London; he lived relatively modestly. Those who know more than I do tell me that of the $70 billion he allegedly stole, perhaps two or three billions will in the end remain, and he may even have acquired them semilegally. A list of Middle Eastern rulers who have not enriched themselves while in office would be very short indeed.

Under his rule, fewer people were killed than under most other Middle Eastern rulers, certainly fewer than under Nasser (who ruined the Egyptian economy). When Nasser died, many Egyptian were weeping, not when Mubarrak left. He was an autocrat and a stupid man and was out of touch with the feelings of his people. He outstayed his welcome by ten or fifteen years, which happens frequently to old people who stay too long in power—even Churchill, de Gaulle, and Adenauer did. But he was not a monster. Under him, the Egyptian economy grew by 5–6 percent a year, and the Gini coefficient was less than that in America, Russia, or China. (The Gini coefficient indicates the inequality of income and property in a country.)

Why the fears about the future? Not because of war with Israel. There are no territorial disputes between the two countries. Israel would love to pass Gaza to Egypt, but Egypt understandably does not want it.

Furthermore, Egypt more than any other country is strategically vulnerable (the Nile installations), and it would be very reluctant to expose itself on behalf of others.

Not because of the Muslim Brotherhood. It remains a danger in the longer run, not immediately, and the head of the Central Intelligence Agency (CIA) is quite misinformed telling the American Congress that it has become secular. It stands for a theocracy that still has wide popular support in Egypt, especially outside Cairo. The elections in six months (if they will take place) may show this. The Brotherhood is led by old men who are not in a hurry. But it has always produced more radical groups (who tried to kill Nasser and Mubarak and did assassinate Sadat). They assume that the present power vacuum will lead to deterioration of the situation, and in such a situation, their hour may come.

The Egyptian problem is twofold: The opposition has never been able to agree for any length of time, and this refers not only to the presence of the Islamists. And there is no good reason that this time it will be any different.

The correspondents who have been congregating on Midan al-Tahrir where the demonstrations took place have not visited the city of the dead, the cemeteries where millions make their living and survive on three or four dollars a day, nor to poor suburbs and cities like Shubra El-Kheima or al-Mahalla al-Kubra where many more millions live.

It has escaped them how poor a country Egypt really is and how few resources it has. The young people twitting are only a small part of Egypt, and they want good jobs so that they can marry; they want a welfare state with free education, a health service, and unemployment benefits and social security. How will they achieve it?

When I visited Egypt first, King Farouk was still in power, and it had about thirty million inhabitants. I attended an international conference, and I went along for a walk with a wise European elder statesman Count Mihaly Karolyi (1875–1955) of Hungary, foreign minister of his country—soon to be ousted by the Communists.

We went along Qasr el-Nil, Cairo's richest street. My Arabic was good enough to give him some explanations and act as interpreter, but he did not need them. He looked to the poor side streets and said, "Young man, this story will not end well." The situation has not basically changed since, except that there were thirty million then and there are eighty-one now.

The new wisdom is: If you want to liberate a society, just give them the Internet. It would be far more correct to say that Facebook and the Internet will change nothing in a country like Egypt unless you have a message that tells people how to build a free and just society, how to make the country more prosperous, and how to give satisfactory jobs to young people. No one has come with such a message as yet.

(February 2011)

Arab Autumn

As autumn approaches, economic problems such as the debt crisis and the future of the Euro will dominate European politics. If it would not be for this, it would be the Middle East crisis.

During the first weeks of the Arab spring, optimism about the democratic future of the Middle East could have hardly been higher. The tyrants had been overthrown, and the people had triumphed in the struggle for freedom and democracy, against repression and corruption. It had been a truly glorious revolution, an inspiration for freedom fighters the world over.

And now? Instead of an Arab spring, there is a Middle East crisis and the only certainty is that the prices of oil and gas will remain high. Nine months have passed, and the Western correspondents have left, except for a few covering the search for Khaddafi. The optimism has disappeared, as it had been based on two basic misunderstandings: On one hand, a misreading of the general situation in the Middle East and North Africa and its political prospects. Secondly, on a basic misunderstanding of what revolutions are. A nineteenth-century cynic once said that a revolution is the replacement of a bad government by one that is worse.

This may be too pessimistic a point of view, but it is certainly true that democracy and freedom do not necessarily follow from the overthrow of a tyrannical government that has been in power for too long and lost credibility and legitimacy. Whatever the achievements of the great French Revolution, it did not bring freedom to France, nor did the Russian Revolution make Russia a democratic country. The Shah was overthrown, but what followed we all know—the list could be prolonged.

As we approach the autumn, power in Tunisia, Libya, and Egypt is in the hands of transitional governments that have promised elections. Whether democratic parties will prevail in these elections is very uncertain; in Egypt, more than forty political parties are competing and even more in Tunisia. The democratic forces in all these countries want to postpone elections as long as possible.

Given the many conflicting interests in Libya represented by a multitude of tribes and clans, it seems that only a strong government may keep the country together, and at present, it is not clear where such leadership could come from. Western governments have been talking about the need of economic help especially in the case of Egypt. But economic help, however much needed, will not solve the political problems facing these countries.

Syria and Yemen are virtually in a civil war and no end is in sight. The centrifugal forces in both countries are strong, but for a fairly strong central government, chances are that the country may fall apart.

Some Middle Eastern powers such as Saudi Arabia are vitally interested in the restoration of stability and peace in the region; others such as Iran are vitally interested in disorder. But how stable are Iran and Saudi Arabia? The revolutionary enthusiasts in the Middle East believe their job has been only half done. Morocco and Algeria are not yet democratic and neither of course are Jordan and Saudi Arabia and a few others. But where are the democrats who would bring about such a change toward greater freedom? The Islamists perhaps?

September and October could be critical months for Israel and the Palestinian authority. There could be a new Intifada, or the Israeli settlers could provoke clashes. Since there is so little national solidarity in Egypt, perhaps national unity could emerge as a result of a war against Israel. Iran certainly would be very much interested, they will fight to the last Egyptian soldier and push Syria to take part. But enthusiasm for such a war in Egypt is not that great; when the Islamists called last month for an anti-Israeli demonstration of a million, only a few hundreds came and the military told them this is not the right time. Israel has to be shown that Mubarak is no longer in power in Cairo. But a big war would be a disaster.

The problem of the Arab world is that natural resources are very unequally distributed; the small countries have oil and a lot of money, while the populous countries such as Egypt have very little. The young people have no jobs and will get no jobs commensurate with their aspirations and their training. A little money from the West will not solve this problem. But unless it is solved, there will be no real, lasting progress in the Arab world. Elections and parliaments will not remedy the situation. Some say a Khalifat will, a union of all Muslim countries.

But the rich do not want to share with the poor and such a super state would include such disparate elements and conflicting interests that it is bound to lead to internal war rather than peace.

Perhaps, salvation will come from somewhere, quite unexpected.

At present, however hard we look, no such savior can be seen on the horizon.

(October 2011)

Revolution in the Middle East?

It is only a month ago that the uprisings in the Middle East were hailed as the greatest good thing that happened in recent history in this part of the world. It was the beginning of a democratic revolution that would eventually change the world for the better—it would affect China as well as India, and it would be the overture to a global democratic revolution, sweeping away dictators and autocratic regimes.

And now? Little has remained of such optimism, a few dictators have been deposed, but who and what is replacing them?

Half of Egypt is striking, and the economic situation is quickly deteriorating. The country depends to a considerable extent on tourism, but only a few tourists want to see the Pyramids now. Libya is in a state of civil war, and Yemen is about to disintegrate into two or three parts. There may be more trouble to come in other places. The European Union (EU) and Washington are under pressure to intervene in Libya. But if they were to do this there would be a great outcry all over the Middle East: "Imperialist aggression!" Why the EU, why not Turkey that has declared itself as the new leading power in the Middle East—and they have been in Libya before in recent history.

Revolutions are periods of lawlessness and violence. Perhaps, one should not be too perturbed by the attacks in Egypt on women demonstrating for women's rights and on minorities such as Christians. Perhaps, order will be restored after the elections in six months, which with the help of the twitters and Facebook users will bring freedom and democracy.

However, the prospects are not brilliant. The ruling military officers have said that they will not wait one day longer with the elections they have promised. But now the civilian leaders of the revolt negotiating with the military have cold feet: How to establish political parties in such a short time (only five months are now left) in order to build a democratic system that is solid and will not collapse in a few months? Of course, one could have elections also without political parties—but a democratic system will not emerge in such conditions.

In recent decades, a new middle class has emerged in Egypt and also liberal and democratic groups, but they are still weak, and these in any case are not the forces likely to mount the barricades and to fight in the streets except perhaps for a day or two. Many Western journalists expected far too much from the Facebook as agents of democratization in the Middle East.

It is of course true that the West has supported for decades dictators in the Middle East. But given the heavy dependence of Europe from Middle Eastern oil and gas, what were the alternatives? The West had little freedom of maneuver: It could have tried to reduce its dependence in various ways, but there were no major efforts made to do so. Now, the tide has turned, and some of the dictators have been ousted from power. Western governments are advised to support at long last the forces fighting for freedom and democracy.

Unfortunately, it is not at all clear who will emerge victorious in the struggle for power in the Middle East. It could well be that new dictators will emerge, who are less old fashioned and autocratic, more populist, and demagogic in approach. Some of those demanding reform do not necessarily want democratic reform and they certainly are not friends of the West.

Or, to put it more precisely, many would not mind living in the West but they believe that Western institutions are not suited for their countries. When a few years ago the American government announced a lottery to distribute a number of green cards entitling the winners to immigrate to the United States, eight million young Egyptians applied. Hundreds of thousands of Arab immigrants now live in Europe, who are legal and illegal immigrants. However, America and Europe will not absorb eight millions but only a small number.

The basic social problem of the Middle East is the "youth bulge," the fact that there are many millions of young people who are unemployed or underemployed. This is true for Egypt as much as for Yemen and even for Saudi Arabia and other Arab countries. In all these countries, 60 percent or more of the population is under thirty years of age. And it is precisely in these countries with a youth bulge that the great majority of political conflicts in the world are occurring.

Given the low level of the education system, there is no possible way to turn Egypt or Yemen into a second Singapore, and in any case, high technology does not employ that many people.

But finding employment for young people is the basic social problem in the Middle East. Without finding a solution, all the talk about democratic reform will remain mere talk and the Middle East will remain a region of unrest and conflict for many years to come. And unless the European dependence on Middle Eastern oil and gas is reduced, Europe will have to deal with whoever will be in power.

(Summer 2011)

Cassandra in Cairo

The old order has crumbled in the Middle East, and it will never be the same again. But what will the new order be? What made it crumble? The silence of fear had been shattered. The experts who had been arguing that this was a listless generation that did not care about freedom and democracy, which, if it was politically active at all, tended to follow the lead of the Islamists had been proved wrong. It was the victory of youth, the generation that was believed to be lost, which, free of fear, overthrew the corrupt dictators and brought about the revolution. This was yesterday's uplifting story, but it is as yet the beginning, not the end. President Obama congratulated them and so did the Muslim Brotherhood and the Teheran government.

Once upon a time, the Middle East (the term had not as yet been invented) was ruled by elderly men, who were wise (or believed to be wise) people of substance and had a standing in society. The exceptions were young officers occasionally swept to power by a military coup d'etat. This seems to have been so since the beginning; even the Prophet Mohammed was in his fifties when he moved from Mecca to Medina, the event considered to be the beginning of the history of Islam. The two major figures that were carried by the popular uprising in Egypt to the most prominent place were Sheikh Yusuf al-Qaradawi, who is the preacher of Al Jezeera television station with an audience of forty million is in his eighties, and Tariq al-Bishri, a well-known former judge, philosopher, and historian who is close to eighty. We shall have to return to al-Bishri, a key figure in the present events later on in our narrative.

The intellectual history of Egypt, on the other hand, has been essentially the story of young elites, certainly during the last century and it is to this aspect that we shall turn next: For if the revolutionaries of 2011 have an ideology, it can be understood, if at all, only against the background of the political beliefs of their fathers and grandfathers.

There were, broadly speaking, four stages in Egyptian political thinking in recent history—Fascism before the outbreak of the Second

World War, Marxism during the decade thereafter, Arab nationalism (Nasserism) during the following two or three decades, and eventually Islamism. It goes without saying that not all, probably not the majority subscribed to these tenets, but these were considered the most advanced ideological groups at the time, and it was believed that the future belonged to them.

The protagonists of Egyptian Fascism Misr al-Fatat—Young Egypt, the Green Shirts) were indeed very young people. Ahmad Husain, the leader, was a lawyer in his twenties. He was certainly a radical but had no sympathy whatsoever for the Muslim Brotherhood founded during the decade before; he used to call them Brotherhood of bandits or robbers. Ahmad Hussein was more interested in the Pharaonic than the Islamic tradition of his country. (Later in life, he seems to have discovered Islam and embraced it.) It was a secular party with fairly close ties with Nazi Germany more than with fascist Italy. Their influence was limited at the time but should not be underrated; many of the young officers such as Nasser and Sadat who carried out the coup of 1952, which led to the deposition of King Farouk, started their political career in these circles. The Green Shirts (Misr al-Fatat) were banned on the eve of World War Two. During the last twenty years, attempts were made to resurrect the party under a variety of names but without much success. Ahmad Husain was no longer involved in these initiatives, he dropped out of politics and died more or less forgotten in Cairo in the 1970s.

With the defeat of the Axis, Fascism lost its appeal and Marxism became the fashion. The movement was split into half a dozen Communist and Trotskyite sects; Jews of foreign origin played a leading role in the beginning in some of them, but there were also a growing number of Muslims and Christians, especially from among artist circles. The common language was French rather than Arabic, hardly the best way to gain influence among the working class of Egypt.

The subsequent fate of some of these early militants is fascinating. Henri Curiel, whose family owned at the time a well-known Cairo department store, was expelled from Egypt, became a third-world activist in Paris, and was assassinated in a mysterious circumstance in Paris in 1978. Curiel's biographer describes him as something of a Dostoevskian figure reading out Proust to Cairo prostitutes. His group transferred its activities to Rome and for a while supported the coup carried out by Nasser and his companions. Curiel's deputy Joyce Blau ("Colette" in the underground) became a distinguished Paris professor specializing in Kurdish literature and modern history. Curiel's son, the French journalist Alain Gresh, became editor of *Le Monde Diplomatique*, a radical left-wing pro-Castrist journal. *Le Monde Diplomatique* is funded by a legacy made by a German-Jewish émigré of the extreme right, Guenter Holzmann, nicknamed Akela of the Jungle Book fame, incidentally a native of my home town. In his later years following a prolonged stay in Latin America, he underwent an ideological conversion and moved to the far left or rather anti-Gringoism (and also successful prospecting in the field of mining).

The identity of the killers of Curiel has never been established, but there is reason to assume that they were contract killers belonging to the Abu Nidal group, which, at the time, engaged in a killing spree against a small group of people that had initiated meetings between Arab and Israeli of the far left in an attempt to work for a peaceful settlement of the conflict. However, it is not known who had commissioned the Abu Nidal killers.

Arturo Schwarz, on the other hand, a leading young Trotskyite from Alexandria went to Italy and became one of the world's leading experts on the history of Surrealism and Dadaism, author of monographs of Marcel Duchamp, Man Ray, and Andre Breton. He was also a major collector; part of his collection ended up in the Israel museum in Jerusalem. In his later years, he became preoccupied with the Kabbalah and his own Jewish identity. He received an honorary doctorate from Tel Aviv University and his most recent book is entitled *Sono ebrei, anche*.

However, there were also Muslims of irreproachable background such as Adel Husain, Ahmed Husain's younger brother, and another formidable young intellectual, a budding judge named Tariq al-Bishri— who happens to be the man chosen in January 2011 by the Egyptian army command to head the committee preparing a new constitution, or at least to modify the present one.

There was a fascist wave among European intellectuals in the 1930s and Marxism was very popular, not only in France and Italy after the war; seen in this light, developments in Egypt and incidentally also in some other countries such as Sudan were by no means extraordinary. What is of more than ordinary interest is the ease and the relative speed with which these young intellectuals moved from one camp to the other. Some of them were opportunists, but others were definitely not: Adel Husain must have spent close to ten years in prisons for his convictions and activities.

They all were, in their youth, severe critics of Islamism and the Muslim Brotherhood and ended up in the camp of those they had ridiculed and despised in their younger years. Al-Bishri, in his early books, attacked the Brotherhood because of its reactionary views, opportunism, and ideological obscurity. He called it proto-fascist and maintained that introducing the Shari'a would not change anything in Egyptian society. Formally, these ex-critics may not now be members of the Brotherhood just as they might not have been paid up members of the Communist party in their youth. But there was no mistake about the ideological shift that had taken place not only in Egypt but also in other Muslim countries, especially in North Africa and in Turkey.

What caused the exodus from the Marxist camp and what attracted them to Islamism? Marxism lost many adherents also in Europe in the 1960s and 1970s but for different reasons. The decline of Marxism in the West had to do, to a considerable extent, with developments in the Soviet Union. However, the Muslim intellectuals did not know much about the Soviet Union and cared even less. If, for instance, Aleksandr Solzhenitsyn's books had a tremendous impact in France, they were virtually ignored in the Arab world; I doubt whether they were ever translated. The mass escape from the Marxist camp might have had to do with the pervasive anti-Westernism in the Muslim world, and Marxism, however radical, was after all a Western creation.

It could well be that national pride played a certain role, and they wanted authenticity (a magic word in these circles), an ideology that was homegrown, and which could be a reason of pride, national rather than international socialism. In the case of Adel Husain, nationalism obviously did play a role. Having been an internationalist for many years he wrote a book in his post-Marxist phase entitled "The Zionist Plan for Economic Hegemony" (1984), which might have been inspired by the famous *Protocols of the Elders of Zion*. Zionism, no doubt, can be charged with many sins, but given the wealth of the oil rich Arab countries, the idea that it wanted (or could) establish economic hegemony in the Middle East seems somewhat far fetched—to put it mildly.

Why did the mass conversion to Islamism not occur earlier on?

The explanation seems obvious. In the 1950s and 1960s, the revival of Islamism had not yet come under way and Nasserism was going strong. The masses listened to the *Sawt al Arab* (Voice of the Arabs), the powerful radio station in Cairo preaching from Cairo; the hour of Qaradawi had not yet struck. Adel Husain writes somewhere that his friend Tariq al-Bishri, even as a young man and a leading public intellectual, did not realize at the time in which direction the wind was blowing.

Perhaps, the most important motive was the realization that Marxism would never appeal to broad masses of people and would leave the public intellectuals in isolation. Islam, on the other hand, stood for social justice too, was opposed to capitalism, and had the ability to mobilize the masses. Adel Hussain established the Islamic Labor party in the 1970s. It was not much of a political success and even annoyed to some extent the Muslim Brotherhood because it was not under their direct control. But it certainly showed how far the conversion of Husain and his former Marxist colleagues had proceeded. To a certain extent, the phenomenon reminds one of a similar development among the Jews and above all in Israel known as *"hosrim be'tshuva,"* or secularists seeing the religious light and adopting the religion of their fathers with great zeal. But whereas in the Muslim world, the phenomenon was by and large restricted to the intelligentsia, in Israel, it was only seldom found among intellectuals.

In some cases, the return to militant religion might have been at least a return to family tradition and filial piety—al-Bishri's grandfather had been head of Al-Azhar, the world famous Islamic teaching institution and the highest religious authority in the land. He was a wunderkind, and at the age of six, he was reported to know the Koran by heart. Tariq al-Bishri's father was a well-known judge too, although he was more interested in writing on humorous subjects than religious topics.

The case of al-Bishri might explain some cases of conversion, but the phenomenon is certainly much wider. The military junta introduced him as a universally respected figure which, broadly speaking, is not entirely true. The Copts reject him; al-Bishri who has written frequently about the Copts blamed the Coptic Church rather than the Islamic fundamentalists for the growing alienation between the two communities. Egyptian spokeswomen and secularists in general were also concerned about his appointment because of his Islamist views. He is bitterly anti-Israeli, but this attitude is shared by many Egyptian intellectuals and hardly affects his popularity. It is most unlikely that he will suggest to abolish paragraph two in the Egyptian Constitution, which bases it on the Shari'a, but this too seems to be the desire of most Egyptians, according to the opinion polls. He has always been in favor of an independent judiciary, but in this respect there could be conflicts with the Brotherhood, which stand for wilayat al-fakih—the idea that (Islamist) jurists should be the supreme authority in an Islamic society.

But why bother about al-Bishri and the Brotherhood, and why should they be considered relevant? Everyone says that the young in Egypt do not hear what they are saying, do not even know about them, and they do not read anything but the Facebook. Over the last decades, a sizeable young generation grew up, the children of liberal capitalism (the term most frequently used), which lives in a different world. Recent events have shown that they can mobilize hundreds of thousands on short notice. True enough, but the others, the majority have not disappeared. The Brotherhood and the less-well-organized Salafis have also undergone a process of rejuvenation, and they are not the same any more. The twitter crowd can get hundreds of thousand together—but what staying power do they have? What do they want, and what political experience do they have? Is their medium the message?

There has been, for a long time, a political opposition in Egypt, be it legal, semi-legal, and underground, but it has never been united and the question arises whether cooperation between the various groups will be likely in future. There was the Muslim Brotherhood, banned much of the time, but active under various other labels. There is no need to deal with it in any detail nor with its most popular (albeit unofficial) protagonist al-Qaradawi, the television preacher with a mass audience. Their history has been the subject of many books and articles; their program can be found easily, and their attitudes toward women, gays, minorities, and the nature of an Islamic state is well known and heavily documented. It has been argued by Western journalists that the Brotherhood is not what it used to be; it has become more bourgeois, more sedate, and moderate in most respects. The head of CIA said the same but corrected himself after a few days. It is true up to a point, and moreover, vagueness on all issues but religious has been traditionally the great strength of the Brotherhood; well wishers and critics can usually find in the many and contradictory statements of the *Ikhwan* whatever suits their preconceived notions.

Some Middle Eastern experts such as Olivier Roy have been arguing that Islamism was on the way out for the last twenty years. They may well be right: It is only a question of time until people realize that Islam does not have the answer for all questions (as the *Ikhwan* claims), but it may take a long, long time. It is true that Qaradawi, in his speech on Midan al-Tahrir, has welcomed the Copts and Christians in general, which would not have happened a few years ago. However, the Copts, who have been the victims of some major attacks in recent months, do not yet quite trust them. The Brotherhood now stands for a civil society and parliamentary democracy with Islamic foundations.

What precisely are Islamic foundations? This remains unclear, probably deliberately so. Yusuf al-Qaradawi was persona non grata in the United States and the United Kingdom, which, his well wishers argue, was a mistake, for he condemned terrorism *expressis verbis* and especially suicide terrorism, except in the case of Israel, where civilians too are legitimate targets. If he called for jihad in the West, he meant (according to his well wishers' interpretation) cultural rather than physical jihad, persuasion rather than bombs. One could accept this as a very commendable showing of moderation. But some puzzling questions remain—why the exception of Israel? Was it because of a particular hatred, *odium theologicum*, or was it because Israel seemed a relatively easy target in contrast to other countries where, as he saw it, Muslims were persecuted, from the Caucasus to Kashmir and Sinkiang, not to mention Western Europe. And was it not likely that jihad against Israel would be broadened against other enemies of Islam, strong today but perhaps more vulnerable in future? As for cultural jihad, Mohammed Gudie, a veterinary surgeon by training and the Supreme Guide of the Brotherhood declared a few months ago that "our objectives should be obtained by raising a jihadi generation that pursues death just as our enemies pursue life." Why should those engaging in cultural jihad have to pursue death?

Somewhat closer to the moderate camp than the Brotherhood is *Hizb al-Wasat* (Center party) and a relatively new group named *al Hizb al Arabi al Dimokrati* (Nasserist, national socialist), which also existed under Mubaraq. A new organization is the "January 25th Youth," also called the Coalition of the Youth of the Revolution, the April 6th movement, and several others. This very loose alliance of some fifteen groups includes the youth organization of the Muslim Brotherhood but also some small Trotskyite sects assiduously hiding their identity and various other groups based on Facebook activities. They want a government of experts trusted by the people. As for the policy followed by such a government, everyone has tried hard not to be too specific, but once these issues are decided, dissent will recur. However, the Egyptian left, such as it is, seem to be willing to make far reaching concessions to Islamism and Arab nationalism. They follow the time honored policy of "entrism," believing that the Brotherhood is by and large a populist and progressive movement. Its religious excesses may be regrettable and sometimes embarrassing, but they will no doubt gradually weaken or fade in time. Hope springs eternally.

It is difficult to see how these inchoate groups of political activists will turn in the foreseeable future into a working parliamentary democracy. There is, at present, a Dignity party, a Conciliation party, and half a dozen youth parties. Some exist largely on paper, and others consist of notables, old and young, with a small office, but only the Brotherhood has, at the present time, a functioning grass-root organization. It could be that one or two of the other organizations will turn into a well-functioning political party. But the lack of any clarity as to what policy a new government should pursue, which is the precondition for establishing a democratic system, does not at present exist and will not come into existence in six or nine months. For this reason, if for no other military rule, direct or by proxy, may last for a long time, and the Brotherhood will probably remain the strongest single force.

Just ten days passed between the publication of two headlines in *Al Ahram*, Egypt's leading daily newspaper. The first said: "Millions ask Mubarrak to stay." The second said: "The people chases the regime away." But had the regime been ousted? Doubts began to creep in both inside Egypt and among the foreign media, which had been carried away in the heady days of the Midan el Tahrir demonstrations. Earlier on, the feeling had been one of "Bliss was it to be alive but to be young was very heaven"—as Wordsworth wrote at the time of the French Revolution, and as Michel Foucault might have said at the time of his memorable visit to Tehran to welcome the Khomeini Revolution.

The euphoria gave way to reflections about the difficulties of transition and the problems of transformation.

Had the regime vanished or was it merely the disappearance of one man and those closest to him? Was it not like the Revolution of 1848, which brought about the ouster of Louis Philippe I, King of France and Metternich, but otherwise ended in failure? True. Gradually, democracy prevailed in Europe during the decades that followed, but there were major setbacks, and it took more than a hundred more years and a world war to defeat Fascism and Communism to collapse.

Why Tunis, why Cairo? A great many explanations were offered. Most agreed that these had been autocratic and corrupt regimes and that an educated young generation wanted freedom and a better life. Kefaya (enough) had been the name of one of the leading opposition groups founded in 2004. These explanations were correct as far as they went, but there were also other explanations such as the one offered by Bashar Hafez al-Assad, the Syrian President: Only pro-Western regimes have reason to be afraid. Had the Egyptian and Tunisian regimes been the worst in the region, the most repressive and corrupt? To argue this was not easy—the list of Middle Eastern rulers who have not enriched themselves while in power is a very short one and the Egyptian dictatorship was less harsh than the Iranian or the Syrian to give but two examples. There is much reason to assume that Saddam Hussein would have died in bed and not on gallows but for the war; given the size and strength of the Iraqi organs of repression, a popular uprising could not have succeeded. Could a book like *The Yacoubian Building* (or the movie based on it) have been produced in any other Arab country—could the books of al-Bishri (such as *Egypt in Decay*) have appeared elsewhere in the Middle East? Or was it perhaps mainly because the rulers of these countries out of touch with popular opinion had outstayed their welcome by many years?

Among the main factors generating the Egyptian uprising, the social media were mentioned in the beginning perhaps more often than any other. The Egyptian youth (it was claimed) was both more tolerant than their elders and far more techno savvy, hence the ease with which masses had been mobilized. The internet and twitter, it was said, would reshape Egyptian politics.

But again, as time passed, these certainties faded. Twitter was indeed helpful for mobilizing masses, but it changed neither the facts on the ground nor the mentality of people; it was usually preaching to the converted. However often twitter was used, Egypt still remained a poor country and this narrowly restricted the prospects of young Egyptians (and Tunisians and Yemenites) to find jobs commensurate with their expectations. Seen in this light, the social media in a poor, overpopulated country like Egypt or Yemen may lead eventually not to freedom and democracy but to chaos and despair. For given the poverty of these countries and the lack of resources, what policy could possibly give the young people what they wanted? True, the distance between poor and rich in Egypt is very great, indicated by the difference between the slums and the gated communities of the rich with fancy names such as City Views, Palm Hills, and Palm Beach. The Gini coefficient (indicating the difference in income equality and inequality) may tell us that the differential between rich and poor is less in Egypt than in the United States, Russia, or China. But whatever Gini says, perception is at least as important, and on the "Corruption Perceptions Index" (of Transparency International) Egypt appears on place 111 of 146. Corruption in other Arab and Middle Eastern countries may have been as great or greater than in Egypt, but it was more obvious in Egypt, and this was what eventually helped to bring down the Mubarrak regime.

However, even if there was no corruption and if the riches of the billionaires and multimillionaires were seized or taxed away, there would still be the youth bulge, which feeds pessimism about the future of the country. It is easier to feel optimism about the future of Libya, a country of some six million inhabitants (given sensible political leadership) and the largest oil reserves in Africa, provided the revenues are not spent on harebrained schemes as Khadafi did over many years. But even Libya and Tunis have witnessed, so far, much more chaos than was hoped. And above all, it is difficult to feel optimism about Egypt with its more than eighty million inhabitants.

The essential facts about the youth bulge have been known for a long time. The birthrate is declining all over the world but least of all in the Middle East; in this region, 65 percent of the population is under the age of thirty-five, and many of them are poor and frustrated with no work or only part-time work. It is also known that in recent decades, 80 percent or more of all conflicts, internal and external, occurred in countries in which 60 percent of the population was under the age of thirty.

It may be possible to find work for the cohort of the young in the oil rich countries. But what solution is there in the others? When, in 2006, the US government announced the distribution of green cards by way of a lottery, eight million young Egyptians applied. Hundreds of thousands of young Egyptians now live in countries of the European Union. Following the overthrowing of the Ali regime in Tunis, thousands of young Tunisians fled to Italy via Lampedusa, and this may have been only the beginning of mass emigration. However, there is mass unemployment in Europe at the present time, and the new arrivals often do not have the necessary education or professional training to succeed. Those who remain in North Africa are those who have found a niche in the system, or those who have no hope to succeed in the first place. The Egyptian educational system has deteriorated over the years, and there is no chance of building a new Singapore in the country. (And high technology, in any case, employs only relatively few people.) Egypt, perhaps more than any other country in the world invests in private tutoring. But what if at the end of the road, there are still no jobs?

The Egyptian economy has shown progress during the last decade, the GNP grew between 4 and 7 percent, figures that compare favorably with most other Middle Eastern countries of similar size and population. By the middle of this century, the youth bulge in Egypt will probably have shrunk and the problem may gradually become manageable. But no one has a realistic plan how to solve the problem of the next few decades. And since the hopes from January 2011 were so high, the despair could be equally great. The road to freedom and democracy will be long.

(Summer 2011)

An Interview

Rubin: Within a week of the beginning of the Cairo demonstrations last year, you wrote a series of articles which appeared under the general title "Cassandra in Cairo." They were published wholly or in part in several European newspapers, and also, I believe, in part in the *Democracy Digest* and the *New Republic*. They were in stark contrast to most comments at the time.

Laqueur: What I wrote at the time was very briefly this (and I quote): Of all the headlines covering the Egyptian situation, I found only one with which I could fully agree—"Jubilation today, future uncertain." It is not tactful to play Cassandra in the middle of universal rejoicing, but I fear that the high expectations of today will lead to bitter disappointment for the following reason.

What happened in Egypt was not a revolution, certainly not so far. It brought about the deposition of one man who was a dictator but by no means the worst in the Middle East. The worst dictators will not be attacked by *Al Jazeera* because they are (rightly) afraid of them. Mubarak probably misappropriated state funds, but all that has been found so far is one house in London. He lived relatively modestly. Those who know more than I do, tell me that of the $70 billion he allegedly stole, much less will in the end remain, and he may even have acquired this semilegally.

A list of Middle East rulers who have not enriched themselves in office would be very short indeed. Under Mubarak's rule, fewer people were killed than under most other Middle Eastern rulers, certainly fewer than under Nasser, who in addition ruined the Egyptian economy. When Nasser died, many Egyptians were weeping, but not when Mubarak left. He was an autocrat and a stupid man, out of touch with the feelings of his people. He outstayed his welcome by ten or fifteen years, which happens frequently to old people who stay too long in power—even Churchill, de Gaulle, and Adenauer did.

But he was not a monster. Under him, the Egyptian economy grew by 5–6 percent a year and the Gini coefficient—a key indicator of inequality—was less than [that] in the United States, Russia, or China.

Rubin: What led you to such pessimist conclusions?

Laqueur: My early steps as a political commentator were in this field. I lived for several years among Arabs—not politicians, not intellectuals, but simple people; fellaheen, Bedouin, poor town people. True, my Arabic was not very good, and I have forgotten most since. (I did acquire a reasonable knowledge of Arab words and phrases not found in dictionaries.) I visited Egypt as a young journalist when King Farouk was still in power. My first book, titled *Communism and Nationalism in the Middle East*, appeared in 1956. It was bound to be an amateurish effort, but it was a pioneering study and widely read and commented on at the time.

Rubin: Do you still stand by your evaluation of 1956?

Laqueur: Yes and no. I overrated the prospects of Communism in the Middle East, but not by very much, and I also noted that the appeal of Marxism was really skin deep. I underrated the appeal of religion, but I was in good company—everyone did that. At that time religion was simply not a very important political factor—this came only thirty years later. I noted that the quest for an universal faith was very strong, and if Communism had an appeal, it was that of a secular religion. Nationalism seemed to be the wave of the future; the great breakthrough of Islamism (the Muslim Brotherhood) came only after nationalism—in the case of Egypt, Nasserism—had failed and Communism had declined. In the late 1950s, many Arab and North African intellectuals flirted with Communism—Fascism was out of fashion following the defeat of Nazi Germany and Fascist Italy. It is striking how many of them ended up in the Muslim Brotherhood or its periphery.

There have been some interesting individual studies, but the general picture remains to be presented. I wish someone would write the story of Ahmad Husain (of Misr al-Fatat—Young Egypt—fame in the late thirties). In his fascist period, Ahmad Husain was very hostile to the Ikhwan. Later, he sympathized with them. His younger brother, who died a year or two ago, spent years in prison as a Communist. But he, too, ended up a fellow traveler of the Ikhwan and became the darling of the Egyptian intelligentsia. These were quite typical stories and they deserve to be retold in detail.

Rubin: To move on to more recent events: Why the pessimism concerning the chances of the Arab spring—in Egypt and elsewhere?

Laqueur: My evaluation had more to do with my experience as historian of revolutions than the Middle East. (I was the author of the entry "revolution" in the penultimate edition of the *Encyclopedia of Social Sciences*.) Talking about a "stolen revolution" is a bit of a joke for there had been no revolution in any of these countries, merely the deposition of unloved authoritarian rulers who had outstayed their welcome. The secular revolutionaries were relatively few and split the extreme left. Various Trotskyite sects endorsed the Muslim Brotherhood which, after all, was an anti-imperialist movement. The power of the traditional structures and ideologies was greatly underrated. All the attention was focused on Midan al-Tahrir. I don't think any of the foreign observers went to al-Mahalla al-Kubra, or Shubra El-Kheima, or Cairo's mega slum, Manshiet Nasser (also known as Rubbish City), home to a million unfortunate people, or the many other places where the great majority of Egyptians live. Nor did they pay attention to the fact that a great many people had benefited from the Mubarak regime, millions of state employees—but this is a different story.

Rubin: The US government obviously prefers the Muslim Brotherhood to the SCAF—the generals. Why?

Laqueur: Who knows? I do not understand the cogent need to choose between two antidemocratic forces. Perhaps, they know something we don't. Perhaps, they think the Brotherhood will eventually prevail and will feel gratitude towards Washington. Perhaps they believe the Ikhwan have changed their character and will become even more moderate when in power.

Rubin: There is obviously a great deal of ferment in Egypt—the young people relatively qualified who cannot find jobs commensurate with their training and expectations. In what direction will they turn?

Laqueur: It is a real tragedy. Egypt is a very poor country as far as natural resources are concerned. The Brotherhood has neither a vision nor a program, except "Islam is the answer." The situation has greatly deteriorated since the outbreak of the Arab spring and the number of unemployed has risen. There has been a flight of capital from Egypt; tourism has greatly declined. The Egyptian pound has lost its value; inflation has risen significantly. I do not know how much money the government has for the import of essential foods. It cannot be more than a few months (three months according to government spokesmen). Unless Egypt gets a handout of a few billion dollars immediately, there will be starvation. Can a disaster be averted? I doubt it. It may coincide with a similar breakdown in Sudan. Help from the oil-rich Arab countries? This would be a real sensation.

Rubin: In view of all this, how to explain the great optimism of the Western media beginning with the Arab spring in January 2011 concerning the prospects of the democratic-revolutionary movement—the dawn of a new glorious age?

Laqueur: I wish I had an answer. To read now the comments of the correspondents of the *New York Times* reminds one of Alice in Wonderland. They were so utterly mistaken. It is probably unfair to single out one specific newspaper because the illusions were so widely shared even by the experts. In part, the roots of the misunderstandings were, of course, psychological. For so long, reports from the Middle East had been negative and depressing: autocratic governments, riots, terrorism, corruption, civil wars, and so on. And now suddenly, there was this great, intoxicating promise of freedom and progress—a beacon of light to the whole world. . . .

There was a total misreading of the Egyptian situation and the prospect and the reasons should be examined very, very carefully. (summer 2012).

Part 4
Israel and Jewish Affairs

The New Million

Professional photographers have a sharp eye for their surroundings. Oded Balilty is one of them, an Israeli Pulitzer prize winner, he thought that he knew well the country in which he was born and had grown up. But as he was commissioned to produce a series on Russian Jews in Israel, he realized that he was dealing with a world whose existence he had never been aware of. This was certainly not a unique case; historians and political scientists in their books about Israel usually mention, only in passing (if at all), the community that "changed the Middle East to the core," according to Mrs. Lily Galili and Mr. Roman Bronfman. The title of their new book probably constitutes a slight exaggeration, but the Russian aliya of the last two decades has been (and continues to be) of great importance. If so, why is so little attention paid to it?

This is mainly perhaps because native Israelis were not that much interested in a community that kept itself apart from the mainstream, culturally, socially, and eventually also politically. But this is certainly not the whole story and it is the great merit of this book to provide, for the first time, a comprehensive attempt to explain the character of this community.

Mrs. Galili is a well-known journalist who was, for many years, on the staff of *Haaretz* and who followed the mixed fortunes of the Russian aliya in Israel. Bronfman, who arrived in Israel in 1980, had been a community activist, and he served as a member of the Knesset but later on left politics for business.

Most of the newcomers arrived in Israel in the early 1990s, and their absorption went through the usual difficulties facing every wave of immigrants. How to find work for (to give but two examples) the many physicians and musicians who came? The number of ex-Soviet physicians was about twice as large as the number of Israeli doctors practicing in the country at the time. Given these and many other problems, namely the relatively high number of elderly people and other newcomers not considered productive by the Israelis, it seems surprising in retrospect that the absorption was not a failure.

It is frequently forgotten today that there were high expectations on the part of the yishuv. Following the disappearance of European Jewry, the great majority of newcomers arrived from North Africa and Muslim countries. There was no other human reservoir and the feeling was, as President Peres put it in an interview with the authors of this book, "if they (the Russian Jews) would not have come we would have been lost."

Nevertheless, however welcome the arrival of the immigrants from the Muslim countries, strengthening the demographic base of the young state, this was hardly the "much needed human material" that Herzl and his successors had envisaged as the founders and builders of the new state. The Russian immigration wave, on the other hand (it was hoped), would bring those above all needed, scientists and technologists those who would establish a modern country, European style. (America at the time was outside Herzl's purview.) There was considerable opposition on the part of Arabs, Palestinian, and others, who tried to bring pressure on Moscow to stop the Jewish emigration; the Israeli Black Panthers were also quite unhappy about the strengthening of the Ashkenazi element.

Many of those permitted to leave the Soviet Union in the early years preferred America to Israel, and the percentage of the dropouts on the road via Vienna was embarrassingly high (it was called *neshira* at the time). The economic prospects in America were better and Israel was a dangerous place—there always could be a new war. It was only after the Shamir government had persuaded Washington to limit the entry of Russian Jews into the United States that the flow of immigrants increased in numbers. As an Israeli minister put it at the time, it was a case of robust Zionist indoctrination. Many of the newcomers, perhaps as much as 30 percent, were technically not Jews in the halachic sense with non-Jewish mothers or even only one Jewish grandparent. This caused endless friction with the orthodox rabbis who were the authorities deciding on marriage, burials, and many other issues.

A significant number of immigrants, perhaps 100,000, left the country in subsequent years. This was by no means a unique phenomenon and a manifestation of failure. It had happened in all earlier immigration waves even the second aliya (1905–1914), which consisted of confirmed

Zionists. It is one of the few shortcomings of this book that the authors hardly ever refer to the experiences of earlier immigrants, which had been in some respects quite similar. They too initially encountered opposition, tended to keep themselves apart, complained about discrimination, and eventually established political parties in defense of their interests—*Aliya Chadasha* in the case of the immigrants from Central Europe and *Shas*, which found its supporters almost entirely among olim with a North-African background.

A personal recollection comes to mind: In the late 1950s, during an extended visit to Jerusalem, an unexpected visitor appeared in our apartment in Gaza Road. I was in bed running a high temperature; the visitor entered the room pushing my wife firmly aside and did not introduce himself but said that he had been commissioned by his boss to ask me a few questions. It had come to Ben Gurion's knowledge that being active in the field of Soviet studies, I had been several times to Russia of late, which was quite rare in those years. My visitor, a blunt man, did not hide his doubts: it was not quite clear to him what a Jew from Germany (he used a stronger term) could possibly know about Russia that people of his generation (he was born in the then Russian empire on the last day of the nineteenth century) did not know. Be that as it might. Shaul (he volunteered that much information) had been asked to get my views on the prospects of immigration from the Soviet Union—if a massive effort was undertaken, how many would come? How angry would the Soviet leaders be? And could I suggest perhaps a few people suitable to work in a campaign scheduled to expedite this process. What I told him in my feverish state I do not exactly recall nor is it of historical importance whether any of my views and recommendations played a role in the subsequent deliberations. I know that some of the people I suggested became active in the campaign. Manny Litvinov, the British writer, was among them; he died not long ago in London aged ninety-six.

In the years that followed, I encountered on occasion Shaul and those working for him in the Soviet Union and abroad and was impressed by their work against heavy odds.

I also met some of the immigrants; there was a great deal of difference between the *refuseniks* and those who came later when the gates were opened. In retrospect, those who were fighting for the Russian aliya were not fully aware of how far that generation had moved from Jewish (let alone Zionist) traditions. This was in many ways a natural process that equally applied to Jewish communities in Europe and

America. There were strong ties with Russia; even in the writings of an earlier generation of Russian Zionists from Moshe Smilanski to Abba Achimeir, we find longings for the Russian landscape and especially the forest. But the Russian olim were many and self-confident, and in view of the lack of interest of the Israelis in their interests, values, and heritage, it was only natural that they should keep to themselves; they thought Israeli culture provincial and preferred to stick to their own traditions.

I thought this pride in their specific identity legitimate and on occasion touching, if sometimes, a little idealized. Visiting Russian language bookshops in Israel, I encountered more Pikul than Pasternak, more books by my late dubious friend Julian Semyonov than Mandelstam. I saw Russian translations of Leo Strauss and even of Levinas but also a great deal of rubbish.

However, they were great readers and theater goers, and they added very much not only to the standing of Israel in the world of chess but also the world of music. They contributed greatly not only to Israeli night life at various levels of sophistication but also established newspapers and television channels of their own (Arutz 9), the theater (*Gesher*) and sports (especially track and field and gymnastics). They were overrepresented in the fighting units of the Israeli army and played a very important role in the development of Israeli computer technology. It is difficult to think of a single field in which they failed to make a significant contribution.

This is one side of the coin, a very impressive one, but there remain questions to which I have not always found satisfactory answers. The immigrants who came to Israel were products of the Soviet system however much they disliked and suffered from it. In what way was the culture and way of life they brought to Israel different from the one they had absorbed at home and in school in their country of origin, and in what way was their Israel an extension of the old and new Russia? An unfair question perhaps—the Jewish state envisaged by Herzl was not specifically Jewish either but simply a modern society consisting of Jews from Europe (and also some Arabs). Why blame Russian Jews for not mastering Hebrew? (As the saying in Israel goes, how do you define a person mastering three languages? A trilingual. Two languages? Bilingual, and one language? An Anglo-Saxon). It is recalled that Ivrit makes no appearance in Herzl's *Altneuland*. There are countries ranging from Canada to Switzerland where different cultures and languages peacefully coexist.

However, these are the exceptions; some common cultural ground seems to be needed in the modern world to keep a society together to provide a minimum of national solidarity. To accept this, one need not be a firm believer in fashionable theories on identity politics. The issues go deeper; they concern the identity of individuals and societies. To illustrate this dilemma, I want to refer to a person who does not appear in the Galili Bronfman book. Alexander Rosenbaum is not known outside the community of Russian speakers, but within that community, it certainly is a name to conjure with. He was born in Leningrad and became one of the best known and most popular "bards." Now in his sixties, he is still going strong. Many millions love his *valse*—Boston and other songs, particularly those devoted to the criminal underworld—*blatnoi*. Rosenbaum was in Israel and is something like an honorary member of *Yisrael Beiteinu*; in the election campaign of 2009, he was invited to sing the party theme song. His Yerushalayim (readily accessible on Youtube) is showing him walking the narrow streets of the old city, invoking all the right associations and symbols including Palmah and Entebbe.

Rosenbaum was also a member of the Russian parliament (the Duma) representing Putin's party, acting as the deputy head of the Duma cultural committee. Two years ago, his *Romance Kolchak* (also accessible on Youtube) became a bestseller. Admiral Kolchak was an Arctic explorer, but he is better known as one of the heads of the White counterrevolutionary movement in 1918/19 who was defeated and eventually executed by the Bolsheviks. The Romance, a moving and sympathetic song, is devoted to his thoughts and feelings during the last minutes prior to this execution.

Yerushalayim and Aleksander Vasilevich Kolchak (1874–1920) is a strange synthesis and not a shocking one. The admiral, for all we know, was no more an anti-Semite than the current president of Russia; perhaps, with a little effort, some common denominators can be found for Kolchak, Putin, and Lieberman. Galili and Bronfman are in fact trying to find parallels between the latter two, yet it is a puzzling combination and it is at this point that the question of identity obtrudes itself. Russian and Israeli patriotism, Kolchak, Putin, and Lieberman—what a fascinating combination, but how will it all add up in the end?

The politics of the Russian aliya is the most controversial issue in this context. The first Russian party (Israel be'aliya) headed by Natan Sharanski came into being in the early 1990s. Sharanski had been a true hero in his homeland, but he was not a great success in politics after his departure. His party moved from center to the right, and eventually, he was pushed aside by Lieberman who moved even further to the right and became a major player in Israeli politics.

The politics of the Russian community is often explained against the background of its Soviet origins, admittedly not the ideal preparatory school for a democratic education. This explains at best part of the phenomenon. Do we know how deep this extremism goes?

Shimon Peres, in the interview mentioned earlier on, put his finger on another, probably a more important aspect. Most of the olim of the 1990s were accustomed to think in terms of great countries and big powers. They believed that Israel was one of them with the Jordan a mighty river like the Volga, and the Golan, which of the magnitude of the Ural or the Caucasus. Russian Jews, like other denizens of the Soviet Union, had been cut off from the outside world, and their knowledge was limited to their home country and it was this naivete that probably shaped their world view and their thoughts on Israeli politics more than any other factor. Many of them never quite understood that equal justice does not so far prevail in international relations and that small countries cannot afford to behave like superpowers except at great risk to their survival. True, such thinking is not a specific Russian-Jewish monopoly; it is shared by a multitude of others.

Kamu gryadeshi? What will be the future of this community? In what direction is it moving? What will be the face of the young generation that was born in Israel, went to local schools, and served in the army? What will be their impact on Israeli society and culture? How will they get along with other groups of olim of the last generation or two? It worked well as the authors note in Netivot, but Netivot is a small town midway between Be'er Sheva and Gaza; will it work equally well elsewhere? They will certainly master the difficult language spoken in Israel. How deep will be their attachment to the country? It would be interesting to know more about "mixed marriages," but these are early days and such information is not yet available. The importance of the Russian language in Israel may well decline. The circulation of *Vesti*, a leading Russian language daily, is now only a third of what it used to be in its heyday, but this is true for all the printed media in Israel and the world in general. The number of Russian-language bloggers in Israel could well be a per-capita world record. However, in many families, the second generation knows hardly any Russian.

In brief, the Russian-Jewish community, like much of Israel, is in flux. In the meantime, one ought to be grateful for this valuable report on its present state.

Lili Galili and Roman Bronfman: *Hamilion she shina et hamisrah hatikhon. Ha aliya hasovietit le' Israel* (**The million which changed the Middle East. The Soviet aliya to Israel**). **Matar, Tel Aviv, 2013. 282 pp.**

The Kibbutz at 100

One hundred years ago, Josef Bussel, Josef Baratz, another eight young men, and two women arrived in Umm Juni on the southern shore of lake Tiberias and established "Kommuna," a small agricultural settlement that was to become the first kibbutz. Bussel was twenty-one at the time (he drowned in the Kineret a few years later) and Baratz the same age. The anniversary has been duly remembered and celebrated in Degania Alef (the name of the settlement) as well as in Tel Aviv and elsewhere in Israel and in a number of books, the most massive (certainly the heaviest) of which is the present volume, much of it encyclopedic in character as each kibbutz receives an entry. It is lavishly and attractively produced with many maps, perhaps too many illustrations and a preface by the President of Israel. It has sections about the development of kibbutz agriculture and industry about kibbutz cultural life, education, and how festivals are celebrated in the kibbutz. It is a work very useful for reference, but it can also serve as a coffee-table book. It is not a history of the kibbutz movement; such a work does not yet exist. The one that comes nearest to it, Henry Near's two volumes, takes the reader up to 1955.

To declare a personal interest, the kibbutz has been part of my life, as a member for a number of years, and as an observer from afar for a long time after. When I arrived in what was then the British mandate of Palestine, the number of kibbutzim was still small, forty or fifty in all compared with 265 today. I visited at least half of them at the time. One could always get a meal in the dining room and a place to sleep somewhere. I remember a trip to Degania, which at the time, was most conveniently reached by rail, how the train did not even stop at Zemah, the local station, but merely slowed down, and how I had to jump from the compartment because the train went on to Damascus. I recall the surprise when meeting some of the founders of the first kibbutz and that these legendary figures were not even very old but men and women in their late forties. I remember the infernal heat in the Jordan valley (no one had heard about air conditioning) and took part in one of the first banana harvests. I recall that some of my coworkers were eating twenty-five, perhaps thirty, bananas a day, a remarkable feat, even though the fruit was then relatively small.

Having decided after a number of years that kibbutz life was fascinating (and for me, being the youngest in my group, highly educational) but not the way I wanted to spend the rest of my days; I announced my departure and was given the usual farewell present at the time—five pounds sterling, a mattress, and an iron bed frame.

My attitude since has been one of critical sympathy. I frequently visited my erstwhile comrades there, once or twice, in the company of a Jerusalem neighbor named Gershom Scholem, whose boyhood friends lived in Bet Sera (originally called Markenhof—the early pioneers had trained in a farm named Markenhof near Freiburg in Southern Germany). Conditions were primitive and there was an acute housing problem. Even in my time, couples frequently had to share their tent with a third member of the collective called a "primus" for reasons unknown to me (even the kibbutz dictionary section in this book is not certain about the origin of the term). But then, I noticed the changes over the years—how people moved from life in tents to a room in a wooden shack (also called a lift or a zrif) and later yet to a room in a house of stone, and subsequently to two rooms with a little kitchen—creeping privatization in retrospect.

These then were the early "heroic" days of tower and stockade (homa umigdal), of Hora Nahalal, and a variety of "fantasiot"; everyone was poor and sometimes went to bed hungry, but the atmosphere was one of optimism, being part of a great and growing movement, engaging in a major social project, which had never been tried before. There was no feeling of loneliness, for every week with every ship anchoring in Haifa reinforcements arrived. The war brought a halt to all this, but the feeling was that at its end, everything would continue as before. The news about the great tragedy in Europe came only toward the end of the war, and it took even longer to understand its full meaning.

I was no longer a member when the War of Independence came, but my work as a young war correspondent led me to kibbutzim in the north and south of the country. Reflecting on the course of events in later years as a historian who had also been an eye witness I never doubted that without the Palmah, essentially a little kibbutz army, the

War of Independence would not have ended as it did. I was not and did not become a military expert but still realized that much of what I saw was amateurish and fatal mistakes were committed but what was lacking in experience was compensated by enthusiasm.

The tribulations of the kibbutz movement began with the establishment of the state. This process has frequently been described and analyzed. The kibbutz was neither able nor willing to absorb the masses of new immigrants who did not share their idealism and their values, and the spirit of sacrifice and pioneering.

At the same time, it no longer attracted many young Israelis from outside kibbutz, as it had done in earlier years. Members left and this led to a diminution of the specific weight of the kibbutz in Israeli society. There were splits; there are now two settlements named Givat Haim or Ashdot Ya'akov; had it to do with Stalin or with Israeli domestic policies in the 1950s? Today, hardly anyone remembers the reasons for the splits, but at the time, the conflicts were quite bitter.

These were the years of zena (austerity); the country suffered from an economic crisis and so did the kibbutz. The kibbutz aged, and living conditions that had seemed almost normal at the age of twenty were no longer acceptable thirty years later. Agriculture, even though its professional level had immensely improved, could not provide the basis for a higher living standard. The kibbutz had to look for other, more profitable sources of income such as industry and tourism, but it was slow to do so in the beginning. All over the world, there was a crisis of agriculture and the state had to step in and help. In this respect, the Israeli situation was by no means unique, but it led to the dependence of the kibbutz on the state, and as governments unfriendly to the kibbutz or even hostile came to power, the situation aggravated.

Gradually, an anti-kibbutz ideology developed. The kibbutz had been an Utopian enterprise; the kibbutzniks were parasites. Socialism had been Israel's great misfortune, and it had been holding back the Israeli economy. If the laws of the market had prevailed, if there had been competition, the economy of the country would have been much stronger, and many more people could have been absorbed. Many of the six millions who perished could have been saved.

Some of this criticism was correct, and some was arrant nonsense. The kibbutz was, of course, an Utopian undertaking based on a radical egalitarian ethos, so it could work only for the idealistic elite. But there was not that much Jewish money around at the time, and those who had it preferred to invest it elsewhere. The 1930s were a period of economic crisis all over the world, and the number of the immigration certificates issued depended on the good will of the British mandatory government, not the state of the economy. In brief, there was no market alternative to the kibbutz and other "socialist" enterprises.

The kibbutz's crisis reached its climax in the 1980s against the background of a general crisis affecting Israeli economy—with an inflation rate of 400 percent. The kibbutz management acted foolishly and irresponsibly when it took out bank loans; debts and interest were blown up by the inflation. When the economic situation changed, the dust had settled and the banks performed their legerdemain; what with high real interest, the kibbutzim found themselves saddled with a debt of six billion dollars. It took more than a decade to agree how to restructure debts and these were the years when the kibbutz changed out of recognition—three quarters of the kibbutzim gave up their old egalitarian way of life, differential wages were introduced. Private property became the rule, and meals and everything else had to be paid for, but a safety net was kept for hardship cases. The new kibbutz (*kibbutz mithadesh*—a euphemism) came into being.

I suspect the process of privatization would have come under the way in any case because there was a growing realization that the old kibbutz no longer fitted into the new world that had arisen. Voluntary collectivism was on the way out, and most realized that self-interest was not a capitalist prejudice but part of human nature—at least for the time being in the process of human evolution. But the transition would have been slower and less acrimonious but for the economic crisis.

In the 1980s and 1990s, the epitaph of the kibbutz was written. As late as 2007, Gary Becker, a Chicago professor and Nobel Prize winner in economics, summarized his impressions of a few days' visit—it was inevitable that the classical kibbutz system would fade. (A socialist professor, Franz Oppenheimer, had predicted this in 1926.) It was a perspicacious summary; training as an economist seems to sharpen one's powers of observation; Becker also noticed that there was a fair amount of promiscuity (email from a kibbutz: more than elsewhere? Rubbish).

Only a few years have passed, but I suspect an updated article by Professor Becker would reach slightly more cautious conclusions, not because he changed his views about "from each according to his or her ability." (I always thought the phrase was coined by Louis Blanc in 1840—Becker attributes it to Marx several decades later.) The perspective of 2011/12 has changed because we have witnessed, off late, far more massive debt crises, not just in Greece, Ireland, and Portugal but most of Europe, not just in California but in these nonsocialist United States. The sums involved are no longer measured in millions but trillions. Was it the fault of the market or of capitalism? The kibbutz may offer some lessons how to confront a debt crisis.

The new form of settlement shows no sign of disappearing. Five years ago, I visited Kibbutz Hama'apil, once Israeli volleyball champion, to see old friends. The number of members had shrunk to 197, and it looked to me like an old age home what with a median age of sixty-two. Today, it has 317 members and the average age is considerably lower (Email from Kibbutz Lehavot Habashan in Galilee: We have now over 150 young families as private settlers, more than kibbutz members). It will take no more than a few years before the two parts will merge into a *yishuv kehilati* (community settlement). This is not mere anecdotal evidence; thousands of people have joined the new kibbutz (or whatever we call it), some *banim chosrim* (kibbutz children returning from town), and others for any number of reasons that have nothing to do with A. D. Gordon or Ber Borokhov; the air is better and so is the security situation; education for the children is also often preferable and there are many other attractions. The new setup seems to work.

The economic situation is no longer desperate. I was a member of Kibbutz Shamir for a year in 1940, and I remember how desperately the secretary of the kibbutz tried to obtain a loan of a few hundred pounds and how demeaning it was to apply for such small sums. Today, Shamir, located in Upper Galilee, is one of the leading global producers of contact lenses with a turnover of hundreds of millions; its shares are traded at the New York stock exchange and it employs some 1,400 people. Ma'agan Michael and Sassa employ even more, and Na'an and Mishmar Ha'Emeq are also big employers. They produce rubber and plastic products for irrigation and other purposes, vegetarian and baby food, ornamental fish for Japan, and other products for which quite obviously there is a market. Less than 2 percent of the population of Israel now live in kibbutzim, but their share in industrial and agricultural exports is ten times as much or more.

Not everyone has prospered and profited in equal measure. Some years ago, Kibbutz Ha'ogen was considered the most successful entrepreneur, but it has fallen back, while Ma'abarot on the old Haifa-Tel Aviv Road, which did not do too well, does now belong, I am told, to the club of millionaires. Economic success was not the main ambition of the generation of the founders, but it is a precondition of survival in the modern world. Epitaphs in the circumstances seem premature: The old kibbutz is history, and its post-Utopian successor may last a long time.

(Elieser Saks (ed.), *100 Shnot Kibbutz. Sipura shel ha'tnua hakibbutzit.*[100 years of Kibbutz. The story of the kibbutz movement]. 416 pp. Coordinata. Tel Aviv 2011.)

Recollections of Jerusalem

I would like to talk tonight about Jerusalem, a city I have known reasonably well for sixty-five years during which I have not been able to make up my mind whether I like or dislike it.

Ben Gurion writes in his diary sometime in spring of 1948 following the visit of David Shaltiel, the commander of the Jewish forces in that city, that 20 percent of the inhabitants of the city are normal people, and further 20 percent are connected to the university in one way or another and are also normal (Shmuel Agnon may not have agreed with this as appears from his novels *Tmol Shilshom* and *Shira*), but the rest are mostly weird. Ben Gurion, needless to say, wrote about the Jews not the Arabs. It is a shocking, at the very least, highly subjective statement, but there must be a reason why he jotted down these words, and while I do not pretend to have a conclusive answer, I shall try to shed some light.

My own contact with the city goes back to November 1938 when I arrived in an armored bus from Tel Aviv around lunch time. It took more than three hours; there were many British army control posts on the narrow road. It was fairly warm—a welcome contrast to dark and rainy Europe, which I had left a few days earlier; this was the week of the Kristall Nacht. It was a good feeling to be out of Europe, even though I was hungry and thirsty and did not know where I would stay that night.

The entrance to Jerusalem was anything but impressive—ugly low buildings, narrow roads that were not too clean. After a few minutes, we came to a halt at a market, which I later learned was called Mahane Yehuda. There was a terrific noise of a rusty pump next to the bus, but there was no pump only a donkey who was braying. But then I had never heard a donkey before in my seventeen years. There were a lot of people in the street, a strange mixture—Arabs with a kefiya and with a tarbush. Orthodox Jews, such as I had never before seen, but also Jews with short trousers, English policemen and soldiers, and monks of various denominations, verily a multicultural society. The shops looked as if they had been transplanted from a small town in Eastern Europe or Anatolia. The central bus station was on Jaffa Road in those days. The light was much brighter than that in Europe, the smells were quite different, and the noise level higher. In brief, it was a strange experience, and not being *religiously musikalisch* (to use an expression coined by Max Weber), I cannot say that I was overwhelmed. However, I doubt whether even a deep religious believer would have experienced a shock of recognition, a deep spiritual experience at this first encounter. I have read countless accounts of visitors to Jerusalem who came to the city holy to three religions and who were not favorably impressed. One of the few exceptions was young Benjamin Disraeli who visited the city in 1831. But he was a young man (aged twenty-six at the time) of tremendous imagination and an enormous capacity for enthusiasm who could ignore the sad and ugly realities confronting him. His impressions of the city are reflected in some of his novels such as *Tancred*.

I spent several years in Jerusalem during the following period, and I have been back almost every year, sometimes for a few weeks, and sometimes for longer. I lived in many parts of the town and also in Arab neighborhoods such as Issawiya and the German Colony, which prior to 1948 was predominantly Arab. I learned Ivrit relatively quickly and acquired a working knowledge of spoken Arabic. I was intrigued by many parts of the city, but I felt at home only in certain neighborhoods such as Rehavia and Talbiye, and these were usually the districts I could not afford at the time.

When I first arrived, Jerusalem had about 140,000 inhabitants, of which 90,000 were Jews. There had been a Jewish majority since the middle of the nineteenth century. After the siege of 1948, the number declined to less than hundred thousand. Today, Jerusalem is the most populous city in Israel (Greater Tel Aviv has of course more inhabitants). The number of Jewish residents has grown fourfold, but the Arab population even slightly more and amounts now to about 30 percent. There has been a steady Palestinian influx into Jerusalem from neighboring villages and above all from Hebron. There was an exodus of Christian Arabs, but the Hebronites are quite influential not only in the markets of the Old City. There is an exodus from among the Jewish community, especially the younger and secular elements. The population growth in the Jewish part of the city took place mainly as the result of the expansion of Mea Shearim, the ultra orthodox element.

When I arrived in 1938, there were only a handful yeshivot mainly south of Bate Ungarim. Today, there are scores, big and small, and three or four pages in the local telephone directory. Some, I am told, are bogus; like Gogol's Dead Souls, they exist on paper only—a trick to obtain financial support from the government. According to a recent report, the managers of one of these nonexisting religious schools have shown a sense of humor, giving the parking lot of the local income tax office as its official address.

Mea Shearim has expanded in most directions—from about a thousand or two thousand before the Second World War it has grown to about 130,000, and a recent mayor of Jerusalem was one of them. As for the real number of those attending the yeshivot, we have only rough estimates; the numbers of attendants are artificially inflated so as to get higher subsidies. The problem is going back to the Turkish days—what number of Jews living in the old city should be given? If one inflated their number, this meant that the community had to pay higher taxes, but if one understated the number, the prospects of getting support from Jewish communities in Europe (chaluka) diminished.

This expansion has caused, as we know, a great many social, economic, and political problems, but while this impinges on the state of Jerusalem, it is not the main subject of my talk tonight.

That Zion played a crucial role in Jewish religion goes without saying, and *Next Year in Jerusalem* appears in the prayers. However, most Zionist leaders from Herzl and Ahad Ha'am to Weizmann and Nahum Goldman were appalled when they first came to Jerusalem and not one of them decided to settle there. This has been the case until fairly recently—not only among the Left and secular but also the nationalist Right. It appears, for instance, in the poems of Uri Zvi Greenberg. Until about twenty years ago, most of the ministers let alone members of the Knesset would come on Sunday morning to Jerusalem and stay there up to Thursday, but very few lived there.

Why? Because Jerusalem constituted all that Zionism wanted to dissociate itself from—the Wailing Wall, the lack of idealism and public spirit, and the tradition of lachrymose Jewish history. Jerusalem was anything but a pioneering city and had no interest in the building of a new society. It was right wing and nationalist—Irgun and Stern Gang were more popular there than in any other city in Palestine; the local soccer team Betar had certainly a very patriotic following, but whether tJerusalem was a Zionist city was and is doubtful. I joined a Kibbutz for a few years, but then my Kibbutz movement decided to establish a daily newspaper, and I became its Jerusalem correspondent, which was about the most interesting job available because politics were concentrated in that city—the Jewish Agency and the Vaad Leumi were there, tie Higher Arab Committee, and of course the Mandatory Government. But in addition, we had to deal with local affairs, crime, archaeology, municipal affairs, terrorism—you name it, never a dull moment. I had the good fortune to have as assistants some of the very young men who became later quite prominent, such as Sabi (Shabtai Tevet), the biographer of Ben Gurion; Amos Eilon the well-known journalist; and Naqdimon Rogel, one of the founders of Israeli television, and so on.

Thus, one met, at a daily press conference and privately too, the leading political figures—Ben Gurion who discussed with me Zionist history (when I worked on the history of Zionism), Shertok-Sharett who wanted to persuade me to change my name to Yakir, then Golda Meir, and others. One also met, more formally, some of the leading Arab figures, some of the Husseini and Khaldis, one of whom was Auni Bey Abdul Hadi; at that time, Palestinian political life was very much a monopoly of a few leading families—including for instance Mussa Alami, for whom I had the greatest respect. He was a man of integrity and character, intelligent, dynamic, and a true patriot. I think in retrospect he was the most farsighted, but it did not help him very much in his political career.

Among the Jews, I was particularly interested in *Brit Shalom* (which changed its name several times). They believed in bi-nationalism but unfortunately did not find interlocutors at the time on the other side. Kalvariski was the most experienced among them, a Russian Jew who had studied agriculture in France and arrived in Palestine in the 1890s. His approach was, however, a little onesided; he thought that bakshish was a panacea, and when I challenged him with great indignation, he smiled and said that the Middle East was not Scandinavia and that I still had a great deal to learn. J. L. Magnes, the President of the Hebrew university, was the most imposing figure, fearless, independent-minded, and truly idealistic, but there was something of a child in him, a truly naïve man who thought that everyone was as broadminded, tolerant, and idealistic as he was. I once asked David Ben-Gurion whom from among the American Zionist leaders he held in highest esteem. His answer was Magnes. Very surprised, I said, "But he stands for all the things you oppose." "Quite true," Ben Gurion said, "but he is the only one who came and settled in this country."

The professors on Mount Scopus should be mentioned, along with Artur Ruppin—who was disenchanted early on as far as the prospects of an understanding with the Arabs was concerned and Hans Kohn but

Kohn left Palestine and had a successful academic career in the United States. Robert Weltsch was a friend of mine, and he tended toward pessimism early on—the way things had developed in Jewish Palestine were not according to his liking. He left after the Second World War, first as a correspondent at the Nuremberg Trials and later in London. All these men—I cannot recall more than one or two women—were people of great learning and sterling character, and they have been derided by later-day publicists without justification. There was no monolithic party line. Martin Buber, for instance, became exceedingly critical of Israeli politics (which may not have been unconnected with the fact that he was much less appreciated in Israel than in Europe or America), whereas Gershom Scholem with all his criticism was a patriotic citizen of the new state. The person who coordinated all these efforts was a youngish ex-student of Arabic at the Hebrew university named Gavriel Stern, a native of the Rhineland who has undeservedly been forgotten. Brith Shalom or Ichud, as it was later called, had no office; its correspondence and archive was in the leather bag that Stern carried around—he saw visitors in the backroom of a bookshop named He'atid at the corner of Jaffa and Havazelet street—at that time, Jerusalem's Fleet street. The book shop is now a fast-food establishment and the street changed its name several times. Let me mention in passing that I never quite understood why a university city the size of Jerusalem should not have one decent major bookshop.

My recollections of Jerusalem at that time are many and very vivid. I hate to stop in the middle so to speak. But time being limited, let us now proceed to the question and answer period.

Bloodlands—The Snyder Version

Timothy Snyder, a Yale professor of history, has written a book on Eastern Europe and the holocaust, which has created a stir well beyond the circle of specialists. It has been translated into eighteen languages. For his admirers, it is the most important work for years, which opens up entirely new perspectives not only as far as the holocaust is concerned but also about Hitler, Stalin, the Second World War, and the crimes of the two dictators. According to his critics, there is little in this book that was not known before, the claims of opening up new vista are exaggerated, and the approach of the author is limited and often wrong.

There is truth in both these judgments. It is a work of importance but also considerable weaknesses, and this for the following reasons. Snyder feels that the suffering of Eastern Europe during the World War Two has not been paid sufficient attention, whereas the holocaust, the murder of the Jews, has been singled out and documented in very great detail. He is in no way a holocaust denier but believes that the non-Jewish victims of the Nazi and Communist dictatorships have been largely ignored. This started with Stalin's liquidation of kulaks as a class and the systematic starving of the Ukraine in the early 1930s (the *Holodomor*), in which hundreds of thousands lost their lives.

It is clear why in Eastern Europe until fairly recently, the Nazi persecutions were given considerable publicity(except the mass murder of Jews) but not the crimes of the Soviet occupation power; Eastern Europe was under Soviet rule for four decades. This has changed since the 1990s, and the victims of the postwar period are certainly no longer ignored today. They have become part of the national tradition of these countries. It is also true that the native recruits of the Waffen-SS have been honored in the Baltic republics and the fact that a considerable number of Eastern European citizens participated in the killing of Jews is played down or ignored altogether.

True, even today, more attention is paid to the murder of Jews; the museums and similar institutions in Jerusalem, Washington, and New York are keeping the memory as is the eighteen-volume official German documentation about the murder of the Jews. There are no similar institutional arrangements dedicated to the other victims of Nazi and Soviet terror, no big museums, no days of commemorations, and so on.

However, the reasons for such neglect should not be looked for in the Western world. Snyder should have inquired in Warsaw and other East European capitals why no greater efforts have been made to commemorate these tragic years—few museums, hardly any research institutes, not much teaching in schools and universities. Andrzej Wajda produced a movie about Katyn, and some old books have been republished about Poles in the Gulag but not much beyond this. He should have asked in the Kremlin why the only museum dealing with the Gulag age—not a very imposing one—can be found off the beaten track in the city of Perm—not in Moscow or St. Petersburg. Official institutions seem to have neither the interest nor the means to concern themselves with keeping the memory alive. The only initiative has come from small voluntary groups such as Memorial with very limited budgets. Even the memory of the Russian prisoners of war who perished in German camps of which there were more than two millions is not kept awake. One does not know whether such official neglect has political or other reasons.

Millions were killed or starved to death in the "Bloodlands." But the fate of European Jews was still unique in some crucial respects; Snyder and some others find it difficult to fully accept this.

Hitler and the other Nazi leaders intended to eradicate the Jews altogether, without exception. As for the Slavic peoples and those considered racially inferior, they were to be expelled within the framework of the "new order" to create space (lebensraum) for German settlers. Many of the educated people among them were killed, but the very existence of these peoples was not put into question. They were *untermenschen*—but they still were *menschen* (human beings) to serve those racially superior. The Jews were not human beings but vermin.

The war and the occupation, the bloodletting, were a tragedy, which was a major trauma for Poland. Prewar Poland counted thirty-four million citizens, contemporary Poland counts thirty-eight. However, the Jewish communities that existed there before the World War Two no longer exist. Prewar Warsaw had 1.3 million inhabitants, a third of them were Jews. Today, the number of Jews in the whole of Poland amounts to about a thousand.

There has been genocide throughout history, and some of it may have caused more victims than the holocaust. There were the massacres in Cambodia under Pol Pot and the mass killings in Central Africa, to mention only two examples from recent history. The number of Russian and Ukrainian civilians who perished in the Second World War (perhaps fourteen million) was certainly larger than the number of Jewish victims of the holocaust. But in no other case was there the intention or a detailed plan of the wholesale liquidation of the people. There was no systematic indoctrination aiming at a specific, violent hatred. There was no anti-Slavic organ similar to the *Stuermer*. There were occasional brochures about the racially inferior Slavs, but at the same time, military collaboration was welcomed with Russian and Ukrainian units such as the Vlasov Army.

The Sinti and Roma were considered by the Nazis as racially inferior and harmful and many were killed. But the policy toward them was by no means consistent. In the beginning, only the "mixed elements" among them were persecuted, pure gypsies were not in view of the alleged Indian (Aryan?) origins. This changed only later on. In some occupied European countries, they were subject to violent persecution, and in others, they were not. Django Reinhardt, the famous Sinti jazz violinist, entertained German military units in France. It is unthinkable that Yehudi Menuhin would have been invited for such occasions.

The story of East European mass murder starts with Ukrainian holodomor in the early 1930s. It is less known that roughly during the same period and in similar circumstances 1.5 million people perished in Kazakhstan. About 700,000 were shot during the Stalinist purges, and more died in the Gulag. About a million Polish civilians were killed by German special units. Two to three million Soviet prisoners of war died in German camps; the majority was starved to death and the others were shot. About a million German prisoners of war died in Russian camps.

These figures are frightening as they are; unfortunately, there are frequent exaggerations, even until quite recently. Guenter Grass, in a recent interview, mentioned a figure of six million German prisoners of war who allegedly perished in Soviet camps. There have been exaggerations concerning the number of Roma and Sinti who were murdered. The figures given by Snyder are cautious, on the conservative side.

The book concludes with the description of the expulsion of millions of Germans from Eastern Europe in the course of which again many died. The author also mentions the Soviet antisemitic campaign in the early 1950s, but in this case, there were only few victims, usually prominent artists, because the dictator died before he was able to carry out his plans.

Snyder frequently refers to an "interaction" between the two totalitarian regimes, but the meaning of the term is not quite clear. The policy of genocide was carried out quite independently by both and they had no need to learn from each other. One of the few exceptions was the handing over by the Soviet secret police of German communist emigrants to the Gestapo in 1939/40 the years of the Molotov-Ribbentrop pact. It is Snyder's merit to describe the events of these years on the basis of research in many languages. He complains that most of his colleagues had based their work mainly or exclusively on German sources. But German sources remain the main sources—the contribution to our knowledge in say Bulgarian or Slovak publications;languages mentioned by Snyder are very limited. It is difficult to fault Snyder inasmuch as facts are concerned, his book is well-written and the evidence of witnesses is well-chosen.

Had this book been published a quarter of a century earlier, it would have received much less praise. Many would have condemned it as a product of the Cold War; the consensus in the academic world at the time was that a work like Snyder's was tendentious and one sided. It was misguided to engage in comparisons between Stalin and Hitler, that is, Nazism and the Soviet Union. Without Stalin's hard line in the 1930s, the Soviet Union would not have been able to resist the German onslaught in 1941. It was not denied at the time that innocent people had been affected, but the dictatorship had to steel itself for the coming trials. Furthermore, it was frequently argued at the time in academic circles that the number of victims in the Gulag and during the purges was exaggerated—a byproduct of the Cold War mentality.

Today, voices are again heard not only in Putin's Russia according to which without Stalin and Stalinism, the Soviet Union would have been defeated in the war, and for this reason, it was wrong to blame the ruler and his system. When the French *Black Book of Communism* appeared a few years ago (a work admittedly not free of certain exaggerations), there was again a good deal of criticism of such coldwarish allegations.

The fact that Snyder's work received a great deal of assent points to a change in the Zeitgeist. There is some irony in the fact that Snyder's book and articles have been strongly promoted by the *New York Review of Books*, a periodical earlier on leading in its criticism of the "cold war mentality" and works such as Snyder's. His book certainly appeared at the right time.

However, those specializing in the research of Stalinist Russia on one hand and the holocaust on the other will hardly find much necessitating far reaching revaluation and revision of their views. Robert Conquest's pioneering book about the hunger in the Ukraine had been published decades earlier and the same is true concerning other aspects of Snyder's work. In some ways, the great echo generated by his book reminds one of the reception of Solzhenitsyn work on the Gulag. The facts had been widely known from many sources, but they had not reached a wider public. There is a famous Schiller poem according to which the fact that a professor had discovered and published certain facts did not mean that everyone would now know about them. Both Solzhenitsyn and Snyder benefitted, to repeat once again, from a change in the Zeitgeist.

What of Snyder's historical perspective as far as the holocaust is concerned? He and some of his supporters believe that it is revolutionary and "revisionist in the best sense." Snyder persuaded himself that up to the publication of his work all (or almost all) works were onesided, limited in scope by a nationalist bias. Writers had focused on Auschwitz forgetting (or suppressing) that there had been many other victims in the bloodlands. Only with the appearance of this book, a truly objective work appeared doing justice to all sides. But this is not the case; perhaps there will be such a work in a hundred years when passions will have died down.

Such exaggerated claims undermine the value of a work that has its merits. Snyder has produced, to repeat it once again, a work in which he deals with the hitherto often neglected victims of Hitler and Stalin. In *Bloodlands*, he has provided the Polish Ukrainian version of events in Eastern Europe. This was a necessary, long overdue endeavor and praise is due to the author. But it is certainly not, as he suggests, the first postnationalist work.

In his effort to restore somehow a balance (as he sees it), he overemphasized perhaps by necessity one side—the one that was neglected in the past. In the process, he sees only light in events in which there was both light and shadow. About the Jewish victims, there had been a great deal of literature in the past—some believe too much of it. Furthermore, at this point the question raised earlier on is reappearing: was the Nazi holocaust of the Jews something specific in a category of its own, or has it been overemphasized—a nationalist presentation of one group of victims at the expense of others? Is it enlightening (and legitimate) to equate the murder of the Jews with the hunger in Ukraine?

The answer seems clear. The holocaust was sui generis not because of numbers but because it aimed at the total annihilation of a group of people. It was sui generis because it happened in twentieth-century Europe and not among cavemen. It was sui generis because the preparations and execution of the mass murder as well as the consequences were different not only from the Ukrainian Holodorm but all other known cases of genocide practiced hitherto. This, it would appear, is the author unwilling to accept.

(Timothy Snyder: *Bloodlands. Europe between Hitler and Stalin.* Basic Books, New York 2011).

George Mosse: Berlin to Madison

George L. Mosse was one of the most influential historians of his generation; the contributions in this volume written by colleagues and students who belong to the leaders in their profession provide ample evidence. His interests spanned various countries and periods—seventeenth-century England and nineteenth-century Germany, the two world wars and cultural history. Later on, his attention was devoted to the nationalization of the masses and the cult of dead heroes, Fascism, German-Jewish history, and the Holocaust. The question why historians opt for the study of one topic and not another is of interest; not only accident plays a role but also intellectual influences experienced at university, travel, a sudden discovery in a library, or the archives as well as apparently a certain predisposition and a fascination with a certain subject, which is difficult to trace but still very real. In his autobiography, George occasionally hints at what made him opt for one topic and then to another.

Perhaps, one should not try to analyze these questions too deeply because in the final analysis, they are not of paramount importance and the historian might have been unaware, at least in part, of the impulses steering him in a certain direction. That George should eventually devote most of the years of his creative life to issues of the twentieth century does certainly not come as a surprise. For the impact of the events of the 1930s and 1940s was overwhelming on those who lived through them.

It is the assignment of the writer of a preface or a postface to summarize the contents of a book, but this is next to impossible in the present case because George was a man of many (and sometimes disparate) parts and also because this has been done by the contributors in the essays that follow, which admirably combine a survey of the state of their specialized fields and George Mosse's contribution.

I shall recall instead George's role as the editor of the *Journal of Contemporary History*, which over thirty-five years has served as a platform in the field of twentieth-century history and published well over a thousand articles with the emphasis on European political and cultural history in the age of Fascism. When I asked George to be the coeditor, I did so not because of personal friendship or because we agreed on all essential issues. The reasons were more prosaic; George was deeply involved in and loved university life, went to many conferences, was a member of many committees, and knew virtually everyone who was someone. My own inclinations and interests were and have remained different. I had certain ideas as to the directions in which we should proceed, but I fear that without George's knowledge of who was who and who could do what, these ideas would have remained, for the better part, a dead letter.

At the time we first met, our interests were close. George worked on his German Ideology, and I worked on the history of the German youth movement. The Jugendbewegung was not exactly identical with the German voelkisch tradition but parts of it were, and in any case, it was an important section of life reform, a topic close to George's heart. We had reached our topics in very different ways. George began professional life as a historian of early modern English history, which was of no interest to me. I had never even heard about the Holy Pretence, let alone of Sir Thomas Smith and Sir Edward Cooke. I had attended a school in Nazi Germany and graduated in 1938. Much of the Zeitgeist, many of the books (above all third rate novels reflecting prevailing mood) that George studied with such gusto at the time, I had absorbed in my teens.

We were more or less the first in our respective fields, the Jugendbewegung had been forgotten and the voelkisch movement was generally regarded as a disreputable and not very important part of the German intellectual tradition. It was only in the subsequent years that dozens, if not hundreds, of books on these subjects were written, and that conferences and exhibitions were arranged dealing with these topics. To be present at the creation had its recompensation, even though the immediate reception of George's book in Germany was not overwhelming. In my own case, I was warned that in view of my background, I was less than ideally suited to understand a phenomenon that was so essentially German that no foreigner could fathom and describe it. However, I cannot complain about the subsequent reactions that were, without exception, friendly and positive, if with a admixture of some regret—why was an outsider needed to write the definitive story of such a quintessential German movement?

In the years that followed, our interest parted: George became interested in the nationalization of the masses; in the history of sexuality, he worked on his cultural history of modern Europe and eventually pioneered work in fields that seemed strange and incomprehensible to me—why this morbid preoccupation with military cemeteries? My own interest was in the field of Russian history and political violence. There was, to be sure, a certain coalescence with George studying Max Nordau and me Zionist history in general.

To make an embarrassing admission, I leafed through George's books of the 1970s and 1980s, but I did not read them and I suspect that he did not closely study mine. This could perhaps explain the fact that we never quarreled in our collaboration over decades. It was not only the sweetness of his character and my own great tolerance (or unwillingness to mount the barricades because of one article or another).

However, this is not the end of the story. For it was precisely in the months after George's death that I became preoccupied with what he had written about "fallen heroes," which helped to shed light on certain contemporary issues such as the cult of suicide terrorists not only in the Arab world but also, even more prominently, in Sri Lanka and other countries. The cult of fallen heroes goes back to time immemorial; it can be found in earliest Greek history (Simonides on the fallen Spartans at Thermophylae), the Jewish zealots who fought at Massada, the Nordic sagas that deal with little but acts of heroism dying in battle and being taken to Asgard, the palace of the Gods, with 540 doors. The legends of the early Middle Ages are in a similar vein with the Chanson de Roland as a prominent example. The mixture of religion and nationalism as far as motives are concerned is interesting: they were fighting not only for *la douce France* but also for their religion against the pagans. Legends of this kind from Wilhelm Tell to Ivan Susanin can be found in the history of every person about heroism and martyrdom, and it was only in the age of the enlightenment that these traditions went out of fashion, but not for long, for in the romantic age, they returned with a vengeance with Germany again as an obvious example. George quotes Theodor Koerner who wrote on the eve of a battle against Napoleon in which he lost his life: Happiness lies in sacrifical death. Friedrich Hölderlin was a greater poet than Koerner and he was not known as an aggressive militarist but in an earlier poem (1797) entitled "Death for the Fatherland," he wrote exactly in the same vain.

I remember the inscription *Dulce et decorum est pro patria mori* (from Horace's Odes—it is sweet and right to die for one's country) in the assembly hall of our school in Breslau, and I suspect that there was the same inscription all over Germany. This was in remembrance, above all, of the heroes of Langemarck (November 1914) when many thousands of young students had tried to storm the enemy lines in Flanders singing "Deutschland Deutschland ueber alles" at a time when this was not even the national anthem.

Indoctrination (then and now) was to create the impression that the fallen symbolized the triumph of youth but that the fallen were not really dead but merely sleeping in the lap of Christ (or Muhammad). Graves and cemeteries became shrines of national worship.

The heroes had not died in vein; they lived on in eternal life in the tradition of "Ich hatt einen Kameraden," Ludwig Uhland's famous poem (1809), which ended with "Kann dir die Hand nicht geben Bleib du im ewigen Leben" (bringing up the idea of eternal life), just as the Horst Wessel song maintains that those who were shot by the enemies continue to march with the living brown shirts in their columns, in spirit, if not in body.

Under Nazism, the heroic tradition involving self-sacrifice became central to the essence of the regime and this perhaps more than anything else led analysts interpret Nazism as a political religion.

At the same time, Nazi propagandists were given instructions to explain to the bereaved that there was no need to mourn which was not good for national morale; one should be grateful that that their dearest had been given a chance to make the supreme sacrifice for a higher ideal. They were not suffering pain but were living on in eternity.

These ideas found their reflection in hundreds of poems not only written by party hacks but also by more serious writers such as Ernst Bertram, the friend of Thomas Mann and one of the leading Germanists of the age. The cult of the fallen heroes also figures prominently in the ideology and practice of other Fascist movement, particularly the Rumanian Iron Guard and in the writings of Jose Primo de Rivera. It takes a central place in the writings of post war neo-Fascists such as Julius Evola, one of their many gurus. It was customary on ritual occasions that when the list of those assembled was read out, the fallen were included and someone answered with "present" when the name was called.

The similarity with the cult of suicide bombers at present time is startling. The Koran and the Hadith warn against mourning the fallen heroes, as their sacrifice is a joyous occasion, and the families should be proud and not dejected. There is the same belief that they were warriors in a holy struggle, that their group was cruelly oppressed, and that their sacrifice was not just desirable but imperative. Common was the belief that the collective (the religion, the sect, the nation, the race) were infinitely more important than the fate of the individual. A whole generation had been indoctrinated in this spirit and many followed the call to give their life when it came. It was not limited to one specific culture—mention has been made to the Liberation Tigers of Eelam (Sri Lanka), and the Kamikaze pilots could serve as an earlier example.

Kamikaze missions were seldom if ever decisive; they prevented neither German defeat in the First and Second World Wars nor the Japanese in the Second World War, and they were unlikely to succeed in terrorist campaigns.

There are other intriguing phenomena that would have been of great interest to George Mosse, a student of the history of sexuality. This refers to the awards waiting for the fallen warrior, for paradise as the Hadith says, is under the shade of the sword. The martyrs were not only entitled to intercede for seventy of their relations to enable them to join them in paradise, which was described as a place of wonderful gardens, streams with clear water, and above it a jeweled dome of pearls and rubies extending from Damascus to Southern Yemen. The martyrs were reclining on thrones and eating and drinking meats and fruit with happiness with many servants at their beck and call. Above all there were seventy (or perhaps seventy-two) virgins ready for them on top of the wives they had had on Earth.

The issue of the virgins has become, off late, a matter of dispute. The Koran and the Hadith are very explicit about this; the virgins are described as doe-eyed and full-breasted. Some of the commentators such as Jalal al-Din al-Suyuti, an Egyptian who lived in the fifteenth century, provided even more details. But what would a normal young man do with seventy virgins? According to Suyuti, his penis would never weaken; he would have an eternal erection and the sensation he experienced would be so powerful and delicious that if one would undergo it on Earth, one would faint. The virgins, it was noted in passing, would have the most appetizing vaginas.

These descriptions of the carnal awards of the martyrs have been an embarrassment to some of the contemporary exegists of the Koran and the Hadith. Some have translated "virgins" as "angels," but this did not make sense in the context. The book of German students of the Islamic tradition published recently (Christoph Luxenberg, Die Syrisch Aramaeische Lesart des Koran, Berlin 2000) made some revolutionary suggestions. He argued that many parts of the Koran were obscure or even incomprehensible if one stuck to the Arab language, but many of the obscurities disappeared if these passages were read as being of Syrian rather than Arab provenience. Seen in this light, the virgins became white raisins of crystal clarity. This new approach would solve a few problems but create many others. To make any change in the holy texts is of course anathema to a believer; it would invalidate much that has been written by way of exegesis in more than a thousand years; orthodox believers would not touch Dr. Luxenberg with a bargepole. Furthermore, eating white raisins might not be an overwhelming attraction, and in any case, the young man indoctrinated in the fundamentalist religious schools were reading (and learning by heart) the Koran in its traditional version and not in the light of the Luxenberg revisions.

Those who have grown up in the post-heroic age find it difficult to understand the issue of the fallen warriors and their cult. It is George Mosse's merit to have given much thought to these problems, to religion, and to the patriotic uses of the cult of the fallen heroes and to have done pioneering spade work at a time when they seemed of little contemporary relevance.

Guttentag: Breslau to Cochabamba

Not long before the German invasion of the Netherlands, where he had found temporary shelter, a German-Jewish refugee, nineteen years of age, arrived in Bolivia from the war-torn continent. He was lucky as only a few managed to escape almost certain death in the nick of time. His name was Werner Guttentag and he decided to settle in Cochabamba, the second largest city in the country where his parents had found a home not long before. His prospects were less than brilliant. He was penniless, knew no Spanish, and perhaps worst of all, he was wearing shorts. This was the custom in the radical youth movement of his native Germany—a group similar in outlook to the Boy Scouts and the Wandervogel but heavily political in inspiration. In Latin America at the time, wearing short trousers was considered scandalous behavior, and he was urgently advised to change his attire. But unfortunately, there was no shop selling trousers in Cochabamba.

Sixty years later, the name of this refugee had become a household word in his adopted land. He had opened a little bookshop, which grew in size and later had branches in the major cities of the country. He built up a publishing house. Mario Vargas Llosa, the most influential Latin American writer, called him a friend; Vargas had spent many years of his youth in Cochabamba. Guttentag established a literary prize, the first and only one in the country that gave many, who later became famous, their first chance and indeed the breakthrough. The highest order of the country, the *Condor de los Andes*, had been bestowed on him. He became an honorary citizen of his hometown and honorary member of a variety of organizations. There was even a postage stamp in his honor, something Henry Kissinger had not achieved. (Hannah Arendt did appear on a stamp but she belonged to a somewhat older generation and it happened in the country of her birth.)

The remarkable story of Werner Guttentag is related, in considerable detail, in a book based on many interviews with the foreigner who had done more than anyone else for the culture of his adopted country. Having been a witness myself, albeit from a certain distance, of the events related in the first part of this account, the German years—some of the dramatics personae were neighbors, others class mates, or friends—I came more than once to ask myself how a biographer belonging to another generation and hailing from another country (Switzerland) could have possibly known certain minute details?

These were the years of dictatorship and quite often of illegality, and one got accustomed, even at an early age, not to keep records. One example should suffice. Ignazio Silone's *Fontamara*, probably the most powerful anti-Fascist novel ever written, had just been published in Switzerland, and some of the leading members of the group living in Prague at the time had decided that copies of the book should be smuggled into Nazi Germany where it might have considerable political impact. Less than a dozen people knew about this action at the time; not one is alive any longer. I happened to be the recipient of such a copy, but with bad luck, I stumbled into a raid carried out by the political police a few days later. Fortunately, those who searched me had never heard of the book or its author and let me go. Many years later, over dinner, I reported the story to Silone in Rome who was much less excited than I had been at the time.

However, it is also true that sections of the book dealing with Guttentag's youth are pure fantasy. Esteban, one of his sons, notes in his preface that his father had been a great reader and in the end found it difficult to differentiate between what he had read and what had really happened. Nor was it a good idea on the part of the biographer to render in direct speech over many pages conversations that had allegedly taken place eighty years earlier. Such practices are out of place in a work of nonfiction. But in this case, it does not greatly affect the general picture, nor detract from the reliability of the account.

Contemplating at the present time, decades after the exodus, the fate of the younger members of this wave of refugees from Nazi Germany, there is the temptation to focus on those who made it—from rags to riches, from anonymity to fame. However, this is only part of a complex story. Many did not manage to emigrate in time, were caught in a murderous trap, and died an early and miserable death. Those lucky enough to escape faced overwhelming odds for these were the years of a global economic crisis and mass unemployment. Their expectations were high, and their abilities were very limited. No one needed and wanted teenagers with an unfinished education; their chances of advancement and of being accepted by society were exceedingly limited. Their upbringing had not prepared them for life in alien civilizations, and the local upper class looked down upon them, even despised the poor newcomers; for the majority of the population, they remained unwanted intruders. They had to live by their wits, there was no safety net in the case of failure.

To survive, let alone to succeed, in these circumstances demanded a high measure of adaptability: One young man became a leading member of the Benedictines, representing the order at the Vatican; another ended his days as a much respected and indeed revered figure among the monks in what is now Sri Lanka. A young Jewish woman from Guttentag's home town and hailing from the same circles ended her days as a martyr of the church; years later, she was beatified and canonized. A young man whom the vagaries of emigration had taken to Nigeria became an honorary chief of the Yoruba, and also a chief expert and the main promoter of Yoruba art. Neither family upbringing nor school had prepared them for a career in the higher echelons of the Washington bureaucracy or for survival in Moscow at the time of the purges and the terror. But it was in these extreme and unfamiliar surroundings that some found themselves, survived, and some even made their way to the top.

Guttentag, a contemporary of mine lived just around the corner. His family was middle class ("petty bourgeois" he used to define his background). He had to leave school at fourteen—these were the early years of Nazi rule; for a while, he worked as a clerk, and later he trained as a locksmith. He belonged to the KPO (Kommunistische Partei Opposition), a small but very active Communist splinter group known as the right-wing Brandler-Thalheimer faction. (Bukharin was their guru in Soviet politics). Self-educated, Guttentag was an avid reader and supplied me with much illegal literature. I admired his great energy and optimism, but there were also times of despair. I remember a letter from Luxemburg shortly after his emigration looking down on a railway line from a bridge above and discussing the pros and cons of suicide.

The illegal work in Germany, the life with danger, the great courage, and the sacrifices had been admirable, but they rested on a fanciful assumption: That the German working class was in any way receptive to the message of a group of Jewish (or half Jewish) young Marxists. They had, in fact, not the slightest interest in their pamphlets, and thus, the sacrifices had been in vain—the death of young men and women who had been caught, the many years in prison, and concentration camps. One of them who had escaped to the Soviet Union was extradited to Nazi Germany; another, the leader of the Breslau group, miraculously survived concentration camps but only because, while detained, he rejoined the Communist Party and thus was protected by "Aryan" party comrades, whose positions of influence in the camp administration enabled them to take decisions on who of the fold should be protected. He stayed on in East Germany after the war but never rose beyond a modest position because as an erstwhile oppositionist, he remained under a cloud.

On Christmas day in 1939, Guttentag arrived in Arica, a port in Northern Chile and the gate to Bolivia, this being a landlocked country. Why Bolivia? This has remained a riddle to this day. Those who wanted to escape Europe in the late 1930s faced a very limited choice of destinations; they had to make up their mind between the Dominican Republic and Shanghai—then a no man's land in international law. However, in mid-1938, the President of Bolivia (whose name was German Busch, of German rather than North American extraction) suddenly decided to open the gates of his country to all able bodied individuals. It is not quite clear why; according to one version, Bolivia had not done well in the Chaco war with Paraguay (1932–1935), and the president thought that this had happened because the border area (this being the bone of contention) was too sparsely settled and immigrants were therefore welcome. This liberal interval did not however last long; less than two years later, the immigration of Chinese, Blacks, and Jews was banned.

With the war going on in Europe and the Nazi military victories, young Guttentag felt it his duty to participate in the anti-Fascist struggle. He still thought of himself a socialist but one without illusions. There was a substantial German colony in Bolivia, some of them militant Nazis. A group of young antifascists to whom the newcomer belonged engaged in putting glue in the key holes of shops belonging to these Nazis and poisoning their dogs, activities that Guttentag in later years thought childish and silly. In the years after the war, refugee Nazis having escaped from Germany found a shelter in Bolivia including, most prominently, Klaus Barbie, the butcher of Lyons, who was eventually extradited to France. Guttentag who knew Barbie in Bolivia as a client under the name "Altmann" and eventually learned about his true identity appears as a witness in Marcel Ophüls' powerful documentary *Hotel Terminus: The Life and Times of Klaus Barbie*. Guttentag had a personal interest in this case, for Barbie had been responsible for the murder of some of the friends of his years in Holland.

In the early post-war decades, Bolivia witnessed more than a few military dictatorships and whenever this happened, *Amigos del Libro*, Guttentag's publishing house, faced trouble and the owner was arrested but never for more than a few days. Sometimes, this happened for political reasons, once on the suspicion of hoarding matches and selling them at astronomic prices. Denunciations by personal enemies were frequent; life in Bolivia in these years was not without danger. Guttentag believed that he was let off lightly because the officers were not interested in books. Equally likely, he was thought to be a Bolivian patriot—after all he had stayed on in the country that he had come to like, whereas most of the other refugees from Europe had left.

Guttentag's politics were still of the Left, but he had mellowed. He published a considerable amount of left-wing literature, but he also had friends on the Right. His hero among literary figures was Commissaire Jules Maigret, not a leading Marxist either. He founded a Maigret circle in Cochabamba. In collaboration with some friends, he wrote a Maigret novel taking place in Bolivia.

The Bolivian intelligentsia, such as it was (many of whom were Guttentag's friends), was mainly interested in left-wing literature. But it was also deeply split. Some sympathized with Che Guevara who having shaved of his beard and dyed his hair grey, had appeared in Bolivia in 1966 in an attempt to launch a guerrilla movement. Others including the Communist Party thought his actions foolhardy and harmful. Che found himself at sea among the *indigenos* with whom, quite literally, he had no common language and whom eventually he tried to terrorize into cooperation. This attempt spectacularly failed and eventually led to Guevara's capture and execution. But the Trotskyites too were divided into a variety of sects and subsects. When Guttentag published his eighty-volume *Enciclopedia Boliviana*, he invited his great friend, the novelist Jesus Lara, to devote four tomes to the history of the Bolivian labor movement. However, as Guttentag realized that far from being a history, this project degenerated into an internal Trotskyite polemic, he refused to publish it; the responsibility of the editor weighed more heavily on him than personal friendship, however close.

For many years he refrained from commenting on Bolivian domestic affairs. Bolivia had saved his life and for this reason alone he felt inhibited to criticize and condemn. He was a lifelong fighter against repression and welcomed therefore the gradual development after 1982 of the country toward free elections and democracy. He lived to witness the emergence of a government under the first indigeno president (Evo Morales in 2005). But he was by no means uncritical; in an interview a year before his death in 2008, he spoke scathingly about the so-called democrats who had been no more efficient and not less corrupt than their predecessors.

The Guttentag phenomenon is less interesting for its politics than for his achievement in the educational and cultural field. He published 1,200 books over the years, including the *Enciclopedia Boliviana* and his particular pride, the annual bibliography of all books published in the country. All this in the beginning almost single-handedly and in a country in which the great majority of the population was illiterate. There was no firm financial basis for the various undertakings. Those receiving the annual literary award were frequently told in a whisper not to cash the check too quickly because it was not covered.

While the 1970s and 1980s were good years for those producing and selling books in Bolivia, this was not the case in the years after. This had partly to do with the general economic situation (the country witnessed a horrific inflation) and a dozen other circumstances including the high price of paper and the appearance in the streets of many pirated editions selling for a fraction of the price of books in the shops.

Guttentag loved books and was a believer, often a naïve believer, in the importance of books and their potential to produce change, not just in society but even in the human condition. There were not many like him in any country at any time, and their number has dwindled in the days of the computer. He was a strange man, an idealist in an age when idealism had become a rare commodity. He had much in common with the greatest hero in Spanish literature—the one fighting windmills. His strangeness attracted many with whom he came in touch. Not only was he one of the few who came to love and respect the country that had given him shelter, with his eccentricities, his mercurial mood, and his uncertain heavily accented Spanish but he was also accepted, respected, and beloved by so many and not only among the intelligentsia of his adopted country.

Bolivia, since 2005, the "plurinational state of Bolivia" is no longer the country which Guttentag came to know when he arrived there seventy-three years earlier. His beloved Cochabamba, the sleepy little town in which he looked in vain for a shop selling trousers (or clothes in general), is now home to about a million inhabitants in its metropolitan area. It is served by some twenty television stations, and on Avenida Ayacucho, near the town center, there still is the bookshop that Guttentag founded and where his life work began.

Guttentag had to leave school early which he always regretted. Things Jewish were of little intellectual interest to him, but he was probably not aware to what extent the Jewish tradition was part of his mental makeup. He was neither Zionist nor anti-Israeli. He did not want his son to go through the bar mitzvah ceremony. But in the last months of his life, when frequent fantasies plagued him both in his sleep and when he was awake; one of the strange recurrent dreams was about a group of old Jews coming to see him, "but I do not understand what they are saying..." This happened time and time again and clearly worried him.

There were some major achievers in Guttentag's generation. But it sometimes occurs to me that getting a Nobel Prize might have been child's play in comparison with what this man did at this time and in these circumstances.

Stefan Gurtner, Guttentag. Das Leben des Juedischen Verlegers Werner Guttentag Zwischen Deutschland und Bolivien. Verlag Edition AV Lich/Hessen 2012. 542 pp.

The Kaiser's Spy, Jihad, and the Jewish Nazis

In 1789, a seventeen-year-old Jew in the German city of Bonn founded a bank that eventually became one of Europe's largest private banks (if not the very largest) with assets of 138 billion euros, which is more than the GNP of many member states of the United Nations. Several years ago, the bank was acquired by the Deutsche Bank, one of the world's largest, but the family remains involved in the ownership. The family was ennobled in the nineteenth century, but this did not prevent difficulties in the Nazi era, for according to the racialist Nazi ideology (once a Jew always a Jew), it was suspect and undesirable. But in view of its very size and international importance, it could not simply be taken over by the new rulers.

The history of this bank (which has been written before) is very interesting, but it is not the subject of the present book, which deals with one member of the family—the great grandson of the founder, Max von Oppenheim (1860–1946). While Max is not unknown to students of the Middle East and specifically Middle Eastern archaeology, he is the subject of a full-scale biography by Lionel Gossman, a Princeton professor. Max von Oppenheim studied law, but when it appeared that he would not be the leading figure in the management of the bank, he traveled widely, was fascinated by North Africa and the Arab world, and eventually settled in Cairo. He became a prominent fixture of Cairo's social life in the years before and after the First World War. He entertained lavishly and came to know everyone who was someone and everyone knew him. According to contemporaries, he was a charming man and no mean self-promoter; his great ambition was to enter the diplomatic service. But his application was turned down time and again despite the strong support he had; the main reason as appears from the files was anti-Semitism; someone of Jewish (or even part Jewish) origin was undesirable. But this was probably not the only reason, for at the same time, Bernard Dernburg (1863–1937) was appointed secretary (minister) of colonial affairs. Their background was similar; Dernburg was Jewish from his father's side, both hailed from banking families—Dernburg was a Protestant, whereas Oppenheim was a Catholic. After many futile attempts, Oppenheim was made an attachee, not a permanent, regular member of the diplomatic service but only loosely connected. Perhaps, the fact that he was very rich counted against Oppenheim, and the suspicion that he somehow could buy himself a position, even if the issue at stake was a lowly *Legationsrat*. Bismarck's son even thought Oppenheim's name ridiculous, a hindrance to a career in the foreign service, though the name Oppenheim does not really inspire greater hilarity than Bismarck.

Max Oppenheim became a passionate archaeologist having visited Tel Halaf, a place some 200 kilometers from Cairo, so much so that he resigned from the diplomatic service a year after the excavations began in earnest in 1909. He was in touch with fellow archaeologists such as T. E. Lawrence (who thought him stupid and disliked him), published his findings, participated in professional conferences, and a considerable part of the items excavated found their way to Berlin museums. He had not been trained as an archaeologist, and some of his interpretations were disputed by leading figures in the field. However, Tel Halaf remained close to this heart, perhaps his most abiding cause up to the end of his life. Oppenheim also had a great interest in the customs and manners of the Bedouin tribes, and he published and edited widely on this subject.

Soon after the outbreak of the First World War, Oppenheim submitted his famous Jihad memorandum (*Denkschrift*) about enlisting pan-Islamism in the struggle against Britain (and also Russia). Pan-Islamism had been discussed (and preached) for a number of years before the outbreak of the war, but it was not at all clear how important a political factor it was likely to be in the struggle.

However, if Oppenheim is still remembered today, it is not because of his excavations and his ethnographic studies but as a promoter, albeit not very successful in jihad, and this is also the main topic of Gossman's biography. He is remembered as the author of the second *Denkschrift* in 1940. It was submitted to the German government of the day and suggested that use should be made of Pan-Islamism and Jihad as a major weapon in the war against Germany's enemies. Oppenheim, it would appear, had not only India in mind but also the Arab Peninsula (as T. E. Lawrence). However, Turkey, the Ottoman empire, was the leading Muslim power at the time. It was an ally of Germany in the First World War and neutral in the Second. In the First World War, the Sultan in Constantinople was the supreme authority for most Muslims. This constituted a major obstacle for political campaigns such as the one suggested by Oppenheim. Moreover, not all German policy makers were enthusiastic about the prospects of such a course of action. The 1914 memorandum was, as Oppenheim later wrote, a failure—a *Schlag ins Wasser*.

If the issue continued to intrigue observers of the Middle Eastern scene in later years, it was mainly perhaps because it was believed to be one of the many manoeuvers in the murky world of oriental political intrigue. It was widely thought that John Buchan's hugely successful thriller *Greenmantle* (that mysterious preacher of Jihadism, 1916) was somehow based on Oppenheim's activities. But the differences between the fictitious *Greenmantle* and the real Oppenheim were huge and Buchan, when he wrote his novel, as we now know, had never heard about the German amateur archaeologist and his salon and lavish parties in Cairo.

The second memorandum dated July 1940, that is, after the defeat of France, complained about the lack of German support (the "cautious hesitation") for the anti-British forces in the Middle East such as the Grand Mufti of Jerusalem, Rashid Ali in Iraq, and the Lebanese politician Shaqib Arslan, residing in Switzerland, who was a personal friend of Oppenheim. In his memorandum, Oppenheim mentioned his lifelong involvement in Middle Eastern affairs and his close personal relationship with (anti-British) Muslim politicians. He specifically mentioned Palestine where the struggle against the British and the Jews was to be taken up as energetically as possible. In fact, some Nazi support was given to the Arab politicians mentioned by Oppenheim at the time. But on the whole, German foreign ministry's attitudes were far more skeptical with regard to the help expected on the part of the Muslims and particularly the Arabs than asserted by Oppenheim. This view was also shared by Hitler; Italian interests had to be taken into account, and there was the hope that an agreement with Britain could somehow be reached. After 1941, Germany suffered military setbacks in North Africa and Nazi planning for the future of the Middle East was considered premature to say the least. Oppenheim's memorandum was shelved.

The second Oppenheim *Denkschrift* became of interest in later years for very different reasons: How to explain the extreme views of a person of part Jewish extraction who had suffered discrimination in Wilhelmian Germany and *a fortiori* in the Nazi Reich where he was considered a Mischling, hence a person of inferior racial background? This has been difficult to understand by those not quite familiar with Nazi theory and practice in this field that was far from consistent. It is a complicated issue and has often led to wrong explanations.

As for Oppenheim's motives, he did not greatly suffer after 1933. People of a background similar to Oppenheim's were ashamed of their Jewish (or part Jewish) origins and were hiding it from their offspring. Others thought it unimportant and more or less successfully suppressed it. The nineteenth-century Jewish establishment in its majority no longer felt Jewish and to a considerable extent converted to Christianity. The percentage of mixed marriages was high and rising. Judaism was not intellectually or emotionally attractive and constituted a hindrance in most careers—the state service, the armed forces, academia, and elsewhere. The motives were not always ignoble and careerist. Judaism, as the walls of the ghetto, came down as an ossified religion considered by many inferior to other creeds. Jewish intellectuals in central but also often in Eastern Europe unsurprisingly preferred *Faust to Fishke der Chigger*.

Max Oppenheim felt not in the least Jewish. In letters after 1945, he blamed Hitler for having caused the death of millions of German soldiers, and the fate of the Jews was not mentioned with a single word. His German patriotism was intense, and since not all accepted him as a fully fledged bona fide German aristocrat, he may have felt doubly motivated to prove his patriotism. He truly believed in German conservatism and belonged to all the right-wing clubs and political organizations of that world both before and after the First World War. Such radical assimilation sometimes led to anti-Semitism. But for Oppenheim, the whole issue was apparently so irrelevant that he did not even become an anti-Semite.

All this was, by no means, a specific German phenomenon. An interesting similar case is that of Daniel Halevy (1872–1962), a French historian and man of letters and a close friend of Marcel Proust who became an ideologist of the extreme Right and a propagandist of the Vichy regime. Another fascinating case was Bertrand de Jouvenel (1903–1987), a person of considerably greater political acumen than Oppenheim. A son of Sarah Boas, prior to the Second World War, he became the right hand of the Fascist leader Jacques Doriot.

He realized, however, relatively early on that he had backed the wrong horse and worked his way back to political respectability. Marc Bloch (*les rois thaumaturges*) was one of the great medievalists of his time, and he was shot by the Germans for his resistance activities. He wrote, in 1941, about the more recent Jewish arrivals in France that their problem was not his.

Tsarist Russia was not propitious ground for Jewish assimilation, but the cases of Boris Pasternak and Semyon Frank were by no means unique. They believed that total identification with Russia and Russian culture implied embracing the Orthodox Church. Pasternak's father, the painter Leonid, had already converted (as had Anton Rubinstein, the nineteenth-century pianist and composer). But Pasternak junior went further recommending that all Jews should convert.

A list of leading Polish writers makes interesting reading: Moshe Agatstein became Mieczyslaw Jastrun, Wiktor Zisman is better known as Bruno Jasienski, Aizik Wagman was transformed into Adam Wazyk, Boleslaw Lesman polonized his name slightly but significantly, and Wiktor Lesman ended up as Jan Brzechwa. Juiian Tuwim did not convert or change his name, but what he wrote about his fellow Jews prior to the Second World War was not complimentary. This is not to denigrate any of them; it was a general trend, the Zeitgeist and not a German-Jewish peculiarity.

Max Oppenheim was by no means a dyed-in-the-wool Nazi, though he was not critical of the new regime either. His post-1945 denigration of the Nazi regime was quite dishonest, but this was a fairly frequent phenomenon in Germany. Why did the Nazis with their relentless persecution of the Jews spare him, perhaps even make use of him? Nazi policy toward half and quarter Jews (*Mischlinge* of the first and second degrees) was contradictory and changed from time to time. Half Jews, who were not brought up as Jews (*Geltungsjuden*), were not deported and killed. There were legal problems and Hitler, who did not want to be bothered by lawyers and legal problems, declared that he would take a binding decision only after the final victory. Those of military age had to serve in the army at the beginning of the war and its end when the armed forces were depleted. But in between, they were excluded from military service and in any case were not permitted to serve in positions of command. It was quite common for half Jews to try to improve their status by becoming quarter Jews and for quarter Jews to turn into complete Aryans simply by claiming that their non-Aryan father or grandfather was not their biological predecessor—in this respect, Nazi authorities were quite liberal in helping to improve the records (Hermann Goering's famous "I will decide who is a Jew").

In 1943, Berlin Goebbels had the male partners in mixed marriages arrested in order to have them deported and killed. But there were spontaneous mass protests (the famous Rosenstrasse incident), and he had to beat a hasty retreat. There were a few who escaped the net of persecution—among them the Jewish doctor who had been treating Hitler's mother in her illness. There was the case of Leo Blech a world-famous conductor who, owing to the intervention of Goering, was permitted to emigrate from Riga to Sweden in the middle of the war. There was no more rabid anti-Semite than Goebbels in his later years. But when he was told that an enthusiastic racial researcher had established, beyond any shadow of doubt, that the great grandfather of Johann Strauss had been a Hungarian Jew, he ordered the evidence to be suppressed: "For if we go on like this, all we shall be left with of our racially pure cultural heritage will be Alfred Rosenberg (his pet aversion among fellow Nazi leaders) and this may not be enough..."

Those who did not live through that period and had no personal experience of life in a totalitarian state are bound to find it difficult to make sense of these currents and crosscurrents especially at the time of war. This has given rise to all kinds of explanations, sometimes very offensive but more often rooted in ignorance rather than ill will. Why, it was frequently asked, did Germans (and Austrian and Czech Jews) not leave their country hurriedly at any price in view of the horrible fate awaiting them? The brief answer is of course that Auschwitz did not yet exist in 1933 not even in 1936 and that there was the false hope that Nazi policy vis-a-vis the Jews would improve or at least not become harsher. Some authors blamed Jewish leaders in Germany (especially Zionists) for having negotiated with the Nazi government to facilitate Jewish immigration—as if there would have been an alternative approach to get Jews out of Germany. Central European Jewry consisted, to a large extent, of elderly people, neither mentally nor physically capable of envisaging a new life in another country. These were the years of a global economic crisis and mass unemployment—no one wanted immigrants, especially not Jewish immigrants.

All this should have been obvious, but instead, a literature was forthcoming sometimes malevolent, more often ignorant and breathtakingly obtuse in its conclusions. One such study about "Hitler's

Jewish soldiers" (not less than 150,000 of them) accepted the Nazi racialist definition of being a Jew and even went beyond it. It is a racist argument: If someone were to declare that he (or she) does not belong to a certain people or religion, this would be accepted. But not in the case of a Jew. It is no longer "once a Jew, always a Jew"—but "once a quarter Jew—always a full Jew." But even if one added all the male half and quarter Jews of military age and even those one-eighth Jewish according to the Nuremberg laws, the total figure was closer to 15,000 than 150,000, and even this was probably an exaggeration.

On a personal note, I experienced many of these issues in my own family. Half, perhaps more, had been converted a long time ago, and there were half and quarter Jews and not a few mixed marriages. The Jewish partner in a mixed marriage would usually survive—but during the war, no one could be sure. There was my cousin Hans Bodlé, a few years older, who coached me in mathematics, my weakest subject in school. His father of Huguenot extraction had been killed on the Western front during the last year of the First World War. Hans was in and out of the German army according to the changing Nazi policy. Toward the end of the Second World War with a fanatical commander in charge of the defense of our home town, Hans Bodlé had to again join the army, which of course he hated. He was killed in Breslau on the very last day of the Second World War.

Having written an excellent biography of Max Oppenheim with sovereign mastery of the sources and fairness in his approach, Gossman toward the end deals with "Oppenheim's relations with the National Socialist regime in context." This section deals with several Jewish personalities and organizations that (the author believes) also showed pronounced Nazi sympathies. What context? Somewhere, the author notes that the case of Oppenheim may well have been *sui generis*. If so, what does the author want to prove? Oppenheim was not a Jew, except in accordance with Nazi doctrine. He was as much identified with Judaism as with Buddhism, probably less so, for he must have felt resentful about his Jewish antecedents, which caused political and social difficulties in his career which Buddhism did not. It should be noted in passing that other members of the family, that is, Oppenheim's cousins and second cousins, who were half and quarter Jews according to Nazi doctrine and being staunch German patriots and conservatives, behaved on the whole decently during the third Reich. Some were arrested and persecuted. They helped Jewish business partners to escape Germany during the war, even at a certain risk to their own life. In later years, the Israeli government noted such decent behavior and included them in the list of righteous gentiles.

The politics of German Jews were centrist or left of center; some were Communists, but these had usually left the community or in any case were no longer active in it. A handful belonged to the extreme Right and their writings quoted by Gossman make very embarrassing reading—for instance, those of Hans Joachim Schoeps, a student of theology. (The author should perhaps have mentioned that Schoeps was in his early twenties at the time.) He emigrated to Sweden; both his parents perished in Nazi camps. After the war, he became a professor at Erlangen University. He continued to denigrate parliamentary democracy, believed in the Prussian spirit, and was a monarchist at heart.

Most space is devoted to Nikolaus Pevsner who went probably furthest expressing sympathy for Nazism. However, Pevsner left Germany for England in 1933, having been baptized at the age of nineteen; he was not a Jew and since his father was holding Russian nationality, he was probably not a German either. In England, he became a celebrity and something of a national treasure. In more than forty volumes, he listed all buildings of historical or architectural interest. His history of European architecture became a bestseller, selling more than a million copies, and Pevsner was eventually knighted. The history professor Hans Rothfels, a student of Meinecke, also mentioned by Gossman as a witness for the prosecution was perilously close to being a Nazi fellow traveler. Gossman calls him a Jew, even though he converted at the age of nineteen.

Numbers four and five in the author's list of villains were the medievalist Ernst Kantorowicz ("Eka") and Edith Landmann, a philosopher married to a well-known economist. Eka is by far the most interesting of the lot; both belonged to the inner circle of the poet Stefan George. George's esoteric and powerful poetry attracted people of very different views and background. There were anti-Semites among them, but the brothers Stauffenberg, who almost managed to kill Hitler in July 1944, were also part of this circle. About a quarter of the members were Jews. What attracted Jews to this cult (George was always the master for them) is a fascinating question. It rested on the famous German-Jewish symbiosis, which was a fatal, one-sided misunderstanding, as Gershom Scholem later put it. But George was not a Nazi—when he wrote about *das Reich*, he did not have Hitler's Third Reich in mind. In the year the Nazis came to power, George moved to Switzerland where he died.

He never endorsed the Nazis and rejected the offer to become the head of the German Writers' Academy. Nor did he ever publicly condemn Nazism. He did not comment on current affairs; on the First World War, he had written—"this is not our war." His (and Kantorowicz's) cult of a hidden, secret Germany referred to something in the realm of the spirit, not of this world.

To call Kantorowicz a Nazi, as the medievalist Norman Cantor has done, betrays a profound ignorance of German politics and probably politics in general—the difference between conservatives and Nazis. Kantorowicz's main work prior to the Second World War, which made him famous was about the Emperor Friedrich II (1194–1250). However, Kantorowicz admired and probably somewhat idealized him not because he was a great war hero but in view of his chivalry and humanism *avant la lettre*. Contemporaries called him *stupor mundi*, the wonder of the world. At his court in Sicily, he assembled Muslim and Jewish savants to learn from them—this at a time when rulers were not known for their intellectual interests and when religious tolerance was anything but common. Kantorowicz was a conservative and in the words of his friends, a "Draufgaenger," meaning a daredevil. Politically naïve, he would join the unsavory Freikorps after the First World War. But after the Second World War as a tenured professor at Berkeley, this ardent anti-Communist was one of the few who refused to sign an anti-Communist loyalty oath demanded by the university. This was nobody's business, which was an intolerable infringement of privacy and his rights. It cost him his job but he could not care less. He had no difficulty to find another position—at the Princeton Institute of Advanced Studies.

Like Kantorowicz, Edith Landmann was highly educated, but political common sense was not her forte. She wrote George in early 1933 that some of the Nazi views were, in certain respects, close to the ideas she and her friends had expressed earlier on. She had also been an anti-Semite (in her own words), her views about Jews who were less patriotic-German than she was were similar to those of Marc Bloch. Later on, realizing how bad her judgment had been, she became not only a Zionist (as Gossman notes) but a sympathizer of the *Irgun*.

Oppenheim's biographer also deals with some patriotic German-Jewish organizations active in the 1930s in his attempt to provide the wider context toward an understanding of the Kaiser's spy. One is the association of the First World War veterans (RJF), which had at one time 40,000 members, the other is a youth group named *Schwarzes*

Faehnlein. A number of declarations are quoted in which the Reichsbund jüdischer Frontsoldaten (RJF) expressed its loyalty to the government that came to power in 1933; no political declarations were expected from a youth group. (Under pressure from the Gestapo, it was forced to dissolve in summer of 1934.) Since I was a member of both organizations (albeit at the tender age of twelve), I can bear witness that the quotations are correct. And yet the general picture presented is quite misleading. Why? Because there was a world of difference between declarations made, forced or unforced, and what really went on in these organizations. In order to survive, to lead a more or less normal life in a totalitarian regime dissimulation was the first commandment. There is a good description in Czeslaw Milosz's *Captive Mind* about the need to practice dissimulation (*ketman* in the Shi'ite tradition, *taqi'a* among the Sunnis) in such circumstances. But this is difficult, perhaps impossible, to be understood by people who had the good fortune never to be exposed to such pressures in their lives.

There were a few, an infinitesimal minority, who thought like Schoeps, and even they soon realized how wrong they had been. Why did Jews join an organization like the RJF? For the simple reason that those who had served in the army in the First World War enjoyed certain exemptions from the anti-Jewish laws. According to the Nazi version of history, Jews had shirked military service; this was not true, as most had served and 12,000 had been killed. These exemptions did not last long, at most a year or two, but who could blame those who wanted to make use of temporary benefits?

As far as my generation was concerned, the explanation was even easier—the reasons were not ideological but pragmatic: They joined the sports branch of the RJF. True, there was also a Zionist sports organization, but it existed only in a few places and the RJF usually had the better facilities. Since Jews were excluded from German sports groups, it was only natural that most would join associations such as the RJF, where such facilities existed. No ideology was involved, no patriotic speeches, not even the national anthem but soccer, swimming, track and field, and some other sports. There was a legendary boxing trainer in our town named Lachmann; under cover of darkness, non-Jewish boxers came for a workout with him. I served as a sparring partner of men considerably older. They went on to the 1936 Olympic Games such as Buettner and Miner 1 and his brother Miner 2. Some came home with medals. For me, it was certainly a useful experience.

Professor Gossman had the good fortune to attend the Pollokshields primary school in Glasgow and schools in Renfrewshire and Ayrshire and handsomely thank his teachers to whom this book is dedicated. Had he gone to a German school after 1933 as the present writer did, he would have been given an assignment to write an essay on "Ludwig Uhland in the light of National Socialism." It was a demeaning task, but it would have helped to understand life in a totalitarian dictatorship. There was no alternative but to comply with the assignment. The very subject was preposterous; Ludwig Uhland (1787–1862) was a fine poet, but Aryan students too found it difficult to establish any connection between the castle by the sea ("and the moon about it standing and the mists rise solemnly"—translation by Longfellow) and the author of *Mein Kampf*.

The activities of the youth organization were by no means those that were officially stated. Anti-Nazi literature was circulated, including the Communist Manifesto. Groups had their signature songs—ours happened to be the *Warszawianka and Unsterbliche Opfer* (immortal martyrs), that is, left-wing revolutionary statements, not *Volk ans Gewehr*. The head of our group (nicknamed Tom) who became a lifelong friend, suddenly disappeared in early 1934. The Gestapo had made a search at his home and found literature they did not like at all, as well as a revolver. He went to South Africa, became a Liberal party militant, and was arrested for several months. I met him again in Reading and Stirling, Scotland, where Professor Hans Meidner was a distinguished biology professor. He was a labor-party stalwart and a CND militant, fighting for nuclear disarmament.

There were many similar cases, whereas the hyper patriots were very few. One of these few was Guenter Holzmann (nicknamed Akela, derived from *the Jungle book*), at one time, head of the local branch of our little movement and a young man of great personal courage and monumental political stupidity. Soon after the Nazis rose to power, he published an advertisement in a local newspaper making it known that he had nothing in common with the Jewish community. One day in 1933, he decided to pay a visit to the head of the Hitler Youth in Berlin, trying to persuade him to recognize the little movement to which he belonged. He did not stay long in that building; to do him justice, in his autobiography, published many years later, he called this venture one of the stupidest things he ever did (*On dit que j'ai survecu au dela des mers*, 1997).

Guenter Holzmann was probably the closest approximation to the "Oppenheim context." But his story did not end there. He went on to Cambridge to study mineralogy and geology. Later, he emigrated to Peru, worked for a leading company (Hochschild or Patino, I believe), and lived in places where few were willing to stay for any length of time. He made a considerable fortune, which, having become a militant left winger, he left to the *Monde Diplomatique*, the main organ of Castroism, published in around fifteen different languages. On page one or two of this weekly, readers will encounter an announcement expressing gratitude to the *Fondation Guenter Holzmann*, named after a leading anti-Fascist and fighter for the liberation of mankind. It would probably be too much to expect to be told that he was a latecomer to the cause.

Not all Jews living in Germany in 1933 were clear-eyed militant antifascists of pure heart. Many, perhaps most, lacked political understanding, hoping against hope that the Nazi rule would quickly end. There were fools among them and traitors. There were a handful collaborating with the Gestapo. But were there more of them in Germany than elsewhere? I do not know of statistics showing this. Bitter experience made even the most obtuse to mend their ways. There was no "Oppenheim context." It is doubtful whether the story of the Kaiser's spy from Cologne and Cairo teaches anything, except that with greater distance from the age of totalitarian dictatorship it is becoming more and more difficult to understand what life was really like in those far away days.

Lionel Gossman, The passion of Max von Oppenheim. Archaeology and Intrigue in the Middle East from Wilhelm II to Hitler. Open Books Publishers, New York, 2013, 388 pp.

Postscript

To prevent misunderstandings: This review article refers to a number of books dealing with German Jews under Nazism of very different levels of knowledge and insight. Comments referring, for instance, to *Hitler's Jewish Soldiers*, do not apply to the Oppenheim biography.

Part 5
Departure and Arrival

Preface

At no time in my life did I keep a diary. This I came to regret on occasion in later years when I wrote some autobiographical essays, for I had to rely on memory, letters, and conversations. I tried to be truthful, though I never felt the obligation to relate the whole truth. There was a private sphere that I had no urge to share with others. Memory is fallible, and in some instances, in later years, I was no longer certain where my imagination got the better of reality. I was born on a Thursday and my autobiography was therefore entitled *Thursday's Child Has Far to Go*. I thought it a good and original title; only years later did I realize that it was also the title of Eartha Kitt's story of her life and half a dozen of other people. It seems to be impossible to find a title of which someone else has not thought before.

"1938" and "Homecoming" deal with the years of my youth. Only many years after did I fully grasp how lucky I had been to escape the country of my birth just in time. For like my friends and contemporaries, I was living in conditions of a normalcy of sorts, not knowing that it was the calm prior to a major storm. I left home, parents, and friends at the age of seventeen, and most of whom I never saw again.

As the war ended, I had become a journalist, war correspondent, and foreign policy commentator. But there was a major handicap; while I had been to Cairo and Beirut, even to Nicosia and places in between, I had never been to Paris and London, let alone to America and Russia. I had never met the leading people in my field. In other words, my knowledge was largely second hand. A whole dimension (and perhaps two) in my knowledge and experience was missing. I was writing about countries and people of whom I had no first-hand knowledge. If I wanted to continue working in this field and acquire at least a minimum of authority, I had to see the world. I wanted to meet the people I regarded as my teachers and gurus and whom I had known only from afar.

The 1950s and early 1960s became my belated years of apprenticeship, and for much of the time based in London, I was traveling.

Naomi and I visited every European country except Albania, Portugal, and Norway at least once; we went a few times to the United States and Israel but also to West Africa. In connection with my work, I had to be in Paris at least once a month and came to know it fairly well. Work took us to all major German cities; when I left Germany in 1938, I had known only my hometown and Berlin. But above all, we went virtually every year to the Soviet Union in the 1950s and 1960s. This for several reasons: Naomi's father and mother and two of her siblings had emigrated to Russia in 1936 not for political reasons but it happened to be the only country at that time willing to employ him—a distinguished professor of medicine at Frankfurt/Main but with a stiff leg as the result of blood poisoning when he was doing his military service. He was, therefore, considered an invalid, and according to the stringent regulations of the period that permitted the immigration of only able-bodied individuals, he was turned down everywhere as an immigrant. Eventually, his wife managed to obtain an invitation from the Soviet Union; Moscow had no interest in accepting immigrants, but in 1936, an exception was made for a hundred physicians from Germany.

The family arrived in the middle of the notorious purges and Professor Richard Koch was cooling his heels in Moscow until a receptionist at *narkomzdrav* (the ministry of health) took pity of the bewildered innocent foreigner advising him to move away from Moscow as far as he could. This he did settling in Essentuki, a small but fashionable resort in the foothills of northern Caucasus where he found a job, and more importantly, was forgotten, which probably saved his life during subsequent purges.

As a result of our frequent visits, we came to know this part of Russia (as well as Moscow, Leningrad, the Crimea, and a few other places) rather well. In fact, we were apparently among the first foreigners permitted to travel to the Caucasus after the war.

There was yet another reason for my interest in these trips: The Soviet Union had become my main field of study during this period, and the visits gave me an excellent opportunity to become more familiar with the country and its peoples. I was employed as a special correspondent by the *Neue Zuercher Zeitung* (NZZ), one of Europe's leading newspapers. The NZZ had at the time correspondents in every major country but the Soviet Union and China because it refused to operate in countries in which correspondents were subject to censorship. But my reports were always filed after I had left the country and were therefore not subject to censorship. However, there were other considerations that made caution mandatory. I had to consider Naomi's family and take great care not to endanger it. As a result, I wrote about a great many topics such as Soviet daily life—literature, the theater, cinema, and television (then at the beginning), shopping in Soviet cities and villages, food and drink, how Russians were spending their free time and holidays, and how to get married in the Soviet Union. I wrote, over the years, about almost every aspect of Soviet life, except politics, which suited me and probably kept the censors happy.

Over time, I came to know this part of the Caucasus rather well—it is not that near from Chechnya, which became the scene of so much fighting in later years, but not very far from it either. But it was clear to me even then that under the surface of *druzhba narodov* (the friendship between the various nationalities of the Soviet Union), there was great tension, which however in the political conditions then prevailing could not openly manifest themselves.

1938

I was seventeen in 1938. I passed my exams for an Abitur diploma in February, and I left the country in November. I read every newspaper I could lay my hands on—politics vied with sports. I somehow managed an equal interest in Rudolf Harbig, a track star and Rudolf Hess, Hitler's deputy at the time. I listened to more radio broadcasts than was good for me, yet I was barely aware of the connection between politics and everyday life. Politics seemed to be something rather esoteric, which possibly might have some meaning for a few people in Berlin, Paris, and London and which in itself might well be an important subject, like for instance the study of philosophy. However, I felt that the ordinary mortal could not possibly have any influence on politics, and it was therefore best ignored. Life would go on somehow.

At the age of seventeen, as I later discovered with a confused sense of guilt one possesses an astonishing capacity for overlooking unpleasant facts. For me, 1938 was the year of waiting, the year of unsuccessful attempts to train for a profession, the year of cycling tours in the mountains of Taunus and the Riesengebirge (the Giant Mountains), the year in which I did a lot of swimming, fell in love with at least two girls, saw many films, and read countless books.

I am asked sometimes—and indeed I ask myself—how such a life was possible being a young Jew in Germany, on the eve of the Second World War? However incredible this may seem in retrospect, the spring and the summer passed without any real excitement, although the autumn crisis left its mark. Came September, came November. Right into the late summer, I must have been so immersed in my own thoughts and problems that I noticed events around me out of the corner of my eye. The only excuse I can muster is that it was no different for many others, who were older and more experienced than me. The awakening was a slow process.

When I revisited Breslau after the war many years later, I drove out to the stadium by way of the Scheitnig Park. In 1938, it was one of the most modern sports arenas in Europe. It was built in the early 1930s by the father of a classmate of mine named Richard Konwiarz; both father and son, my classmate, were to build many more sports arenas in northern Germany after the war.

Everything seemed unchanged: the Silesian Arena where I had run the 100-meter relay in school sports, the grounds where we had played soccer every Thursday afternoon, and the swimming pool where, as a small boy, it had taken me two hours to summon up sufficient courage to dive off the ten-meter board. Now, the pool was noticeably neglected, the soccer fields overgrown with grass, and in the whole huge sports stadium, there was not a body to be seen. But my mind's eye saw a crowded stadium—thousands of spectators, athletes in track suits, and hot-dog and ice-cream vendors. The last occasion on which I had seen the Hermann-Goering Stadium (as it was then called) was during the Gymnastics and Athletics Festival of July 1938; it was packed to overflowing, and I still remember the monster demonstrations and the public appearance of Hitler, Himmler, and Goebbels.

The official propaganda machine had been preparing the ground for some time beforehand. There was much talk of the "precious blessing of physical fitness," of the big rally in Silesia, and the border land that had for centuries been a living proof of "the binding strength of German blood" and of "the might of the German spirit," where Germans would link up with their brethren regardless of frontiers.

There were many fringe events; at the Municipal Theatre, they were playing Gregor und Heinrich, but what Kolbenheyer had to say about the conflict between Emperor and Pope was of no particular interest to me. Kolbenheyer was one of the favorites of the Nazis, but they never embraced him wholeheartedly because earlier on, he had written a highly laudatory novel about Spinoza.

A cousin of mine, a "half-Jew" serving in the Wehrmacht, was enthusiastic about developments he had seen on the Gandau aerodrome: the new DO-27 (the "flying pencil"), gliders and parachutists, and aerobatics. He talked about Gerd Achgelis, Count Hagenberg, von Lochner, and other famous flyers of the day. He was particularly impressed by the daring maneuvers performed by some of the pilots. Achgelis, in later years, designed a helicopter, and he survived the war and lived to a ripe old age. So, I believe, did most of the other aviation heroes of that day. But my cousin did not. Hans, who coached me in mathematics (my weakest subject in school), had a great and fatal capacity for enthusiasm. His mother was Jewish, and his non-Jewish father had been killed in the First World War. He had to serve in the army, was ousted, and then again re-enlisted. Nazi policy toward half-Jews changed several times during the war. As so many soldiers were killed, the purity of the race became of less importance. He had again to join the army and perished at the beginning of May 1945, one day before the siege of Breslau came to an end—an unhappy wanderer between two worlds who did not know, perhaps could not know, where he belonged.

I went to the stadium on a Saturday. It was "the Day of Community," *der Tag der Gemeinschaft*. There was a full program, though things were a bit chaotic; there had been a heavy thunderstorm in the morning. I well remember the 800-meter race. The favorite, Harbig, was the last to take his place on the starting line where the others were jogging about impatiently. A trainer gave some last-minute advice to one of the runners; two got into the starting position, the starter fired his pistol, and they were off. The pace was not fast, and one could scarcely expect a record time on a track sodden with rain. Harbig occupied the middle position. After the first lap, tension suddenly mounted, and some of the spectators jumped up, while others shouted, "Sit down."

The crowd was shouting "Harbig" as he sprinted and began to overtake the whole field on the outside. He reached the winning-post with a ten-meter lead, but his time was rather slow. This was followed by the ceremony to honor the winners.

It started with a spectacular display by the SS (Schutzstaffel—the Nazi elite para-military unit) and music by massed bands of the Wehrmacht. Himmler and his staff had timed their arrival to coincide with the SS gymnastics.

A little man with a mouse-like face—was this the supreme leader of the fearful elite corps? Then came units of the army parading in historic uniforms—a company of the ancient regiment of the Elector of Brandenburg and a landing corps of the old Imperial Navy. Finally, there followed a sort of war game, a reconstruction of the Battle of Eckernförde (1864, in the war against Denmark). Flags and bunting fluttered, the bands played the Düppeler-Schanzen march, the blue coats smartly turned right and left, and the public was highly edified by it all.

After a brief moment, there was a burst of applause from the many Sudeten Germans present. On the speakers' platform appeared a man in a white shirt and white trousers—Konrad Henlein, the athletics master from Asch. It took several minutes for the cheering and shouts of Heil to subside; finally, he removed his glasses and started his speech.

He was not a great orator and seemed altogether ill at ease.

He said he was immensely impressed by the enormous progress made by the New Germany and that he himself had come from sports and knew how great a contribution athletes had made to the unification of all Germans. "With awe and deep emotion, I stand before the mighty, living work of Adolf Hitler. That we Germans have found our way to this great inner unity is due to one man only, Adolf Hitler."

Thunderous applause.

Henlein left the platform. This was perhaps his finest hour. He did not have much of a political career during the years after. Some Nazi leaders (especially Heydrich) did not like him and thought him too soft, not really a militant Nazi. Some suspected him of contacts with Admiral Canaris and other semiresistants. He committed suicide while in American captivity in Pilsen, a few days after the end of the war.

Now, Dr. Goebbels spoke, and a few sentences were sufficient to make one realize how fully "our Doktor" was accepted by the public. "Certain cultural apostles abroad claim that we in Germany have forgotten how to laugh," the little man said. Gales of laughter swept the stadium. Then, turning to more serious matters, he screamed into the microphone that the enslaved people of 1918 had now become a Great Power. "We are fully conscious of our strength! And we know what we want!" Tumultuous applause. He waved it aside impatiently, and silence returned. Was it not a miracle that the unknown conscript of the World War was today in charge of the destiny of the Reich and of the whole nation? Tomorrow, the Führer was to come to Breslau whose citizens would be inspired to renewed faith and fresh hope by beholding his countenance. More than anyone else, they needed this faith and hope "which you must preserve for the greatness of our nationhood and the honor of our blood." Once again, deafening applause. Press reports next morning were to describe the meeting as "a mighty demonstration of the unity of Germany on both sides of the frontier, which can no longer be sundered by any power in the world." I made my way home in a more thoughtful mood.

Hitler arrived in Breslau, and on the following morning, the huge festive procession wound its way through the streets of the city. I can no longer remember the Führer's speech on this occasion. In three ranks, several kilometres long, ten and twelve abreast, the participants in the Sports Festival marched to the Castle Square, where a colossal rostrum had been erected opposite the opera house. Beneath a large swastika made of oak leaves, Hitler stood with his staff on a platform swathed in red draperies. Beside him were Goebbels, Himmler, and a third man whose name was not very well known at the time: Martin Bormann. I was impressed by the feat of sheer physical endurance; with outstretched hand, Hitler saluted column after column of marchers. The march-past continued for several hours, and the Führer's face became more and more rigid; the effort clearly showed, but he stuck it out. The marchers swarmed through the flagged streets of the town:

> *Es fragen nicht nach Spiel und Tand*
> *Die Männer aus Westfalenland*

(They seek not fun and regalia. The stalwarts of Westphalia.) Then came a troupe of Swabian girls in regional costume:
Wir sind schwäbische Mädels (We are Swabian girls) ...
They chanted, as if anyone could have mistaken them. They were followed by the Austrian athletes, the first contingent since the Anschluss. Twelve abreast they marched past the Führer's platform:

> *Wir sind der Ostmark Söhne*
> *Unser das Land, das schöne.*
> *Unser der Kampf und der Sieg.*

(Sons of the Ostmark [the Nazi name for Austria] are we.
Ours is that beautiful country, Ours the struggle and victory.)
The procession went on and on, until at last came the turn of the hosts, ecstatic faces, sparkling eyes, and tumultuous cheering. From my vantage point on the corner of Schweidnitz street, I heard them singing the local anthem, the Schlesierlied:

> *... wo vor einer Tür mein Mägdlein steht.*
> *Da seufzt sie still, ja still, und flüstert leise*
> *Mein Schlesierland, mein Heimatland.*

(... where my maiden stands by a door. And she sighs and whispers My Silesia, my homeland.) The SS that was responsible for keeping the streets clear had great difficulty in holding back the crowds.
"My Silesia, my homeland, We will meet again on the banks of the Oder."

We shall meet again on the banks of the Oder when roses will be in bloom. Roses have been in bloom for many years now but the banks of the Oder are further away than ever.

The bands were playing the Badenweiler march, the York march, and the Hohenfriedberg march. Then came the Sudeten Germans, thousands of them, who were all clad in white. A group of young girls ran toward the platform, lifting their hands up to Hitler. For several minutes, the Heils and spoken choruses continued:

> *Wir wollen heim ins Reich.*
> *Ein Volk, ein Reich, ein Führer.*

(We want to come home to the Reich.
One nation, one country, one leader.
We want to come home to the Reich.)

Now for the first time, they beheld the man whose countenance would inspire them with renewed faith and fresh hope, as Goebbels had told them the day before. The enthusiasm was boundless: "As through a floodgate, the broad stream of happiness and joy flows between the Führer's platform and the marchers," reported the *Völkischer Beobachter* next day. "Here was an expression of the passionate love of all Germans for the man who is the embodiment of the youthful German people." The march suddenly came to a halt, and the whole procession was threatened with momentary confusion. Himmler left the platform and thanked the Sudeten German girls in Hitler's name, asking them to continue on their way, which they finally did. Further groups marched past and were welcomed enthusiastically, especially the Volksdeutsche (Germans living beyond the borders of Germany) in their white embroidered shirts, with long flowing ribbons, and carrying bouquets of flowers in their hands. Again and again the chanting

> *Wir wollen heim ins Reich...*

I did not watch the march to the stadium in the afternoon. That evening, Hitler flew back to Berlin. When, at a late hour that night, I went to visit a friend in town, I could still hardly make my way through the crowds. Everybody was in high spirits; great events were casting their shadow before them. The Sudeten German brothers would not have to suffer much longer under the "despotism of the licentious Czech soldiery."

During the same period that the Volksdeutsche were clamoring so loudly to come "home to the Reich," several hundred thousand German Jews had no dearer wish than to leave Germany as quickly as possible. They were pariahs in the Third Reich and were living—figuratively speaking—in a ghetto that was closing in on them all the time; many of them were no longer able to carry on with their daily work. In Breslau, for example, almost half the Jewish community had to be supported by Jewish charities. The measures by which the Jews were to be excluded from the life of Germany had by now been in force for over five years, but many thought that this process was still too slow. In February of that year, *Das Schwarze Korps*, the SS newspaper, had devoted an important editorial to the Jewish problem. In answer to the question "Where are the Jews to go?" it said, "We must point out that the Jews have not exactly been seized by a feverish desire to emigrate. The behavior of the Jews in Germany does not give the impression that they are sitting on ready-packed suitcases.

With admirable agility, (the paper continued) the Jews have switched over from retail to wholesale trade, from manufactured goods to raw materials, they have cleverly developed the art of camouflage...." Needless to say, there was not a shred of truth in this statement. I did not know of a single case where Jews had "switched over" to wholesale trading or raw materials, but the intention was unmistakable. The Jews were still too well off and they had not disappeared. What was to be done to hasten their departure? What indeed? Gunter d'Alquen, the editor of the newspaper and a favorite of Himmler, had a good war and an almost trouble-free post war. Charged with incitement to murder, he (among other accusations) had to pay a fine and lost his civic rights for three years. He did lose his pension but did not have to starve being on the board of a textile enterprise. He emphatically denied ever having heard of the plans to exterminate the Jews.

He died in 1998.

The Jews were besieging consulates, administrative offices for Palestine, emigration advice bureaus, and language schools and were preparing themselves hectically for departure.

When I think back to 1938, I still hear some snatches of songs, which have imprinted themselves on my memory. To me, they symbolize a whole era in Germany: *Steige hoch du roter Adler* (Rise, thou red eagle), *Geduld verratne Brueder* (Patience, betrayed brethren), and time and time again *Wir seh'n uns wieder am Oderstrand* (We'll meet again on the banks of the Oder). When I recall the Jewish situation of that summer, certain phrases come to mind; among them is this compulsive advertising jingle, which I can recite by heart to this day—probably because I had to spend several hours waiting in an office where there was nothing else to read:

> *Willst den Wohnsitz du verändern*
> *Sei's auch nach den fernsten Ländern,*
> *ob nach Indien oder China*
> *oder auch nach Palästina*
> *Zieh getrost zum fernsten Ort,*
> *Eckstein bürgt für den Transport.*

(If you're on the move, Let Ecksteins prove
The farthest spot on earth is not too hard to do.
From Timbuctoo To Samarkand or the Holy Land
Eckstein's take care to get you there.)

Most of my acquaintances would have cheerfully moved to the farthest spot on earth with Eckstein's, but certain little difficulties stood in their way. These difficulties could be drily formulated in scientifically precise terms; the clamp-down on the international movement of capital and the crisis in world trade exerted an unfavorable influence on emigration overseas, or to express it more simply and brutally, there was no country in the world waiting for the German Jews (or any other immigrants for that matter).

However, the words that were on everyone's lips and which, in my memory, characterize the whole period, are re-training, livelihood ("create a livelihood" and "a secure lively hood"), certificate of good conduct, Hachsharah (preparation for Palestine), health certificate, police clearance, harbor charges, Affidavit (a necessary condition for obtaining a US visa), Chamada (the same for Brazil), and so on. In addition, there were the many new abbreviations, such as ICA, HIAS, HICEM, ALTREU, and PALTREU, which had suddenly acquired supreme importance. All this must seem rather odd, if not funny; however, it soon turned out that the certificates, affidavits, and chamadas were a matter of life or death. I know a number of people who are by no means of a nervous or sensitive disposition but who, even today over a quarter of a century later, are seized with violent palpitations when entering a consulate, although they have, in the meantime, become unimpeachable citizens of the USA, Israel, or Honduras.

While rummaging through some old papers recently, I came across a hectographed leaflet, yellowed with age, which had been handed to me at an emigration office. The imagination boggles at these extracts:

Luxemburg: frontiers closed to all immigrants and passengers in transit.

Ministry Of Justice, Amsterdam: in future any refugee will be regarded as an undesirable alien.

Notice from the United States Consulate in Berlin: in view of the extraordinarily high number of entry applications, the quota figures for the immediate future are exhausted.

The following are required in the Fiji Islands: a Jewish pastry cook and a single watchmaker who must not be younger than twenty-five or older than thirty. Paraguay was looking for an accomplished, self-employed sweetmeat cook, and British Bechuanaland wanted a qualified tanner, Central Africa an unmarried Jewish butcher (specializing in the manufacture of savory sausages), and San Salvador required a single Jewish engineer for the construction of electrical machinery. The greatest opportunities existed in Manchukuo where there were vacancies for a Jewish cabaret producer/choreographer who had to partner the prima ballerina, together with a troupe of —six to eight ballet dancers able to dance solos. In addition, they wanted a Jewish ladies' orchestra and a pianist able to play the accordion.

There was a peremptory notice from Mexico to the effect that a visa issued by a Mexican consulate did not guarantee official permission to disembark in Mexico.

The Canadian delegate to the Evian Conference on Refugees stated that Canada could not make any binding promises.

The British delegate, Lord Winterton, declared that Britain was faced with heavy unemployment.

Such were the openings for German Jews in the summer of 1938. They could emigrate to the Fiji Islands if they happened to be pastry cooks aged between twenty-five and thirty, or to Manchukuo, if they belonged to the female sex, played an instrument, and were prepared to entertain the Japanese armed forces.

The scenes in these offices are the most harrowing that I can remember. At the same time, as the Athletics Festival was being held at Breslau, an international conference had been convened at Evian on Lake Geneva for the coordination of aid and emigration facilities for refugees. All the delegates expressed their deepest sympathy with the prospective emigrants (who, since the spring of 1938, also included the Jews of Austria). Most Jewish communities held a day of fasting and prayers in the synagogues, but the prayers remained unanswered, for no country in the world was prepared to accept refugees without any means of support, and National Socialist Germany made it impossible, even for those Jews who had any property left, to take their possessions with them. However, one land would have been prepared to welcome them: Palestine, the "Jewish National Home." But in 1936, there had been violent disturbances, and the British had severely limited immigration in order not to jeopardize their relations with the Arabs.

Occasionally, a ray of hope broke through the clouds.

Magic words like "Shanghai" or "Bolivia" appeared on the horizon, or rumors were heard about the Berlin representative of a Central American republic who was selling passports for money and kind words, but above all, for lots of money. The only drawback was the dismal fact that these passports were apparently valid everywhere except in the country that was supposed to have issued them. The desperate economic situation was driving more and more German Jews, with the exception of the old and sick, to emigrate. Large-scale arrests had not yet begun in the summer of 1938, but certain events were casting their shadows: the sad fate of the Viennese Jews during the weeks following the Anschluss, or the series of new rules excluding the Jews from an ever-growing number of occupations. It was at that time when by official edict, all Jews had to change their first name to "typically Jewish names," such as Chava (as a man's name), Kaiphas, Sirach, Celea, Tana, and Rause.

A ridiculous situation, but no one was moved to laughter.

A Jewish cultural association had been founded in 1933. "Admission for Jews only on presentation of pass"—here the unemployed Jewish actors, singers, and other musicians found a modest field of activity. My father once took me to the synagogue where I listened to Joseph Schmidt or perhaps Alexander Kipnis (I cannot quite remember who it was), singing arias by Donizetti and Puccini and from the *Postillion of Longjumeau*. Though the acoustics were far from ideal, there was warm applause. In the summer of 1938, one could attend lectures on "Jewish Emigration—Whither?" "A Biedermeier Evening with Meyerbeer," "The Origin and Nature of the Golem" (a mystical figure of clay endowed with life, that had been the subject of much speculation since medieval times), "Jewish Hellenism as a Cultural Problem," and "What Meaning Can Books Have for Us?" There were also topical revues such as

"From Romeo to the String quartet," "Poor as a church mouse" and "All Aboard Please—a Travel Revue in 21 Tableaux" with Max Ehrlich and Willy Rosen, and "Winterhilfe of the Soul" (Winterhilfe = an officially sponsored German relief organization).

Hotel Frohsinn at Bad Harzburg, it said in a Jewish newspaper, was still offering all mod. cons. Football result: Hakoah I vs. ISK I-17:o. Small ads in the Jewish press offered an "assured income" and "excellent prospects." Mr. Simeon Victor, of Frobenstrasse 5, Breslau 18, promised a carefree old age by means of an annuity insurance paying high benefits: "Pension arrangements to suit every individual requirement."

Thus, here I was, several decades later, trying to take a snapshot of the university from across the river. I found it difficult to hold the camera steady because of the vibrations from the heavy traffic crossing the bridge. A few passersby turned their heads, wondering what I could see worth photographing. On the right, the cathedral with its ruined towers, and on the left a small island in the Oder. I suddenly remembered Anders and Kallenbach, and I told Naomi of the many hours I had spent on this island in that summer of 1938. "On this island?" she asked, "In this weather, in this water?" However, the weather was not always so bad, nor the water so dirty, and in those days, the island had looked so much bigger to me. For bathers, there was a rectangular wooden raft in a tributary of the Oder River, a few lockers and cabins, and an outsized "Nivea" ball. Access to the small island was free of charge. Jews had not been allowed to use the municipal pools for years, and the older generation had no penchant for swimming. So for most of the time, we were by ourselves—a few dozen boys and girls in the same age group and some younger children who were being taught to swim by the bathing superintendent at the end of a line, while others were moving cautiously along the edge in their first attempts to float unaided. If the sun was shining, we arrived early in the morning and stayed for hours; I usually brought some books but never managed to read them. From the water, you could only see the island—nothing of the people, the houses, or the traffic on land. It was easy to succumb to the illusion that civilization was far, far away, but not for long; conversation inevitably returned to the same theme—emigration. Someone had a brother in a kibbutz in Palestine; someone else had discovered a rich relative in America who was willing to help; a boy talked of the difficulties he had to overcome if he was to be accepted at a hotel catering college abroad. E., whom I had known since our days at nursery school together, turned up during his holidays. He was being trained on a farm in Southern Germany where a fairly large group were preparing themselves for work on a kibbutz. He told us that at first, he had found agricultural work very hard, and that his knowledge of the declension of Latin verbs had been no use to him at all, but he was almost aggressive in his optimism.

I had a girlfriend, whom I met here practically every day unless we decided to go cycling together. She had a tyrannical father who had been an officer during the war and was proud of his decorations. He was a member of the *Reichsbund Juedischer Frontsoldaten* (Association of German-Jewish War Veterans). His constant refrain was that the German Jews simply had to stick to their posts "like good soldiers." Soon things would get better. The present measures were mainly directed against the East European Jews. He had forbidden his daughter even to think of emigrating. She rebelled and decided to run away from home, but her mother was in poor health and she did not want to leave her behind. I tried hard to persuade her, but to no avail. Once, we went to the pictures—the Deli or the Gloria Palast, I cannot quite remember now. It was a film about Paris at the turn of the century. I whispered:

"If only one could . . ." An unattainable dream. Romeo and Juliet in the backyard.

She was deported in 1942.

Twenty-five years later, I saw—in what was now called Wroclaw—the Ida Kamenska Ensemble of Warsaw, in a comedy by Goldfaden in the same cinema that had been rebuilt as a theater. The performance in the Yiddish language was impressive, though I missed some of the finer points. Still, I could not bear to sit through the comedy to the end. The doorkeeper was concerned enough to ask whether the play was so unpleasing. It would have been difficult to explain.

The months went by, waiting, waiting. In February, I had passed the Abitur for my higher school certificate a year earlier than usual; the introduction of compulsory labor and military services had resulted in the abolition of the upper sixth. I did not mind; the last few years at school had seemed utterly superfluous to me. At one stage, I had wanted to become an athletics coach, and then again a textile engineer.

I received a written confirmation from my school that I was "eminently suitable" for both occupations; they would probably have given me a similar testimonial for any other career I cared to mention. However, opportunities for career training were diminishing day by day. Originally, I had wanted to study history, but this was now out of the question. One evening, in the spring of that year, I went to a lecture with a friend; a professor from the Hebrew University of Jerusalem was to talk about excavations in Samaria. I had no particular interest in archaeology, but my friend who had heard this speaker on a previous occasion was full of praise; it could have been that I had nothing better to do that evening. The lecturer's German was not perfect, but he knew how to make a fairly dry subject attractive to his listeners.

I was not in a position to judge his eminence as an archaeologist, but he was obviously convinced of the great importance of the excavations, and he succeeded in infecting the audience with his own enthusiasm. He was an entirely different type from the German professors I had heard.

After the lecture, we accompanied him to his hotel; as we were walking along the promenade in the municipal gardens, we passed a monument. I ventured the remark that it was Bucephalus. "Nonsense," he said, "this is Pegasus. Bucephalus did not have wings." He seemed surprised to hear that we did not know of Xenophon's book on horses. Still, he went on to inquire with genuine interest about my plans for the future. "Study history? Like my eldest—if only playing at soldiers would leave him sufficient time . . . Why don't you come and study with us?" I explained to him that I was not yet eighteen, that we had no money, and that I had heard there were very few places available at the Hebrew University. "Dear L.," he replied, "there will always be difficulties, but unlike you German Jews, we are not so easily discouraged. Do apply, I will put in a word for you—who knows, it might help? What is there to lose?" Indeed, I had little to lose. I took my leave of him outside his hotel very late that night.

Ten years later, in December 1947 to be precise, in the backroom of a Jerusalem coffee house named Palatin, it was my duty to introduce the archaeologist Professor Sukenik at a press conference. He reported the finding of certain scrolls near the Dead Sea. Most had not yet been deciphered, but if his assumptions were right, these could well be one of the most important finds of the century. His assumptions were right.

Twenty years later, while attending an Orientalists' Congress at Moscow University, I turned up by mistake in the study group of Near Eastern Archaeology. A lecture was given illustrated with slides; the hall was packed to overflowing. The speaker was reporting on the discovery of papyrus scrolls in caves near the Dead Sea. The father had begun the work, and he continued it.

It was one of the liveliest lectures I had ever heard; sitting next to me was a Korean, who, though apparently unable to understand a single word, appeared to be spellbound. There was great applause. At the conclusion of the lecture, I waited for the usual cluster of inquirers to disperse and finally approached the speaker to tell him that it was thanks to the father that I was able to listen to the son. About the dangers of "playing soldiers," the old gentleman had not been entirely mistaken; the son, Yigael Yadin, had been Chief of Staff of the Israeli Army before returning to academic life.

Then, in the spring of 1938, my student days were still a long way ahead. Time passed slowly, waiting for the postman and queuing at various offices. A little while ago, my daughter asked me why I wait so impatiently for the postman at home in London, when I know well that he calls regularly as clockwork three times a day. I tried to explain that it was a "conditioned reflex"—perhaps she had learned about this at school. In 1938, the post was the link with the outside world and a gateway to the future. The finer points of the postal service were carefully studied. Airmail letters were very expensive, especially if they weighed more than five grams. One had to use very thin paper, which sometimes made the writing illegible and tore easily.

Letters destined for abroad had to be posted at a certain time—for sea mail to Palestine, one depended on the D-126, which left the Central Station on a Tuesday; for air mail, it was necessary to post in special boxes by eight o'clock on a Wednesday night in order to make the connection to Berlin for a KLM or an Imperial Airways plane. I used to wait for the postman outside our front door or if it was raining, by the bay window of our flat from where I could overlook the whole street. I knew he would turn round the corner into the Rossmarkt from the Schlosstrasse at four o'clock or five past at the latest. If he had nothing for me, in my disappointment, I would look enviously at the letters in his hand bearing foreign stamps, addressed to the bank next door or to the city library. Never before or after have letters played such an important role in our lives; while there was mail, there was hope.

My parents' financial situation went from bad to worse. Father hardly spoke, and mother, who was in poor health, grumbled a lot. The business was being gradually wound up, and when my parents moved into a small flat, part of the furniture was sold. Of all this, I wanted to see as little as possible; after all, I could hardly be of any help to them. In April and May of that year, I spent very little time at home; I was an unpaid trainee in a big textile mill at Reichenbach.

One of the workers with whom I had become friendly initiated me into the mysteries of dyeing techniques. In my time off, I tried studying chemistry, but it did not come easily; my heart was not in it. I was living with an uncle at Schweidnitz, nearly an hour's train journey from the mill; I had to get up early in the morning and did not get home till late at night. My grandfather had bought a house on the Ring, the central square at Schweidnitz, and now my uncle was selling spirits from the premises. He was a tiny man, and I especially admired his courage and skill in dealing with drunken haulage workers. His cultural interests were limited, but he possessed a dry sense of humor and a feeling for music. In the old days, he used to play chamber music with his friends at least once a week; now, the other members of the quartet had been unable to come to see him for some considerable time. One of them was a lecturer, the second a tax inspector, and the third worked in the police department. In this small town, everybody knew everybody else.

They would certainly have got into trouble had they continued their music-making with a Jew. As public servants, with pension rights, they had to be careful. Occasionally, one of them would steal into my uncle's flat after nightfall and talk to him for a few minutes. Sometimes, my uncle would ask me to accompany him on his evening walk. I did so reluctantly; it seemed a bore, and I had better things to do; the acquaintances we met during these walks were of no interest to me. Nice elderly folk whose conversation was mainly about whether they had saved up enough money to enable them to retire to an old people's home in Berlin.

These people were too old to emigrate, and I heard them say occasionally that they envied me. I, for my part, envied my friends who had already managed to get out of the country, and their number was mounting from day to day. Behind my uncle's house, there was a steep drop, and it used to be said that his neighbor, a baker, had fallen down there and died instantaneously. I often thought of death and of dying, but the depression did not last long. At night, I was always so tired that I fell asleep at once.

The train arrived at Reichenbach shortly after seven o'clock every morning, so I used to spend some time in the station waiting-room reading the paper: "Take-Over Of Austrian National Bank By The Reich" and "Teruel Reconquered." The *Berliner Illustrirte* was serializing a new novelette: "Must Men Be Like That?" The advertising slogans still remain with me:

"*Sei sparsam Brigitte, nimm Ultra-Schnitte; das ist der neue Name der altbwährten Ullsteinschnitte*" (an advertisement for dress patterns), "The dead can be brought back to life if one lives with them in the spirit" (Hans Schemm), and "Make Trilysin the essence of hair care..."

After work, we used to play soccer in an open field. Sometimes, I stayed overnight; another apprentice had a motorcycle and we would spend the night riding round the mountains. The nights were clear, the weather was nearly always perfect, and there was a ghostly silence. We passed through Langenbielau and Peterswaldau (the two largest villages in old Prussia) right up to the Waldenburg Mountains. This was the setting of, *The Weavers*, Gerhart Hauptmann's radical social drama.

This area, though boasting the largest textile mills in Eastern Germany, had never acquired the genuine status of an industrial region. It was no more than a collection of overgrown mountain villages. Once, in the dark, we nearly ran into an army column on the march.

Our rides through forests and clearings, through abandoned villages, past factories and castle ruins, were an obvious kind of escapism, a fleeting illusion of a freedom to travel wherever and whenever we pleased. Its only tangible result was that back in the factory next morning, I was sleepy and weary and even less attentive than usual. Many years later at an accidental meeting near Albany, I was told that somehow the motorbike and its owner had found their way to Peru and later yet to upstate New York.

After a few weeks of this sort of life, the Arbeitsfront (after all a Nazi organization) foreman considered my presence a nuisance, and that was the end of my term in the dye shop. My uncle asked me what I intended to do, but how could I give him an answer? I took my leave from a few acquaintances; one of them, named Urban, had been a friend of my father's and a devout Catholic. In his spare time, he attended to his bees, and when I was a little boy, he sometimes took me along with him. His family was full of sympathy and advised me that if ever I were in trouble, I should place my trust in the Church, which would help me in word and deed. When I objected that I was not a member, they said this did not matter a bit. "The Church would help everybody...."

Twenty-five years later, I drove along the same road and found Central Silesia scarcely altered (apart, of course, from the new inhabitants). At Schweidnitz, I found the houses around the Ring freshly spruced up, even my grandfather's old house had been renovated. With great effort, it was still possible to decipher his name at a side entrance. I looked for the cemetery, but neither the tourist bureau nor the municipal administrative offices were able to assist me; they said they only knew of Catholic cemeteries. Finally, I entered the first churchyard I could see and enlisted the aid of the watchman, a Ukrainian, who led me across some field paths to an army camp enclosed with barbed wire. Next to it, there was indeed the cemetery. Some of the gravestones had been piled up in a corner, most of which had been overturned. I turned them over till I found one I had been looking for.

There had been small Jewish communities in these towns south of Breslau. The generation of the parents had been shop owners with a sprinkling of physicians. The next generation, more often than not, went to study law, medicine, and various sciences. I have mentioned Schweidnitz—Albert Neisser was born there; he was the discoverer of the causative agents of Gonorhoea and leprosy; Paul Ehrlich, one of the greatest names in bacteriology, was born in Strehlen, less than twenty minutes by car from Schweidnitz; Karl Weigert, another leading figure in the field in Muensterberg, another half hours' distance. They went to the same Breslau high school (Neisser and Ehrlich were classmates, I believe). The list could be prolonged. A geographical-social accident no doubt, but an interesting one all the same.

Reichenbach was more neglected than Schweidnitz. I could not find any of the big textile mills and soon gave up the attempt. At the Ring, looking for a bite to eat, I was unable to find a restaurant. The access roads to the Ring or market square in these towns were rather narrow; now, they had been turned into one-way streets. They all led away from the Ring; in Waldenburg, I had to drive round and round three times before I managed to find a road leading to it. I heard some French spoken; a few thousand Polish miners from Northern France had settled here after the war. We drove past the "Maurice-Thorez Pit"; the soccer club was also named after the French Communist leader. In the hills of the Eulengebirge, I lost my way. All the names had been changed, and the new inhabitants of this area had never heard of Lindenruh or the Sieben-Kurfürsten hut. All the houses were occupied, but there was not a soul to be seen, and we drove on for hours without meeting another vehicle.

After my abortive start as a textile engineer, there was an interlude in a carpenter's workshop in Frankfurt. Several applications for emigration were under way at different consulates, but it might take weeks, if not months, before I would know anything definite. I did not want to hang around at home. At the end of my first day, I knew that I would never really become a carpenter. On the third day, the workshop was closed; there was an outbreak of polio in the city. We started exploring Frankfurt and its surroundings, cycling to Wiesbaden and into the Taunus mountains.

I became friendly with Kurt, who was a few years older than me and a native of Stuttgart and a "half-Aryan," according to the Nuremberg laws. He was a dedicated Zionist who could hardly wait to become a member of a kibbutz. We went for walks along the Kurpromenade in Wiesbaden, visited the Kronberg Castle, climbed the Grosser Feldberg, and discussed the latest events in Palestine, the partition plan, and the Arab terrorist attacks.

I can still see him, broad-shouldered and invariably cheerful.

His dream of a kibbutz life was not to be fulfilled; the last time we met was on a hot summer's afternoon in Palestine, on the road leading through the Jordan valley. He had brought over a group of children from Germany and was going back in order to get yet another group out. I tried to persuade him to stay, argued that he had done his duty, that war seemed unavoidable, and then it might well be too late.

He remained stubborn: one simply could not leave those children in the lurch. As a "half-Jew," he would be able to move about more freely in the Third Reich than his other comrades. I waved goodbye to him on August 20, 1939. Years later, I heard from friends that throughout the war, he had helped to organize an escape route from Holland and Belgium through France to Spain, and by this underground route, many hundreds had found their way to freedom and salvation. He lived a life of hourly danger as an "underground man." Shortly before the Allied invasion, his group was trapped by the Gestapo, but in the general chaos of those months, his personal dossier went astray and he survived the war in prison. A few weeks after the end of the war, he was run over by a car in a Paris street and killed on the spot.

A haze lies over those weeks in Frankfurt, and a feeling of unreality pervaded the whole of my last summer in Germany. We cycled along the Rhein and the Main rivers, ate the local cheese, drank the local cider, when we could afford it, and argued about ways and means of setting the world to rights. At night, we returned to the hostel, too tired to do more than glance at the headlines from which we learned that once again, a crisis was in the offing.

In the middle of September, I received a telephone call from Berlin. Great news—I had been accepted as a student at the University of Jerusalem, the entry permit was on its way, and it would only take "a few more weeks now." It seems that they overlooked, in that pre-computer age, the fact that I was not yet eighteen, apparently a precondition for acceptance. It was one of several fortunate accidents that saved my life. I had graduated at seventeen and not a year or two later because the upper form at school had been abolished because non-Jews were called up; they had to serve in the army.

Meanwhile, I was to present myself at various offices in Berlin: I would also need "a medical." I left the next day. At the central railway station, police were looking for juveniles under eighteen (on account of the polio epidemic, they had been strictly prohibited from leaving Frankfurt). Fortunately, I looked rather older and passed the barrier unmolested.

I do not mean to give a hectic impression; in fact, until the end of September, things were rather quiet; it was as if time stood still. The situation seemed to be at an impasse, and I was living without a plan: somehow, I never felt that I was under pressure. There were idyllically calm days, especially the week I had spent in the Riesengebirge.

We had met by the fountain in front of the Freiburger Railway Station. The Monday morning train was packed—a few winter sports stragglers and soldiers returning to their bases and country people who had spent the weekend in the capital. Our journey went off without a hitch, and we reached the frontier in the early afternoon, reporting first to the German and then the Czech border guards. The customs officials glanced at our rucksacks: "In Ordnung, just be careful with the Czechs. They are in a nasty mood because of Austria—they feel that it will be their turn next...." The Czech official did not even bother to look at us; he stamped our passports, and we were free to go. We proceeded on toward our destination, a farmer's house at Ober-Kleinaupa, a mountain village where we had booked a room. We walked past snow-covered slopes and through fir forests. For as long as I could remember, I had spent summer and winter holidays in the Riesengebirge, first with my parents and later with friends. In our geography lessons at school, we were taught that "the Sudeten range runs from south-east to north-west like a rampart separating the North Bohemian Basin from the Silesian Plain..." The highest part of this rampart is the Riesengebirge, its peaks and ridges rising far above the tree line.

Mountain anemones and Alpine flowers could be found on the high plateaus; tough knee pines struggled for survival between the gigantic blocks of granite. At the foot of the mountains, which formed the frontier, there were many summer and winter resorts catering for all tastes and able to satisfy the most exacting demands. The air was pure, and there were chalybeate springs, traditional German hostelries, good old-fashioned cooking, white slopes, and ski instructors. The frontier was running more or less on top of the mountains. On both sides, there were guest houses, restaurants with a few rooms for those wanting to stay overnight. Some were quite luxurious and not exactly inexpensive, and others quite modest. I loved the German (or Bohemian) Forest, its smell and its silence, and the taste of blueberries and wild raspberries, looking for edible mushrooms. My dream in those years was to live in a little house in a forest or on the sea shore. The proximity of the sea I achieved for a decade but not of the forest. I doubt whether the forest I knew as a child, boy, and young man is still to be found anywhere.

On a rainy weekend, almost twenty-five years later, I revisited the places of my childhood. As we were driving up the steep climbs, our car started to steam like a locomotive, and we just managed the way back to a garage at Hirschberg. A swarm of children clustered round our Volga car, gleefully shouting *Russki kaputt* or something to this effect, but there was no international incident. A policeman chased the children away; the mechanic opened the hood and pronounced his diagnosis in measured tones: we should wait an hour and then fill the radiator with cold water.

All this took place in front of the monument to Zamenhof, the inventor of Esperanto. For the first time, I regretted the fact that the synthetic world language had not become sufficiently established to overcome our difficulties. While the engine was cooling off, we entered a food shop in the Ring, which still lay partly in ruins. I asked the elderly assistant, in Russian, whether he could open a bottle of wine for me as I had no corkscrew. He had forgotten his Russian since his days of service in the Czar's army, he said, but he could open a bottle of wine po polski without a corkscrew.

No sooner said than done: placing the bottle firmly between his thighs, he slapped the bottom of the bottle with his flat hand, and the cork popped out, much to the entertainment of an appreciative audience of customers. Having retrieved our car, we drove along the streetcar lines to Warmbrunn and then further on up into the mountains. In one village, people waved us down; the road was closed for the great international cycle race "Across the Riesengebirge," and the first competitors were due any moment now, and there they were—first the leaders in a small group, followed by the main body and finally a few stragglers. The villagers cheered them on, with a special round of applause for the last few.

The road snaked alongside a torrential stream shaded by tall trees; there was heavy traffic round the many bends, and I had hardly had a chance to enjoy the landscape before we reached the outskirts of

Schreiberhau. A tourist department official took us to the "Snezka" Hotel—I remembered a Hotel Schneekoppe where I had stayed as a little boy with my mother. It was of course the same hotel; the forest began only a few yards away. If one followed the river Zackel, one came to the Josephinenhütte where glass-blowing was still a specialty.

Schreiberhau, not a luxurious but a very pleasant resort—now named Sklarska Potreba—had its moment of fame later on. In November 1947, Zhdanov, the Soviet leader most trusted by Stalin, assembled the East European Communist leaders as well as those from France and Italy telling them that the transition period was over—the East European countries had to follow the Soviet example without deviating one inch in the domestic and foreign policy. The Cold War was now really on, but this was nine years later and it also belongs to a distant past—who remembers these days the Cominform?

Next morning, the sun was brilliant, and from our window, we could see the crest of the mountain range still covered with snow. The season had started: one could hear Polish, Czech, and a little German. For an hour or two, we stretched out in a clearing by the Zackel, where the roar of the water drowned human voices. Toward noon, the rain started again; we drove to Flinsberg and on to Krummhübel (now Karpac). The great attraction there was a wooden church, Kirche Wang. It stood originally in a small place in Northern Norway, but in the 1840s, it was decided to sell it. The Prussian government bought it and it was relocated to this unlikely place.

How the distances had shrunk! The resorts were fairly quiet; only a few hardy holiday makers were braving the rain for a walk on the promenade. In Berutowice (Brückenberg), a huge dog was looking out of a second-floor window.

When I got my camera out to take a snapshot of him, a local policeman advised me against it. A gentleman from Lodz asked me how he could convert Zloty into dollars; we made it clear that this was a subject in which we were not interested. We gave a lift to a young woman waiting at a bus stop. After grumbling about the lack of buses on a Sunday, she inquired why my Polish was so bad. Reassured by my reply, she took us into her confidence and told us she was of German origin married to a Pole.

She had relatives in both the Eastern Zone and in the Federal Republic of Germany, and she had visited them once or twice. "And what was it like over here?" So-so, it was getting bearable now. In the summer, the whole district was crammed with holiday makers, coming from all over Poland. There were not enough hotels and sanatoriums, and many tourists had to find private accommodation. Groups of weekenders often came from Czechoslovakia and even from the German Democratic Republic. "And what was it like in comparison with the old days?" She couldn't say; she was hardly more than a child when the War ended.

In the evening, we went for another walk in the forest. We met groups of people going for strolls, a few drunks, and some courting couples; one could hear folksongs and Polish jazz.

Little remained of the peace and quiet of the Riesengebirge as I remembered it before the invention of the transistor radio. Perhaps, we ought to have gone on a bit further à la recherche du temps perdu, but I had seen what I had come to see, and we were weary. I did not go to the Czech side of the mountain range, but a few weeks ago, I received a picture postcard from my elder daughter who had gone to Prague on a school excursion and had visited Spindlermühle. It meant that we had been in almost shouting distance from each other: she on the Czech and me on the Polish side of the mountain.

It was very pretty, she was well, and she was very busy, but everything was quite different from the description I had given her. She was nearly the same age now as I had been then, yet how different must be her impressions of a journey through mountains in a far-away country of which most English people—as Neville Chamberlain had said twenty-five years ago—knew nothing.

The Consultant in Berlin had Insisted on a Tonsillectomy

"Nowadays," he said, "this is only a matter of three days."

He talked of focal infection and chronic septicemia and of throat inflammations that would have more than nuisance value once one had left the parental home. I felt like objecting, but then I thought of the hot and cold compresses round my neck, the gargling with various chemical substances, the frequent visits to ear-nose-and-throat specialists, the swabs, inhalations, and other unpleasant childhood memories. Anyway, opposition on my part would have been useless; he insisted on the operation. Thus, I presented myself at the Jewish Hospital in Breslau on September 19, 1938, handed in my clothes, and was allocated a bed in the surgical ward. M., a youngish doctor who intended to marry a cousin of mine, visited me that evening and talked of wedding plans and emigration, but the ward sister turned off the light at ten o'clock. A little boy talked in his sleep, an elderly man was groaning, another was telling his neighbor jokes that I, in my then puritan upbringing, found disgusting, and two were playing cards by the weak rays of a flashlight.

The operation would be ridiculously simple, M. had said, and it was "just a routine matter these days." However, there were complications, and I had to stay in hospital longer than anticipated. In the morning, we were awakened early—every hospital has its own routine, but at one point, all these institutions seem to agree, and this conviction is harmful to health, if not downright dangerous, that is, to allow patients to get sufficient sleep. In the semi-darkness, the nurses would start walking about, talking to each other in loud voices. Temperatures were taken, and tea was handed round. M. came to see me briefly after breakfast: "You are not missing anything outside. The hospital is easily one of the healthiest places to be in at the moment. Have you heard the news?" Everybody in the ward was talking politics. Snatches of conversation drifted over to my bed:

"Chamberlain will surely find a way . . . Benes is in a very strong position . . . Ultimatum . . ." With a bit of an effort, I managed to find out what was going on. Before my illness, I had been preoccupied with preparations for my departure and had only glanced at the newspaper headlines. There was a "crisis," this much I knew, but there had been a succession of crises, since the spring almost without pause. At the beginning of September, the situation had become more critical, as Hitler had declared at his annual Nazi congress that he would solve the Sudeten question "one way or another."

On September 15, Chamberlain had gone to Berchtesgaden, and I was lying in bed in the surgical ward, running a temperature.

My parents arrived later in the morning, looking very worried. Father said piously that I must get better as soon as possible. Mother told me the latest news about my schoolmates and friends, who were already abroad, what they had written to their parents, and she mentioned the bedding she had prepared for my emigration. The half hour was painful, and what a time for an operation! Would there be war? My parents had brought me a newspaper in which I read about the "Czech-Jewish-Marxist blood terror," about German mothers-to-be who had been beaten with rubber truncheons by the Czech police. The headlines ran: BLOOD LUST AND HATE PSYCHOSIS RIFE, INCREDIBLE BEASTIALITIES BY CZECH SOLDIERY, UNPARALLELED BRUTALITIES BY CZECH MURDERING BANDITS. Czech children had thrown bottles of petrol on innocent German children, and old people had to run the gauntlet past rows of bayonets. A report from Annaberg said that a Sudeten German mother from Komotau had tried to flee to Germany; at the frontier, she was discovered by Czech officials who tortured her; the poor woman went out of her mind. "Prague threatens Europe with war. . . . The blood of the victims cries for vengeance. . . . Discovery of horrific murder plans by the Communists . . . Steel rods and rubber truncheons used on German workers . . . Moscow assassination commandos with poison gas and explosives are preparing for a bloodbath at Reichenberg. . . ." Amidst the clash of arms, the Muses were not silent:

> *Kein Friede wird ihnen werden, Die Gott zu Kindern uns gab.*
> *Es gibt keinen Frieden auf Erden, Es gibt keinen Frieden im Grab.*
> *Nicht wollen die Hörner wir dämpfen, Es schreitet die Zeit mit Gestampf, Wir kämpfen. Wir kämpfen, wir kampfen Um einen besseren Kampf (Wilm Pleyer)*

(No peace is there on earth, nor is there peace in the grave.
Let us not mute our trumpets, with heavy tread time marches on.
We fight and we fight and we fight on, to make the struggle supreme.)

This kind of rubbish with a strong admixture of mendacity was quite typical for the quasi-heroic Zeitgeist. I remember a photo of a Sudeten German woman with the caption: "This tormented face of a German mother expresses all the misery of mankind." "We want war," so the Czechs are said to have cried. The German Embassy in Prague had lodged sharp protests against Czech border violations at Seidenberg and at the frontier huts.

During the next few days, the mood in the hospital wards was one of utter dejection. Everybody, it seemed, had finally realized how things stood. Newspaper headlines and radio reports were reflected immediately in the mood and behavior of doctors, nurses, and patients. When Chamberlain arrived at Bad Godesberg, there was some tangible improvement in the general atmosphere: there was going to be a compromise, "everything would turn out all right. . . ." The doctors were genial, and the patients no longer difficult. The man in the bed next to me said, "It's a put-up-job-they have pre-arranged everything, and they are staging the whole show just to confuse the masses. . . ." He continued with his never-ending game of cards. I went for little strolls in the hospital garden. The end of that September month had brought warm, sunny days following weeks of rains and floods. The gardener was pottering about his asters and dahlias; in the morning, we were awakened by songbirds.

A deep calm reigned.

Then came the news that, after all, reports of an agreement at Bad Godesberg were premature: Czechoslovakia had rejected the German demands. Hitler made a speech in the Sportpalast and said that the handing over of the Sudeten region was the final German demand. Demonstrations of loyalty everywhere, "Fuehrer, *befiehl—wir folgen* (give the order and we will follow you)!" The propaganda machine was running in high gear:

> This caricature of a State must come to an end . . . children in indescribable misery . . . Czech women as sharp-shooters . . .

In rooms requiring a great deal of lighting, the windows and skylights must be covered in such a manner that no light can be seen from the outside; this may be done with shutters or roller blinds made of wood, fabric, paper, or other materials. Bohemian Woods a living hell for victims of Hussite murderers . . . Announcement of the Happy Event of the Birth of a Son to Henriette von Schirach, née Hoffmann. "This is the Czech: lazy, cowardly and impertinent . . ."

The mood in our hospital ward sunk to new depths of depression; the patients suffered relapses and crises; the doctors were curt, and the nurses irritable (some of them with eyes red from tears). A screen had been placed around the bed of the groaning old man, and now the card player was lying in his bed in complete apathy, staring at the ceiling for hours.

In the bed opposite me, there was an accountant who had undergone a stomach operation. His wife and children came to visit him—the wife looked haggard, care-worn, and badly dressed, and the two little girls, obviously twins, were spruced up in white dresses, patent leather shoes, and colored barrettes in their hair. He told me his story: he had been employed by a large Jewish firm in Upper Silesia who had dismissed him without notice over a year ago, under pressure from the "Labor Front." They had moved to Breslau where they were living somehow in a one-room flat at the Odertor. During this past year, they had gone through all his savings and were now dependent on charity. When his family had left, he said nothing a long time but lay silently, with his face turned to the wall. After supper, he started to talk again; he did not know how it could go on, his wife did not have a single pair of serviceable shoes left, and now he was lying here sick, unable to help. Had he not thought of emigrating? That was impossible for "little men" like him, as he did not even have enough money to travel to Berlin, let alone to far-away countries. If he were twenty years younger and unmarried, then of course he would try. But for people like him, there was only one way out—the gas tap—that is, if the gas had not been cut off already, but for the children, they would have ended it all long ago. On the Saturday, a friend phoned me: "Mensch, the mousetrap might be sprung any moment now. I am getting out of here—on my motorbike—to Constantinople!" Did he have a visa?

No, he would get through one way or another. Next day again, in the paper: "Sudeten German youth caught in the pincers of Czech-Jewish blood terror... The masses of persecuted Germans raise their voices in protest... Rubber truncheons against weeping mothers... All Germans are going to be liquidated, say Czech policemen... Germany's world struggle against lies..."

On that Monday, war seemed inevitable. Had I missed the last train? I envied my friend who was at this moment riding his motorcycle through Czechoslovakia or Hungary.

My parents arrived, tried to comfort me, pretended that in the outside world, nothing had happened, and discussed final preparations for my coming journey. They had bought a special pair of buttonhole scissors for an aunt in Haifa, and I was to take them for her. Several minutes were spent discussing the little scissors. The nurse who brought me my supper had been crying (her fiancé was in South America, she had booked a passage on a boat sailing mid-October, and now she would never see him again). It was a long night, even with sleeping tablets. The old man was louder than ever, and his groans were mixed into the radio's request program called "Nights of Old Vienna."

Nothing seemed to matter. The old man had died during the night, and nobody in the ward felt like talking. Toward noon, we heard the news that Chamberlain was, once again, on his way to Germany and this time to Munich. (His wife had accompanied him to the door of No. 10 Downing Street, the crowd had shouted "Good old Chamberlain, God bless you!"

The old gentleman with the umbrella had made a short speech: "When I was a little boy, I used to repeat, if at first you don't succeed, try, try, try again. That is what I am doing... When I come back I hope I may be able to say as Hotspur says in Henry IV: 'Out of this nettle, danger, we pluck the flower, safety'..." The ward sister came in and attended to the little boy who had been seized with a fit of coughing: "Everything will turn out all right...." There was much visiting between patients from different wards.

All of a sudden, everybody was in a happy mood. There would be no war. We were not trapped. We would all get away. I started to write a hopeful letter, but could not quite manage it and put the pencil aside. On the radio, there was martial music, poetry recitals, and timely reminders: "Nations of Europe, this is the beginning of a Holy Spring...."

A foreign radio station reported that people in Prague were weeping in the streets, but who cared? Good old Chamberlain! All was quiet during the night of Tuesday, and on Wednesday morning, I was discharged from the hospital.

I saw the Jewish hospital again on my visit. On our way back from Poludnia Park, we had to drive past it, and the main street being closed to traffic; we took the long route along the old water tower, opposite that large building of ugly dark red brick. I had assumed that the hospital had been destroyed during the wartime siege of Breslau, but I was mistaken; it was still standing, at least in part, and some public offices had been installed there. I asked my wife if she had been able to read the sign. No, I had been driving too fast. Should one go back? I hesitated for a moment. Was it really worth the trouble?

Six weeks after my discharge from the hospital, my train stopped at Munich en route for Trieste. It was the eighth of November, and the papers reported that Herr von Rath, a German diplomat in Paris, had been assassinated by a Jew.

There were a few young people of my age group in the carriage, and I made friends with a girl from the Rhineland.

In Trieste, no one knew where to stay for the night, but we did not mind. The Lloyd Triestino ship was due to sail the following day; the evenings were still warm, and we would pass the time somehow. The days spent on the boat were a delight. Among my follow passengers, I met a few who were going to study at the University like myself, and others were going to a kibbutz. I went to the cinema in the evening, and I have forgotten the name of the film, but Zarah Leander, the Swedish actress whom Goebbels wanted to transform into a new Marlene Dietrich was singing *Der Wind hat mir ein Lied erzählt*. The ship's radio informed us that there had been "pogroms" in Germany. We felt concerned, but curiously enough, not intensely so. Surely, it could not be all that bad. Then, we sighted Cyprus, and the boat dropped anchor at Famagusta. I tried to tell a girl the story of Othello, but she was not the literary type. Late that night, we packed our things, for it would only be a few hours more. We stood on deck long before land could be seen. An old hand told us that ships used to land at Jaffa in former days, but now they were diverted to Tel Aviv because of the terrorist attacks. Our ship was one of the first to berth in the new harbor. As we approached the shore, the minarets of Jaffa could be seen and finally the white buildings of Tel Aviv. A motor launch came to meet us, and a British police inspector climbed aboard. Evidently, the harbor installations were not yet completed, for our ship had to drop anchor off the shore and groups of us were brought to land in small boats.

In my boat, a student from Cologne had been clutching an old battered case, and when he took out his violin, he started to play gaily, *Bei mir bistu schain*, and then, more formally, standing up, the Hatikvah. One of the Jewish port workers pushed him: "Sit down, you idiot!" The boat rocked, he fell on to the seat, and his violin soaked. It was November 14, 1938. We had come out of the ruins of Europe, and an old world was already half-forgotten.

(1963)

Homecoming (1963)

Years ago, I found myself, one morning, in a somewhat bewildered state on a bench in Park Poludnia in the Polish city of Wroclaw. It was a fine day, sunny but not too warm, and some well-nourished swans were cruising effortlessly on the little lake, a cuckoo was calling, and great plots of pansies, a flower that is to the Poles these days what the shamrock is to the Irish, were in bloom. I had not lost my way; in fact, I knew every little path in that splendid park. I could recall having sat on that very bench twenty-five years before, almost to the day, and listening to what may have been the grandparent of that cuckoo, but then it had been the Suedpark in the German city of Breslau. The city I had known has disappeared like Herculaneum or Pompeii (or as some may prefer, like Sodom and Gomorrah); many landmarks are still the same; the Oder still flows through the town and quite a few streets and buildings look exactly as they did a quarter of a century ago, but then I had parents, acquaintances, and friends in that city. Now, I did not know a soul.

The character of the city had really changed; there were new people around who talked a language that I could understand only with difficulty. I felt somewhat like the hero of H. G. Wells' *The Time Machine*. The combination of the deja vu with the totally unexpected was confusing; it would almost have been easier to accept if the city had disappeared altogether. Even now, I find it difficult to write. I try to concentrate on the present, yet my thoughts return to those days in May 1938. I had just graduated from school, and my future was entirely in the hands of various committees, boards, and consulates.

I had much free time and came to the Suedpark almost every morning; I remember reading here Celine's *Voyage au Bout de la Nuit*. What fascinated me in this story of cynicism and despair I do not know; perhaps, I had an inkling that another journey to the end of the night was about to begin? Or would it be wrong to attribute so prophetic an instinct to one who had not yet turned eighteen? I recall meeting an old teacher of mine one of those mornings in the Suedpark. He was no Nazi and had been forced to retire before he had reached the age limit. He was deeply pessimistic about the future and strongly advised me to clear out as soon as possible. He spoke about very difficult days ahead, about envying my ability to get away, and he ended by asking me to come back when the worst was over.

He turned to go but suddenly seemed to remember something and said, "You will recall that I tried to explain to you, not always with success, the song of the Nibelungen. Do look up Hagen's story one of these days." That was the last I saw of Dr. U., walking away from me with his ebony walking stick. There is no trace of him now, nor of any of his pupils (1921 proved to be a bad year to be born as far as the chances of survival were concerned in those parts of Europe).

I have looked up the story of Hagen, but I am not sure what he meant. He may have referred to Hagen's words before he went to his last battle that everything had happened just as he had forseen ("... es ist auch so ergangen, wie ich mir hatte gedacht"). However, there is another incident in the story of the Nibelungen that has intrigued me for some time: when Hagen crosses the Danube together with King Gunther's armed escort on his way to Attila's court, a party of mermaids tells him that they are all going to perish with the exception of the King's chaplain. To prove them wrong, Hagen pushes the priest into the torrent.

However, the chaplain is carried by the current to the safe shore, while Hagen and his comrades are killed in the battle they foolishly provoked.

The stranger coming to Breslau in the 1930s received a leaflet at the central railway station that told him all he needed to know: that the city was located in the alluvium of the Oder valley, 119.98 meters above sea level, that it was the biggest, the most beautiful, and the most important city of East Germany, with a population of roughly 625,000. He was advised to look at the magnificent baroque buildings as well as the monumental modern structures such as the Jahrhunderthalle, with the largest cupola (and the biggest organ) in the world. He learned that there was "a very active social life," and generally speaking, a very *gemutlich* atmosphere. If he was a philosopher, he could join either the Kant or the Schopenhauer Society, and as a Mason, he would find *Hermann zur Bestaendigkeit* or *Settegast zur deutschen Treue* very hospitable lodges, and the Association of Christian Maidens would take care of young women without relations in the city. Anyway, he was bound to like Breslauer Korn (a local schnaps), and *Schlesisches Himmelreich*, a dish, which (if memory serves me right) consisted mainly of baked fruit. The guide was well-meaning but somewhat misleading. In fact, Breslau did not differ greatly from other cities in Eastern Central Europe. The streets in the older parts of the town were rather narrow and the facades of the houses very much like one another and not only the somber, dark-grey blocks of flats of the working-class quarters. There were large factories and markets. In brief, it was a city of work, not of savoir vivre. There were no aristocracy or high society as in Berlin, no royal merchants as in Hamburg, and no artists' quarter as in Munich. The university was a fairly recent establishment by Central European standards, and the city had not produced any important politician with the single exception of the socialist Ferdinand Lassalle, but of him the burghers preferred not to be reminded. There were some fine actors and musicians, but they went off to Berlin as soon as they had made their names.

There had been some outstanding writers and poets, but that was after the Thirty Years War, a long time ago. People did not travel much in those days and many thought, therefore, that Breslau was simply wonderful. Before 1914, people said, things had been different; my own recollections go back only to the late 1920s, but my father came to Breslau from a little provincial town around the turn of the century, and I remember him and his friends telling me about the "good old days": the colorful parades on the Emperor's birthday; the concerts with Buelow, Nikisch, and Mahler; the Fruehschoppen breakfasts at Hansen, Kempinski, or Brill (dinner a la carte for 75 Pfennig, and what a dinner!); the Sunday morning walks on the promenades along the former city walls and the town moat. They seldom mentioned the other side of the picture: poverty and drunkenness in the working-class quarters; the insipid taste manifested in painting, furniture, and interior decoration; the Byzantine manners and customs of Wilhelminian Germany, led by an aristocracy that had long ago outlived its social function, and an arrogant officer corps that deemed itself far superior to all other mortals. Despite ugliness, poverty, and the lack of fresh air, it must have been a very confident age. Progress was in evidence, prosperity was widespread, and technical advances were made almost each year; amenities that have become known in England only in recent days, such as central heating, were already in general use. There had been no war for forty years and everybody was very optimistic, including those sinister fellows, those radical revolutionaries, and the Social Democrats. The first taxi cabs appeared in front of the central railway station and gradually replaced the horse-drawn carriages; first-class coachmen had white lacquered top hats, and their second-class colleagues wore black hats with silver lace; everybody was very patriotic and in 1914, went off to fight for Kaiser and Vaterland. When the war was over, the province of Posen and parts of Upper Silesia had to be ceded to Poland; Breslau lost much of its Hinterland. There was a feeling of stagnation, of narrowed horizons, and limited prospects, though economic progress continued on a modest scale despite inflation and world economic crisis, yet the former confidence had disappeared; Breslau, once an important junction, had become a terminus. I have some memories of the city as it was around 1930; the crowds of unemployed men in the streets discussing politics, the frequent elections, and the brawls almost every Sunday in which a few people usually got killed. My own interests at the time were directed more to soccer and athletics, in which unfortunately, my hometown never excelled; I remember the terrible thrashing the Everton Liverpool team gave our city eleven. We had half a dozen daily newspapers, and I tried to see all of them, the beginnings of a disease that became chronic in later life: the *Schlesische Zeitung*, arch-reactionary and very proud to have published, in 1813, the King's "appeal to his people" to rise against Napoleon; the democratic *Breslauer Zeitung*, which folded because there were so few liberals left apart from the Jews; the Catholics, the Social Democrats, the Communists, and of course the Nazis had their own papers as well.

Now, the Polish journalists have a magnificent club near the town moat with first-rate abstract paintings on the walls, very good coffee, and modern furniture, but the two newspapers they produce are poorer than the papers of 1930. In the elections of March 5, 1933, the Nationalist Socialist German Workers' Party received 50.2 percent of the votes in Breslau district. What happened subsequently in the city did not differ greatly from events in other parts of Germany. I vividly remember the speeches, the demonstrations, the torchlight parades, which hailed the dawn of a new era. The teachers in the *humanistische Gymnasium* told us, with varying degrees of conviction, what bliss it was to be alive in that dawn.

I wanted to see the house in which I had been born, but had some difficulty in finding the street. The names of the streets had, of course, been changed, but that was not the main problem. I had expected to see a house, or its ruins, or perhaps a new building, but there was nothing, not even a trace that human beings had lived and died there. There was a forlorn signpost in the middle of nowhere marking the spot as *ulica Skwierzynska* crossing *Zelazna*. The rubble had been removed years ago, weeds were sprouting and dandelions, and a few shrubs and a solitary tree had taken root. Some children were playing in a nearby street in which a single house was standing; they did not hurry to let me pass; cars are rarely to be seen in these parts. Half a mile or so further on, St. Carolus Church was standing; a nurse had once taken me there and explained in great detail the horrors of purgatory and hellfire. In a different direction, a few hundred yards away, there were signs of life in a big ugly redbrick building, apparently a school. For a few minutes, I stared at the great sundial and the city coat-of-arms beneath it of course; there were trees in front, and we used to collect chestnuts there! The area would have seemed, to visitors who had not known it before, very peaceful and utterly empty. The effect it had on me was different; nothingness can make a stronger impact than destruction and ruin. In this area, the southern part of the town, tens of thousands of people had once lived, yet the story of its destruction is very brief.

During the first five years of the war, Breslau was a long way from the front. It became, in fact, the air-raid shelter of the Reich at one stage, and its population grew to about a million. In January 1945, with the approach of the Soviet armies, a fanatic Gauleiter Hanke had the defeatist burgomaster hanged in public and organized a last-ditch defense. In this, Hanke was, in a way, successful; it took the Russians about three months to advance a mile and a half. As a reward, Hitler, in his Testament, made him the supreme leader of the S. S. in succession to the traitor Himmler. By that time, the S. S. had, however, ceased to exist. Gauleiter Hanke literally vanished into thin air; he flew out of Breslau a few days before the city capitulated it was the only major German city not to surrender before the armistice. We do not know what became of that efficient Gauleiter. He was never identified but there is reason to believe that he was detained and shot—by mistake.

The price the city had to pay for having been turned into a fortress was appalling; the whole southern and western parts were destroyed, and the center of the town was in shambles. When the surveyors came to assess the damage, they said that 60 percent of the city had been destroyed, which was a lower figure than that for Warsaw and some German cities. I do not know how destruction is measured beyond a certain point; in Breslau, at any rate, unlike Berlin, Kassel, or Nuremberg, it seemed fatal because it coincided with the expulsion of the population of the city. Fewer than 200,000 had stayed there when it became a fortress, and the others had been evacuated during the winter. Then, Breslau became Wroclaw. In the following year, all but a few thousand of the remaining Germans were expelled. Slowly, the immigration of Poles got underway. By 1947, the city again had 200,000 inhabitants; in 1949, it passed the 300,000 mark. The newcomers were people of very different social and cultural backgrounds: peasants from backward Carpathian mountain villages, which had been ceded to Russia; intellectuals from Lvov (Lvov University was transferred to Wroclaw); soldiers from German prisoners of war camps; and re-emigrants from Western Europe.

Russian military administration handed the city over to the Poles; the big railway wagon factory resumed production, and the local theater staged Pygmalion, all while the rats were still feeding on corpses in the streets that had once been a battlefront. Wroclaw remained a rubble heap long after other cities had re-emerged from the ashes.

The leading bookshops were on the West and North Sides of the central city square, opposite the statue of a Prussian king. The statue, needless to say, has been replaced by a new one of Aleksander Fredro, the Polish Moliere. The second-hand bookshop provides a welcome surprise; the employees are knowledgeable and helpful, the prices reasonable, and unlike in Russia, one is permitted to approach the shelves. Many of the books are in German; I even spotted copies of the telephone directory for 1937 (which I bought) and 1942 and similar items of local interest. There are hundreds of books side by side claiming that Silesia and Breslau were "always German," and others that maintain that Wroclaw and Dolny Slask (Lower Silesia) have been Polish from time immemorial. The Germans take the year 1242 as their starting point; the German city of Breslau was founded after the Mongol assault had been repulsed, but "No," say the Poles, "we were there much earlier"; excavations in the city and the suburbs have proved the existence of pre-Slavonic settlements during the early Stone Age. During the Iron Age, the Lusatians lived there, and they were, for sure, the forefathers of the Slavs. The Germans violently disagree. During the excavations for the Autobahn south of the city, they found two big subterranean caves containing tons of amber, which they say "could only have belonged to the Wandalers" (not to be confused with the Vandals). And who were the Wandalers but the forefathers of the Germans? Nobody seems to dispute that. The Poles, however, counter that around the year 1000, Wratislawa was a Polish city. At that time, the Polish kings, the Piasts, called in German settlers to help colonize the country. True enough, the Germans reply, but "the Piasts became Germans by intermarriage, and anyway, who made the miserable village of 1000 AD. what it subsequently became one of the most important towns of medieval Europe, more important as a trading center than Frankfurt, or Berlin, of which hardly anybody had heard at the time."

I have always found these disputations somewhat tedious; how can serious people invest so much time and energy in proving and disproving half-truths? However, the struggle continues unabated, each side insisting on its version of the past. The Germans insist that a great historical injustice has been done them; the Poles conclude that the *German Drang nach Osten* (move to the east) was always aggressive and reactionary. The Poles feel strongly about those Pan-German ideologists who claim that the conquest of territory and the assimilation of the Slavonic people were a "historic trend," one that indicated the "physical and intellectual vigor" of the German nation, and that had "spread civilization in a part of the world in which there existed the necessity to import all elements of culture from Germany."

The quotations I have used are from Karl Marx. I know it is unfair. But the Poles, too, ought to be reminded of some of the facts of life. Like the Russians, they prefer not to rely on what Marx wrote about their country; their heroes are Boleslav Wrymouth, Ladislav the Short, Casimir the Restorer, and the like. These absurd exercises were provoked, it is only fair to add, by generations of German Ostforscher, who proclaimed that the Slavs were and always would be an inferior race. At school, we were never told that there had been any Poles in Silesia, but there was an organization called Bund Deutscher Osten (headed by a Professor Oberlaender from Koenigsberg) that distributed maps and leaflets on the German East with many quotations starting with Tacitus and Procopius and ending with Adolf Hitler. One of them I found again in my Wroclaw bookshop. It ended with the following words: "So let us all remember the old inscription on the Reval town hall: He is right who fights. He who stops fighting has lost all rights. . . ."

It made curious reading that morning in the Polish city of Wroclaw.

I cannot recall having met a Pole when I grew up in Breslau in the 1920s and 1930s. True enough, there were many people with names like Stefanski or Osnojewitch, but this was not uncommon in Germany; the forward line of the German soccer team used to read like an excerpt from a Warsaw telephone directory. Anyway, these bearers of Polish names were completely assimilated; they were 150 percent German. There was a small Polish minority, but somehow, one never met them, or more probably, one did not recognize them; they had been to local schools and they spoke German without an accent. In Upper Silesia the situation was different; east of the Oder there had been a Polish majority, particularly in the villages, until 1914.When the war ended there were some 40,000 people in Breslau who opted for Poland. Some were slave laborers who had worked in the city, and others were Polish prisoners of war, but the majority consisted of local residents. Some had never made a secret of the fact that they belonged to a national minority. Others discovered their Polish patriotism only when faced with the threat of expulsion and loss of property; because they were Catholic, had a Slavonic family name and remembered a few words of Polish, they thought they would pass. (Many of them did pass, but the new authorities had to introduce Polish language courses for them.) The percentage of these autochthoni, small in Wroclaw, was substantial in Gorny Slask (Upper Silesia); the newcomers from Eastern and Central Poland regarded them as Germans, and often as ex-Nazis; there was tension and it continues to this day.

There is a great deal of anti-Polish literature on the shelves of those bookshops, starting with publications of the early years of the century. By their side are the Polish anti-German publications (from Roman Dmowski to the books and magazines of the Polish Western Institute in Poznan). I cannot help thinking that these historians could be more profitably employed. Breslau/Wroclaw has a past that is both German and Slav. But what happened to the city in 1945 has nothing to do with medieval history. Don't we all by now know the causes? All traces of German rule in Breslau have been very carefully removed. This includes statues, inscriptions, memorial tablets, road signs, and so on. Sometimes, the old inscriptions have been erased but nothing put in their place, and the result is confusing (particularly in certain public conveniences). The German language is not heard or seen, except in conversations with strangers who want to help, in the second-hand bookshop just mentioned, and in cemeteries. There was a small German-language newspaper in Wroclaw in the middle 1950s, but it has since disappeared. There was one remaining sign an inscription in Ulica Wlodkowica (Wallstrasse); it indicated that this had been the office of the Jewish community. (It still is of an infinitely smaller Polish Jewish community, which had nothing to do with the German Jewry who had lived in the city.)

The inscription was cut into the stone and so could not have been removed without doing damage to the building. It is a bitter irony and yet somehow it seems appropriate that chance should have singled out the local Jews to bear witness to the German past. There were some

20,000 Jews in Breslau of whom half emigrated in time, the remainder being deported and killed. This comparatively small section of the population had a disproportionate influence on the cultural life of the city and beyond. The assimilation of a large section of German Jewry was very far advanced (much more so than in Britain or the United States). The result of this German-Jewish symbiosis was a culture disapproved of by German nationalists. Nevertheless, it had an impact whose effects can be discerned to the present day. Its influence extended far beyond Breslau, for writers and musicians born in the city who became prominent emigrated to Berlin. There were also physicians, physicists, chemists, botanists, and biologists of world distinction whose origins were in Breslau or the surrounding countryside. Looking through a biographical dictionary of the world's leading scientists recently, I noticed how often the entries read b. Breslau, or even more frequently, b. Lissa (or b. Ostrowo); small villages such as these on the former German-Polish boundaries produced more leading scientists between 1860 and 1910 than any Western capital, with the possible exception of London and Paris. With official careers virtually closed to them in pre-1914 Germany, many bright young German Jews were almost inevitably drawn into the then rapidly expanding sciences. The fact that Breslau became a cultural center in the nineteenth century was, to a great extent, a Jewish achievement. True enough, the German-Jewish symbiosis was a hybrid, and therefore dubious and problematical, but it had outstanding achievements to its credit. Who could have foreseen that it would end as it did, with a few thousand elderly people assembled on the platforms of the central railway station one summer night in 1942? Fortunately, most of them did not know that from this journey, there would be no return. My parents were among them.

As I write these lines in the late hours of the evening in my hotel room, the figure of the city's liberal rabbi comes back to my mind. He lived very near this place, on what is now Kosciuszko Square. Dr. Vogelstein was one of the most widely educated men I have known and one of the kindest; he had written a most erudite book on the history of Rome and had one of the largest private libraries in town. Sometimes, I saw him in the municipal library with an apologetic smile: "I am sure I have that book somewhere at home but I can't find it."

When I went to see him last in 1938, he was a broken man. He had always been a German patriot, bitterly opposed to any Jewish nationalist aspirations; his whole world was now in ruins. These were the days of Hitler's great successes, and we talked about the uncertain future. He was a mild man, yet on that day, there was something of the fire of an Old Testament prophet in him; he quoted Isaiah to me, the passage about the coming day of vengeance, and even Paul's Epistle to the Romans 12.19; I have mentioned that he was a liberal rabbi. When I was already in the corridor, he added as an afterthought, "Though the mills of God grind slowly. . . ." *Gottes Muehlen mahlen langsam, mahlen aber trefflich klein.*

Ob aus Langmut er sich saeumet, bringt mit Schaerf er alles ein. (Friedrich von Logau 1605–1655—another native of Silesia.) Henry Wadsworth Longfellow has translated this as follows:

> Though the mills of God grind slowly
> Yet they grind exceeding small;
> Though with patience he stands waiting
> With exactness grinds he all

I often read with interest the sophisticated travelogues, in magazines like *Holiday*, on the charm of the quaint little streets on the rive gauche, the enchanting corners of the Ile St. Louis, and the appeal of the Champs Elysees on a sunny Sunday afternoon. I wish my task were as easy. All the world loves Paris, but who is interested in Breslau, let alone Wroclaw? A detailed description of the strange charm of the cemetery in Cosel, the exquisite beauty of the abattoir in Ulica Legnica and its surroundings, the splendor of the ruins at the Neumarkt, or the fascination of the desert south of Gartenstrasse would probably create the effect the Spaniards call *contraproduicente*. I did see the sights, but the written word does not seem an adequate means of communication in this context; a film using the flashback technique would perhaps be more appropriate and more convincing.

The "Monopol" had been the best hotel since the turn of the century; it still is, though its name is somewhat provocative for a hotel in a communist country. After 1945, it was renamed Metropol. Its reputation for bad service became legendary; one day, even an otherwise unflappable British ambassador is said to have shown signs of annoyance. It is much better now; a local wit maintains that a few waiters were shot *pour encourager les autres*. It would be almost perfect if only Polish economic planning had made provision for the manufacture of comfortable beds.

To the right of the hotel there was, and is, a big open square, which has changed its name and function several times during the last hundred years. The frequent change of names of streets in my hometown

I find quite enlightening. My last abode was off a little square named Karlsplatz where excellent ice cream was sold. After World War One, it was renamed Lassalleplatz, honoring the great early socialist leader who was born nearby. When the Nazis came to power, it was renamed Karlsplatz and today it is called Bohaterow getta—in honor of the heroes of the Warsaw ghetto.

In the nineteenth century, the local garrison held its exercises on the square adjacent to the hotel. Subsequently, agricultural machinery was sold, and still later, Adolf Hitler used to address mass meetings from the ramp of the castle on the north side of the square. The castle was destroyed, but the square is decorated with little red-and-white flags and it is full of people; a Polish military band plays marches; it is the eighteenth anniversary of the capitulation of Breslau. Beyond the square, there were the enormous courtyards and warehouses built in the nineteenth century; Breslau was then a big center for trade with the East.

The houses now look shabbier and more dilapidated, there is little trade, and children play where carriages and trucks once unloaded enormous bales of cotton and other large freight. It used to be a very orderly city, the tanners had their own little street, and so did the coppersmiths and prostitutes; Krullstrasse lies in ruins, is uninhabited and cordoned off, and one cannot even enter it by car. This is the very center of the town; there are old churches and old inns, most of them in ruins now; whole streets have disappeared, but the house where we lived for some years in the 1930s still stands. I had always thought of it as rather small, dark, and in no way distinguished. Now, it looks much brighter and most imposing because so many buildings in the neighborhood have disappeared. It has become something of a national monument because it was designed by Langhans the Younger, the architect who built the Brandenburg Gate in Berlin.

Someone looks down at me from our old flat; he must be the "specialist in nervous diseases," who, according to the doorplate downstairs, now lives there. Business appears to be slack; Wroclaw's new residents seem to be people with iron nerves. It used to take me twenty minutes to reach school; it should have been half the time, I realize now, but there were so many distractions. Alas, I cannot see any now. Half the buildings have come down, and most of the shops have disappeared. There is hardly any traffic at all in the side streets of most Polish cities, all the life is concentrated in the main thoroughfares. The school is there all right, a very ordinary grey building, smaller than it appeared to me in memory. It is still a school, the Wroclaw Economic High School. Overcoming some strange fear of authority (these things, it seems, last forever), I ventured into the building. The teachers' rest room still gives comfort to tired lecturers, but the colored glass panel commemorating those fallen in World War I (*dulce et decorum est...*) has been removed. The little shops nearby that sold exercise books, toy guns, sweets, and buttermilk have disappeared; there are heaps of coal in the street, an execrable but widespread custom in Polish cities.

I only dimly remember the other things I saw on this day; there were some surprises but no major shocks; one got accustomed to the different character of the town. I went to see Wertheim's, once the big department store, and the city's most modern building, now the *Powszechny Dom Towarowy* (the leading state chain-store). When it was established in 1930, the small businessmen made a terrible fuss; they were going to lose their customers, they said, and they threatened to support the Nazis (which I suppose in the end they did). The outcry was not worthwhile; after 1933, the place was "Aryanised"; in 1945, they "Polonized" the store and very faithfully rebuilt it. The selection and the display compare favorably with Moscow; there are good inexpensive cigars and a lot of well-made (and highly priced) motorcycles. In the olden days, prospective customers were invited to taste the products of new baking mixes and custard powders and what not. The new regimes in Eastern Europe do not believe in free samples; the customer must not be spoiled.

I went to see the hospital near the big water tower in the south. A doctor had decided one day long ago that I would be better off without tonsils; he was right, I suppose, but the timing was all wrong. Some slight complication developed. I had to stay a few days longer than planned. It was September 25, 1938; Chamberlain had just returned from Bad Godesberg to London; war seemed imminent. Never had I felt so helpless; it was like being in a mousetrap about to close. However, I will tell this story later. I went to see the Cathedral, which, dating back to the thirteenth century, was largely destroyed in the last war but has been re-built by the Poles. There were groups of sightseers; the new Silesians are certainly eager to know their new homeland and to grow roots.

There is the university on the other side of the river; nothing much has changed there. The new dean, recently elected, is himself a graduate of the university.

Homecoming (1963)

How curious that while trying to eradicate all traces of the German tradition, the Poles should in some ways be so eager to continue where the Germans left off. The original function and character of many shops, public buildings, and institutions has been preserved. The place where I got my first spectacles still sells them and the C&A shop opposite has merely given way to the Polish "state trust," selling coats and trousers. An old aunt was bound to ask me what became of the *Jahrhunderthalle*, so I went to see it too. It was built in 1913, in commemoration of the war against Napoleon a hundred years earlier; at the time, it was one of the world's seven wonders, a building of concrete and iron covering 10,000 square meters. Gerhard Hauptmann wrote a bad play for its opening; there was also an enormous orchestra and choir of a thousand. Now they call it *Hala Ludowa*; it houses a cinema, the biggest in Poland. Not far off the Oder steamers anchored on their run up river. On sunny afternoons, the steamers were full, so the families went to a big open-air restaurant some miles away, where they spent a few hours by the river, fighting off the gnats, eating huge pieces of cake, and drinking lemonade. There were small motorboats and canoes, and people in all sorts of bathing costumes. The little orchestra played *Nun ade, du mein lieb Heimatland* as the steamer left for the city once again. How peaceful it all seemed. One Sunday evening in 1932, on our way back, a swimmer climbed on to the ship and wiped his bottom with the Black-Red-Gold flag of the Weimar republic. There was a roar of laughter; few of the passengers thought much of the flag. I was a mere boy at the time, but I understood that something was seriously wrong with a country; the gesture by the swimmer produced merely laughter. The tranquility was deceptive.

I was not eager to mention the fact that I was born in Breslau, for whenever a Pole heard about it, there was the inevitable question: "And how do you find the city now?" It was a question I would have preferred not to answer; it involved comparing two different peoples, cultures, ways of life, political regimes, and going on to pass value judgments. German Breslau was not only a bigger city than Polish Wroclaw, but it was also more orderly and prosperous; it had a culture of its own and a certain character, but is it fair to compare the toughs from Carpathian mountain villages who now lounge about the Bluecherplatz with the local intelligentsia of 1910 (or 1930) assembled in the Cafe Fahrig after an evening at the opera? German Breslau was not only efficiency, *Gemuntlichkeit*, and culture.

The head of one of the West German refugee organizations said the other day that most of his compatriots who now visit Wroclaw are not really qualified to judge the present state of the city because they had not known the place in "the old days." Maybe so, but what past does he have in mind? 1910 or 1938 or perhaps April 1945? Does he remember only the Fair on the Eve of St. John? Or also the infamous guillotine in the local Gestapo prison? The frenetic applause when Hitler came to watch the gymnasts in 1938? The deportation and murder of thousands of Jews? The rowdy student demonstrations (Middle Eastern style) against professors who did not display enough enthusiasm for the Nazi cause? "Temporary aberrations," some will say; German history does not begin with Hitler, nor does it end with him. True enough, but for such historic aberrations, nations pay dearly. There is a great and growing literature on the new Wroclaw, and I had bought, in Warsaw, some of the more important publications: the urban survey of 1956, the development plan for the city published in 1961, and Irene Turnau's investigation into the social composition of the new population. They all help one to understand the present state of affairs but only up to a point. Forty years later, there was also an enormous one-volume Breslau encyclopedia, which I decided to buy and carry home despite its heavy weight (probably out of vanity because I had entry in the book).

The cultural and social differences between the planners and many of the local population are simply too great. They have helped to clean up the shambles and to get the factories working again. Their children or grandchildren may make Wroclaw a modern city, which is more than a conglomeration of factories, shops, and schools. It must have been a dreadful place in the early 1950s; even the most orthodox party members tell you that life was grim in those days.

The reconstruction of the city had not yet got under way, but a local underworld had developed drunks, prostitutes, and terrifying criminals. There was nowhere to go in the evening; the general mood was one of gloom and despondency. After October 1956, conditions improved owing to not only the general changes that took place in Poland but also to an able local leadership. Matwin, the party secretary and a liberal by East European standards, has done much to improve living conditions and is genuinely popular; so is Mayor Iwaszkiewicz, a former mathematics professor. The number of inhabitants, less than 200,000 in 1946, is now up to about 450,000; it is expected to reach the half million mark in a year or two, and according to the overall plan, 700,000 in 1985. It was 625,000 in 1939 and 631,000 in 2012. But the

Polish birth rate has steadily gone down and it is no longer a city of the young. The central city square with its baroque Buergerhaeuser has been most faithfully reconstructed, with its gables, portals, and richly decorated attics.

The Gothic town hall has been repaired, and with its triangular gable towers, its turrets, and sculptural ornaments, it is still one of the noblest monuments of Gothic architecture in Europe. There are thirty bookshops, twenty-seven pharmacies, twenty-three cinemas, six theaters (counting the opera), and 650 taxicabs (of which 90 percent are privately owned). Some of the shops too are still in private hands, and about 15 percent of the smaller workshops. The cinemas show films from all over the world; the mark of "Zorro" on the town hall showed the progress of Western civilization. A lethargic elephant in the Zoological Garden may be one of the few survivors from the German era. Perhaps, the SS omitted to kill him in the last days of the siege. Thirty-seven percent of the population of Wroclaw is engaged in industry; employment in machine industry has gone up, while in textile plants, it has gone down. Public transport is mainly by a noisy and not very fast streetcar service and no radical change is envisaged for the future. I am not a city planner, but I foresee certain difficulties. Few people want to live in the inner part of the city; the local intelligentsia lives in such suburbs as Biskupin or Oporow. There are museums, milk bars, and a number of new, very big, and always overcrowded coffeehouses around Kosciuszko Square; old General Tauentzien, one of Frederick the Great's paladins, who is buried there, had to give way. There is an International Press and Book Club where the *Herald-Tribune* is sold, sometimes with only three days' delay (the British press seems in less demand); there are even a few gas stations, though it takes some effort to find them.

According to the city plan, the destroyed quarters in the south of the city will be rebuilt in the next few years; I saw a few surveyors at work. There are many schools; Polish Silesia is demographically a very young country; there are more schoolchildren now in Wroclaw than there were in Breslau.

All this does not sound too bad. It is a real achievement, considering that the Poles started from very nearly nil in 1945. In Silesia, the Poles do not merely want to make their own lives more tolerable; they want to show the Germans that they are capable of building a city as well as, if not better than, the Germans.

One recent autumn evening, during an interval at a conference near Athens, the conversation turned to "the need for roots." We were eight around the table, and it emerged that none of us lived where we were born and that only one would be able to see again the parental home if he went back to his birthplace. (This was a girl who came from a small North Italian village that had been bypassed by the war.) The destruction of houses and the uprooting of many millions of people has been a commonplace on the continent of Europe in our time, and not only there. I envy those who survive and manage never to look back; from the point of view of mental hygiene, I suppose it is the right thing to do. I was glad, nevertheless, that I had come back to my native city despite the unquiet memories. I was even gladder when the visit came to an end.

Wroclaw is now very much a going concern; the recent protests in the West German Bundestag against a documentary film showing the new realities will do no good. I do not doubt that, as a new Polish guide to Wroclaw says, the new citizens have become attached to the town in the pioneering days among the ruins and the wreckage left by the war. In a few decades, the city may be among the finest in Poland; today, much imagination and good will is still needed to envisage such a prospect. The importance that Breslau had in the nineteenth and early twentieth centuries will hardly be regained, if only for the reason that the city was then part of the leading country in Central Europe; the language spoken in Breslau was the lingua franca of all Central, Eastern, and Southeastern Europe.

All this is gone and past help; it should be also past grief. It is also, as far as I am concerned, past personal interest. I will not deny that I was excited when the train that was bringing me to Wroclaw entered it suburbs, and for the benefit of my wife, I gave a running commentary from the open window interrupted only by exclamations, but when we entered the train that was about to leave the city in the early hours of the morning, I took no last look. I went into my empty compartment and almost immediately fell asleep. An utterly confused dream is all I can remember: *Deutschland, Deutschland ueber Alles* played by an enormous brass orchestra, directed by a gentleman in very old-fashioned attire; it must have been my Breslau neighbor, Hoffmann von Fallersleben, who wrote the text, yet the German anthem was soon drowned out by *Jeszcze Polska nie zginela* played by a group of ladies and gentlemen looking even more anachronistic. The trumpets sounded a well-known march: "Poland has not yet perished! March, march Dombrowski!" Among the musicians one excelled, Jankiel the honest Jew, about whom I only know that he was the best performer with the dulcimer at Pan Tadeusz marriage, yet even this touching scene did not last long. The Poles disappeared as on a revolving stage, a calm, measured voice came in, announcing that this was a fine morning in London, and that a gentleman in Asmara had asked the BBC General Overseas Service to play "Abdul, the Bulbul Emir," and so to this cheerful tune, the East European confusion dissolved and gave way to British certainties.

I reached out and turned the dial of the little radio. The train had just passed Opole (Oppeln). I had left my native city for the second and I suppose, last time in my life.

Postscript Homecoming (2002)

I thought at the time that I had been back to the city of my birth for the last time. I was given to understand that the Polish authorities had not liked my article, which had been published in several languages, and that I would not get another entrance visa. However, since I was not particularly eager to visit Breslau in the first place, this did not cause me sleepless nights. However, the ways of providence are inscrutable, and thus, I found myself again in the month of May but thirty-nine years later passing the Suedpart (Park Poludnia) on my way to the center of Breslau. This had been on the initiative of Swedish friends who had suggested a documentary on my youth in that city.

In 2002, we came by car; the trip from Berlin had taken twice as long as it should have as a result of the fiercest and longest hailstorm I ever experienced and that caused a halt to all traffic. Again, we stayed at Hotel Monopol, which had reverted back to its old name having forced to call itself Metropol under Communism. We were given a nice room in which allegedly Jan Kiepura and Marlene Dietrich had once stayed. Altogether, the hotel seemed in far better shape than during our earlier visit.

It was a strenuous stay; filming began on the balcony of the hotel facing the local theatre, a massive building that had been given a new coat of paint. Filming continued at the other end of town in a distant suburb once called Hundsfeld or Deutsch Lissa, where part of the university was located. This had been a Soviet military headquarters at one time but was taken over after the withdrawal of these troops by the university. Breslau still seemed a town of young people perhaps in view of the masses of students—we were told that 100,000 young men and women were studying in various institutions of higher learning.

There was a group of thirty or forty attending my seminar; their families had come from all over Poland. The conversation was in English, and they wanted to know what it was like to grow up in this city in the 1930s. I do not think there would have been much interest in 1963, nor were there many English speakers at the time.

What were my impressions crisscrossing the city that day and on the following days? Breslau was certainly in an infinitely better state than in the early 1960s. The center was in fact in excellent shape, the northern and eastern part alas less so, but this had been the case even in my time. It was chosen cultural capital of Europe for 2016. We went to see the mayor of the city in his office, a highly intelligent and unpretentious man (we shared sandwiches) who showed us models of various new projects. He complained that while West European countries were investing in the city, the Germans did too little. There were elegant and expensive shops in the Swidnica street (Schweidnitzer Strasse)—who could afford these prices for Italian ties and French lingerie? But apparently, there must have been enough customers. The book shops and their displays looked like such shops look everywhere else in the Western world. The food in the restaurants was fine and not too expensive. The macroeconomic statistics may not bear this out, but the city certainly made an impression of relative prosperity, even though individual people complained.

This time, the owners of the apartment at the center where we had lived had been forewarned about our coming; they received us nicely and put up with the inevitable disorder created by a film crew. I was surprised to what extent all the rooms were still familiar—I would have found my way around the kitchen blindfolded. But I was equally astonished how little emotion there was—it could have been another person who had once lived here.

And so we went on filming, in the municipal library next door (now the university library), which had once been my Ersatz university, to the parks in the north where both the zoological garden and the *Jahrhundert Halle*, which I had seen on my earlier visit, were located. We went to a disused railway station (the Freiburger) now something like a railway museum, ideal background scenery for a farewell taking scene in our documentary. It reminded me a bit of *Brief Encounter*, but for the fact that we were the only passengers.

There were interviews with the local newspapers—the return of the prodigal—which I faced with mixed feelings. There was a spirit of enterprise in the air and also of tolerance and an interest in the past of the city, which had not existed forty years earlier. The great majority of the people I saw in the streets had not been born when the Second World War had ended. As far as they were concerned, visitors from afar had also belonged to the past of Breslau/Wroclaw. In fact, they prided themselves that this had once been not another provincial center but home to people of various nationalities, religions, and cultures. It was certainly a manifestation of greater self-confidence.

With all this, the city I had known as a child and a young man had disappeared together with the people who had vanished. The local authorities have made considerable efforts to attract survivors for at least a short visit. It is a laudable effort and they deserve credit for it but I did not avail myself of it.

Caucasian Diary

1961: Reading on a train in the Caucasus I find the following:

> Yesterday evening I arrived in Pyatigorsk and found lodgings on the outskirts of the town, fairly high up at the foot of the Mashuk; if a storm comes the clouds will hide my roof. When I opened the window at five o'clock this morning my room was full of the scent of the flowers in the small garden; cherry blossom gazes into the room and sometimes the wind covers my desk with white petals. The panorama is magnificent: in the west one sees the blue peaks of the five-headed Beshtau ... in the north the Mashuk rises like a Persian fur cap; in the east below me there lies the clean new town; one hears the murmuring of the mineral springs and the voices of the cosmopolitan crowd. Further away the mountains form a kind of amphitheater, blue and hazy in the distance; and on the edge of the horizon one sees the silver chain of the snow-covered summits from Kasbek to Elbruz. It is a pleasure to live in such a place ...

Thus, Mikhail Lermontov's Pechorin, in *A Hero of Our Times*, probably the most astonishing short story by a twenty-five-year-old writer in world literature. The journey to Pyatigorsk has become faster, but the jet age has only recently reached the Caucasus. It takes fifty-four hours by train from Moscow, arriving in the town at midnight in bright moonlight, the traveler feels something of the old romantic magic of the place.

In the early morning, such illusions fly away; the traveler opens the window at five o'clock, awakened not by the murmuring of the mineral springs or the scent of the flowers but by the infernal noise of the Kolkhoz market opposite. The crowd outside is cosmopolitan all right, but the fine gentlemen from Petersburg and Moscow are gone, as are their elegant ladies whom Lermontov saw and fell in love with. It consists of highlanders (gortsi) with their large hats, Kabardines, Georgians and Russians, Armenians, and Ukrainians.

There are no Westerners in this crowd; until recently, they were not allowed in this area at all. Neither the mountains nor the magnificent panorama have changed, but there is a gigantic television mast on the top of the Mashuk and on a single day the indomitable Elbruz was recently climbed by 1,300 Alpinists.

Nowadays, Pyatigorsk is a rather dull provincial town with 60,000 inhabitants (142,511 according to the 2010 census), seven public libraries, fifteen sanatoria, an Institute of Education and a pharmaceutical college, factories where bricks, reinforced concrete, machinery, butter, liqueurs, and chemicals are produced, four cinema theaters, four large and several small bookshops, five restaurants, fifteen nursery schools, and a newspaper and a television station. The traveler can get this and other important information from the telephone book, which very much in contrast to Moscow, he finds in his room. There is a special quality about the only hotel in the place; it appears to date from the period of Pushkin and Lermontov, but the sanitary installations were probably in a better state then. A modern hotel in another part of the town is, however, to be opened shortly, and the traveler cannot complain about bad service, even in the old caravanserai; everyone is courteous, friendly, and obliging. (One has to leave Moscow to become acquainted with Russian hospitality.) In the entrance hall of the hotel, there is a branch post office with large pictures of Lenin, Stalin, and Kalinin. However, in the main post office, which is a modern building, there was only a picture of Khrushchev; there are more portraits, busts, and memorials of Stalin in the Caucasus than anywhere else in the Soviet Union. The local patriots are not prepared to give up the great son of Georgia.

Various queues form in front of the post office counters, including one for telephone coupons (or "talons"). In the Soviet Union, it is not at all easy to ring up somebody in another town, even in the immediate vicinity; first of all, one has to go to the post office (which is impossible at night) and buy coupons for a trunk call. Armed with one of these books, they call at home or from a public phone booth; to avoid the complications, many Russians prefer to send a telegram.

Pyatigorsk is not only a town with sanatoria and factories, but it is also a cultural center. Notices on the walls of the houses announce performances by leading theatrical companies from Moscow, Leningrad, and Saratov who appear in the summer months. Deborah Fantoffel sings arias from "La Traviata" and "Rigoletto." The "Great Waltz" appears twice—as a film and as a ballet. Some other foreign movies are shown

Leslie Caron in "Lili" and Gregory Peck in "Roman Holiday." Comrade Filimonov of the Society for the Propagation of Political and Scientific Knowledge is giving a lecture on "The Cunning Methods of Foreign Espionage Organizations."

Pushkin lived in Pyatigorsk and Tolstoy was stationed here as a young officer. Above all, however, the town is bound up with the life and work of Lermontov who was killed here in 1841 in a duel at the age of twenty-seven. In the presence of a lady, he had called a fellow officer a "highlander (gorets) with a big dagger." Martynov was in Circassian clothes and did have a big dagger, but he took offense and insisted on a duel. Lermontov, who was the first to shoot, fired in the air, but Martynov took good aim. An obelisk has been erected on the spot where the duel took place, and beside it, a large stone plaque on which the events that led to the duel are described; around the obelisk, there stand four stone figures, symbols of mourning. One or two groups of pioneers and Oktyabryat, the youngest members of the communist youth organization, with their red scarves, are here on a visit from their holiday camp. Their leaders tell them "the story of the great Russian poet and his tragic end."

The scene in front of the Lermontov memorial in the town park is different. In the morning, at any rate, the place is quite empty and deserted apart from a young man who, leaning on the pedestal with one hand, recites poems in a loud voice. It is not quite clear whether they are Lermontov's or his own. Then there is a Lermontov Gallery, the Grotto of Diana, the "Restoration" House where the ball took place, which is described in *A Hero of Our Times*, and finally, the building in which Lermontov quarreled with Martynov. *Habent sua fata libelli*—Pechorin, "A Hero of Our Times," was, to put it mildly, a wastrel—his problems were card playing, the seduction of young girls and married women, duels, and above all, how to escape boredom. One might expect that a character like Pechorin would not mean very much to the Pioneers except as a warning. But no one likes renouncing a world-famous work of literature and so the Lermontov Cult is more developed now than ever before. A local writer has just published a long and learned treatise to prove that Lermontov did not die immediately after the duel but lived for another day or two, and his thesis has given rise to a great deal of discussion.

Pyatigorsk is the town of the five hills (the Kabardinian Beshtau); it was formerly the county town but now the administrative center is Stavropol, about 150 kilometers away. There have apparently been few building developments in the town in recent years; there is a housing shortage, though probably not so acute as in Moscow. In the town center and on the road to Essentuki, one can still see houses destroyed by the Nazis or in the fighting, which have not been rebuilt. Pyatigorsk and the other North Caucasian health resorts were taken up by Group A of the German Army under Field Marshal von Kleist in August 1942, but the Wehrmacht did not get much further, and in January 1943, the Red Army returned.

The destruction was light in comparison with the Ukraine or White Russia, but in Mineralnye Vody, the neighboring railway junction and airport, the corpses of thousands of Jews, Russians, and people of other nationalities were found in a kilometer-long ravine. The victims included professors and employees of Leningrad University who had been evacuated here. The extermination task force D, led by Colonel Bierkamp, had been at work with its usual efficiency. No trace of Colonel Bierkamp could be found in 1945. (According to later information, Bierkamp, originally a lawyer, committed suicide a few days after the end of the war in a village near Luebeck.) The people of Pyatigorsk have no fond memories of the Germans.

Though it is the headquarters of the Party and the Government, Moscow adds nothing to the foreigner's knowledge of how Soviet policy is actually made. And as far as everyday life in Soviet Russia is concerned Moscow is certainly not at all typical, far less even than New York or Paris typify the United States or France. A walk through the streets of a provincial town like Pyatigorsk provides more vivid impressions and more significant details of the life of the Soviet citizen than weeks in the capital.

The day begins very early in the provinces; people are already on their feet, or more precisely, in the streets, by seven o'clock. The crowds are greatest in the kolkhoz market and the wooden stalls surrounding it. Men and women with shopping bags stream through the gates of the great market hall adorned with portraits of the party leaders, and inscriptions about the coming victory of Communism. The Soviet authorities are very touchy about the kolkhoz markets and taking photographs there is very much frowned on.

They regard it as a relic of capitalist economy, since the hundreds of peasant women, on their little stools, offering their goods for sale, do so on their own initiative and fix their own prices: it is really a bit of a free market economy inside a completely different economic system. According to the Moscow guides, there are "no longer" any such markets in the capital, but one can see with one's own eyes that this is not true. The Moscow telephone directory contains the addresses of many such institutions.

It is true, however, that the kolkhoz markets have ceased to play an important part in the provisioning of the capital, now that supplies in the State shops have become more adequate. In the provinces, the kolkhoz market is often still the center of the small town—at any rate for some hours of the day.

It is difficult for the foreigner to understand the touchiness of the authorities, since it is obvious that the kolkhoz market is bound to disappear in the course of time. Anyhow, he cannot fathom the economic rationale of these undertakings: how can it possibly pay the women selling their goods to travel a considerable distance by train just to offer for sale six or seven kilos of apples or plums or a few dozen eggs? They themselves or their husbands will know best whether it is worthwhile; the prices of fruits, vegetables, and meat are high, and so long as they do not come down to any considerable extent, the markets are likely to continue. Incidentally, in spite of all its primitive fittings, the market hall is clean and there are no flies. There is no wrapping up either; the buyers bring their own nets or bags or buy a newspaper at the entrance for twenty kopeks, which they use as packing paper.

Not far from the market hall is the large State food shop (Gastronom). The choice and quality of goods is not bad, the prices are high, and the purchasing system exasperating.

To buy bread, butter, and sausage, for example, you have to stand in seven different queues; first of all, you go to the assistant of the particular department, who indicates the price of the commodity; from there, you proceed to the cash desk where you are given vouchers for the desired amount, and finally, you return to the bread, butter, and sausage queues where, after waiting patiently for your turn, you get the goods.

Since, in many cases, man and wife are both out at work all day, the congestion in the shops is the greatest in the early morning and late afternoon. People wait patiently in most of the queues, but sometimes, there are altercations and even something of an affray. (Men, it seems, have a tendency to push themselves forward and are generally more impatient than women.) The police on the street corner, not keen on interfering, look the other way. There is an old Soviet joke about the militia being responsible for order but not for disorder. The passivity of the militia led in 1958 to the establishment of the Drushiny, a kind of

Home Guard with a distinctive red arm band who appear in strength especially in the late afternoon and evening. These men and women enlist on a voluntary basis to fight hooliganism and have done more to restore public order than the militia. Although they are unarmed, they are far more feared than the militia.

The Soviet traffic police are likewise well-known for their vigor and severity. They often stop drivers in the streets without previous warning and subject their vehicles to a pretty thorough inspection.

It is needless to mention that another type of police which, although not in uniform, is fairly easily spotted, even by the untrained foreign visitor. It is said that since Beria, their methods have become "more humane." They endeavor (they say) to work by warning and persuasion rather than terror. People prefer, all the same, not to make their acquaintance. In the small towns, as opposed to Moscow, there are no secrets. Everyone knows where everyone else works.

Opposite the kolkhoz market is the public prosecutor's office and next to it a kiosk where one buys the local morning paper as well as the Rostov edition of the Moscow *Pravda*. By the side of the kiosk, watches are repaired in a small shop: the traveler sees more shoemakers and watchmakers in Russia than anywhere else in the world. Fifteen years ago, a watch was still a rarity; today, they are available in all price ranges, beginning at about 225 roubles (i.e., $22). Part of the road is excavated and gas pipes are being laid. There has been talk of gas supply for years, and the local paper complains that the work is not going ahead fast enough. Demands are growing; until quite recently, there was hardly any public transport, and no private cars at all, yet today, one of the older inhabitants told us that people grumble if they have to walk a mile or two.

Many houses have been supplied with running water, another revolutionary innovation. A little boy proudly showed us his school; first impressions were very good. Then, we learned that there are not enough school buildings in Russia, and some of the schools are run in two or three shifts.

We asked the little boy whether the teachers are allowed to beat their pupils. He looked up at me pitifully and said, "No, they are not even allowed to give lines." Afterward, an adult confirmed that a teacher is liable to lose his diploma if he uses corporal punishment.

Among the adults, however, everything is conducted in a strictly hierarchical fashion; the senior officer in an institution addresses his subordinate as "thou," whereas they have to address him as "you." There has been some opposition to this recently, however. Old party members are an exception and always address one another as "thou."

Many of the women over forty still wear the head shawl, which here, as elsewhere in Russia, marks the older generation off from the modern young girls hurrying to their offices, shops, or factories, many of them with a book under their arm.

On a large red roll of honor in the middle of the square are inscribed the names of citizens who have distinguished themselves at work. Not far away, there is another pillar on which no one cares to see his name: the commander of the local Drushiny is accused of sleeping when he should have been on guard. Another caricature shows a woman (name and address given) with a venomous tongue; she is described as a hooligan and is said to have slandered her fellow lodgers and written anonymous letters. In Khrushchev's Russia it became customary to mobilize public opinion against (unpolitical) evildoers who cannot be prosecuted under the statutes of "socialist legislation"; public denunciations at mock trials specially convened for this purpose are now very much the fashion.

A stay in a Soviet provincial town leaves the visitor with contradictory and conflicting impressions, and a picture that is not absolutely clear. What is certain is that the reality one sees with one's own eyes has little in common with the official propaganda put out especially for foreign countries.

It is equally certain that life is very different from what it used to be in the Stalin era. Russia is in the throes of developments, which may lead in all kinds of directions, but like Gogol's celebrated troika, it is impossible for anyone to say where the road will end.

Essentuki—fields of sunflowers on either side of the road; an imposing building, rather like a fortress, is in fact the mud bath establishment that Tsar Nicholas II had built for himself and that was finished in 1916. The layout of the new part of this little town is pleasant; the streets are lined with flower beds. There is a touch of the Orient about the old part of Essentuki; we are near the frontier between Europe and Asia. We pass a Stanitsa (Cossack settlement) founded about in the middle of the nineteenth century, with a newly painted church at the center.

The main road climbs to about 1,000 meters, and it is not long before we reach Kislovodsk. For the Soviet citizen, Kislovodsk means Narzan, the mineral water that is drunk all over the Union. There is a Narzan street, a Narzan Hotel, a Narzan bookshop, a Narzan art gallery, and needless to say, a Narzan sanatorium and countless other institutions where the name occurs. It comes from the Kabardian and refers to the carbonic drink of the legendary heroic tribe of the Nartens. Nowadays, the mineral water is bathed in by unheroic patients suffering from circulatory or other internal complaints, but plenty of Narzan is still drunk.

Around the original spring in the spa park, which is now mechanized and surrounded by glass, a few young girls in white Russian blouses stand pouring out the Narzan for visitors. The patients subject themselves to a strict regimen, for there are fifteen different diets and baths and innumerable variations in 50 sanatoria. Not without good cause: Soviet doctors think highly of walking as a cure and there are three standard walks ranging from nearly a kilometer for the infirm to many more kilometers for those with no organic disorder. On the road, there are check points where one can have one's pulse and blood pressure measured and where inquiries are made about one's general state of health.

There are references to the hot chalybeate springs of the North Caucasus in medieval times, but one of Peter the Great's physicians, a man called Schobert (or Schubert), was responsible for the first scientific description of them. At the beginning of the nineteenth century, members of the nobility who had made themselves unpopular at Court were sent here.

Patients began to appear when the railway was opened in the 1880s, but the place developed very quickly and revolution and civil war only interrupted activities in the spa for a few years. Nowadays, 150,000 visitors come to Kislovodsk alone every year. The Academy of Sciences, the Uzbek Council of Ministers and many other more or less important organizations have their own sanatoria here. A considerable number of visitors who come to Kislovodsk are, however, in the best of health. They come because so many of their friends and acquaintances spend the summer months in the Caucasus or because they want to get away from the heat of Baku, Erevan, and Tiflis.

It is a mystery where they are all accommodated, since, apart from the sanatoria, there is only one large hotel and three boarding houses in the place. A key to the problem has been provided, however, in an article published in the local paper, Sovietskaya Zdravnitsa, about a man at the railway station who offers to obtain accommodation for visitors in return for a small commission or 15 percent of the charge for board and lodging.

The area around Kislovodsk was described as follows by Lermontov in *A Hero of Our Times*:

> "Solitude pervades the whole place and mystery is everywhere: the deep shade of the avenues of lime trees which lean over the noisy foaming river rushing on from stone to stone through the verdant mountains; and the gorges, misty and silent, branching out in all directions; the fresh aromatic air, impregnated with the fragrance of the tall grasses of the South and the white acacias; the everlasting sweet, drowsy murmuring of the icy streams which meet at the valley's end and race merrily along to their final plunge into the Podkumok."

It was here that Trotsky spent the politically decisive months before and after the death of Lenin, when he allowed Stalin a free hand. When he returned to Moscow, he had already been excluded from the supreme command.

Lermontov was also one of the first propagandists for Narzan, which he called a "boiling fresh water which restores the physical and mental powers," a statement that is naturally quoted by the spa administration on every possible occasion.

Lermontov would not recognize Kislovodsk today. The solitude and stillness and the mystery are all gone. At the Khram Vozducha (the "air temple"), there is a roundabout that never seems to close down; the gigantic rocks around the old castle "Intrigue and Love" are covered with such inscriptions as "Long live peace in the whole world" and "Serge Ivanov was here." Despite the cool weather, hundreds of people bathe and row in the lake and one has to queue to get a free table in the "Tourist," an excellent restaurant, a few miles from town.

The best way to escape the crowds is to follow the little footpaths into the mountains; in the distance, one can see the little mountain villages (Aul) of the Kabardian-Balkar Autonomous Soviet Republic. In 1944, Stalin had all Balkars deported to Central Asia, and it is only in recent years that some of them have returned to the Caucasus. There are still wildcats, foxes, and wolves in these mountains. In winter, they come right up to the edge of the town. Bears and lynxes were hunted here up to a few years ago.

The best place to undertake sociological studies is the spa park where thousands take the prescribed walk in the afternoon or evening. There are the Armenians and Georgians who come with their large families by taxi or in their cars, and there are professors from Moscow, Leningrad, or Kiev with their wives. They used to be the best paid section of Soviet society. Some of them received more than one salary and were paid 10,000, 15,000, or even 20,000 roubles a month. This has now been changed; a professor can now only draw one salary (and one pension) and the maximum is around 5,000 roubles, except in the case of the very few full members of the Academy of Science. But it is possible to manage quite well even on 5,000 roubles, which is six or seven times the average salary. Then, there are actors from the great cities combining the starring part with a holiday at the spa. Finally, there are visitors who really are ill.

What do all these people do in their spare time? In spite of the baths, showers, walks, diathermy, and sunbaths, there is a lot of free time in Kislovodsk and not every Russian plays chess or reads a book all day. In recent times, this problem has begun to be discussed in public. Even *Problems of Philosophy* has published an article which stated that spare-time activities must be better organized; otherwise, there is a danger that some young people may go astray. Whole sections of the population have been seized by a mania for games. Even in the park, you can see them playing cards, dominoes, billiards, and a game, unknown to me, called preference.

Russians have a traditional weakness for games: Pushkin, Tolstoy, and Dostoyevsky. Some of them forget time and the world when they become absorbed in cards or billiards. It is not easy to modify this tradition, but attempts are now being made to offer more light music and organize lectures, not only on the world political situation and the resolutions of the 21st Party Congress but also on such subjects as "Is There Life on the Stars?" and more down to earth, "Problems of Married Life."

The day ends early in Kislovodsk. There is no night life. (2012—I am sure it has changed since).

Dance music can be heard coming from one of the sanatoria, "Soviet jazz," a very widespread and very popular form of light music that is only grudgingly tolerated. The dancing is very slow and except for such recent hits as "Domino," most of the tunes appear to date from the period of "Alexander's Ragtime Band."

The last train from Pyatigorsk brings in a few visitors who queue up in the vain hope of getting a taxi. The last shops have closed; in the food stores, work goes on till late in the evening. The last visitors to the flower exhibition in the pump room have returned. Over a loudspeaker comes the beginning of the news: "Govorit Moskva." In spite of holidays, Narzan and billiards, the voice of Moscow is still audible in the Caucasus.

P. S.

I came to enjoy these resorts, and I have been back a few times. They also taught me that I still had to learn a great deal to understand (let alone to predict the behavior) of this country and its natives. Some thirty years later, my brother-in-law took me to one of the open-air coffee houses in the main street of Mineralnye Vody. Suddenly, a small group of gardeners appeared with ladders and some other implements cleaning up the trees lining the road. My brother-in-law got suddenly agitated. Something important is about to happen . . . I got worried about his mental state: But why? Because of a few gardeners cleaning up the street? You do not begin to understand, he replied. The appearance of the gardeners must have a reason; it could be an event of world historical importance.

My concern about his mental state of health was growing by the minute. But he happened to be quite right for two days later Gorbachev and Chancellor Helmuth Kohl met in this very street and agreed about a common policy vis-a-vis Germany. It was the end of the DDR and the reunification of Germany. I, the former editor of *Survey*, a leading journal of Soviet studies and a Sovietologist of some reputation, still had a great deal to learn, for I had failed to see and interpret some very minor events that had alerted an unpolitical Soviet citizen of an indication of important things to come. They knew this by an instinct that the foreigner, however well read, was lacking.

Index

aboulia (absence of will), 11
Abu Nidal, 111
Achgelis, Gerd, 186
Achimeir, Abba, 130
Action Française, 32, 37
Adenauer, Konrad, 97, 121
Agatstein, Moshe, 171
Agha, Hussein, 7
Agnon, Shmuel, 141
Agony of the American Left, The (Lasch), 38
Ali, Rashid, 169
Alami, Mussa, 144
Alquen, Gunter d,' 191
Alsace-Lorraine, 57, 90–91
Altneuland (Herzl), 130
Amedeo, Carlo Alberto, 71
American Scientist, 3
Amsterdam Institute, 18, 21
Anfang, Der, 34
Anschluss, 194
Arab spring, 4–8, 10, 23, 26, 97–99, 101–103, 105–107, 121–124
Archangel Michael, 32
Arendt, Hannah, 159
Arnold, 36
Aron, Raymond, 72
Aron, Robert, 32
Arslan, Shaqib, 169
Assad, Bashar Hafez al-, 117
Atlas Shrugged (Rand), 14

Baden-Powell, Robert, 45–46
Badiou, Alain, 16
Bakunin, Mikhail, 18–19, 42
Balibar, Étienne, 16
Balilty, Oded, 127
Baratz, Josef, 135

Barbie, Klaus, 162–163
Barrès, Maurice, 37
Barroso, Jose Manuel, 63
Bauermeister, Friedrich, 34
Bawerk Böhm, Eugen, 21
Becher, Johannes R., 37
Becker, Gary, 138–139
Ben Gurion, David, 129, 141, 144
Benjamin, Walter, 34, 47
Bernstein, Eduard, 16–17
Bertram, Ernst, 156
Bezmotivniki, 34
Bierkamp, Colonel, 236
Bishri, Tariq al-, 109, 111–114, 117
Black Book of Communism, 150
Black Hand, 80
Blanc, Louis, 138–139
Blau, Joyce, 110–111
Blech, Leo, 172
Bleriot, Louis, 12
Bloch, Marc, 171, 175
Boas, Sarah, 170
Bodlé, Hans, 173
Bolivar, Simon, 76
Bolsheviks, 86
Bormann, Martin, 189
Borokhov, Ber, 139
Bouin, Jean, 84
Boy Scouts, 45–46, 48
Brandt, Willy, 47
Breslau/Wroclaw, 213–231
Brezhnev era, 8
BRIC countries, 72
Brit Shalom, 144–145
Bronfman, Roman, 127, 131
Brzechwa, Jan, 171
Buber, Martin, 24, 74, 145
Buchan, John, 169

Buende, 46
Bukharin, Nikolai 87, 161
Burschenschaften, 30, 33
Busch, German, 162
Bussel, Josef, 135

Cantor, Norman, 175
Capitalism and Freedom (Friedman), 14
Captive Mind (Milosz), 176
Carlyle, Thomas, 36
Caron, Leslie, 235
Caucasus, 233–243
Celine, Louis Ferdinand, 213
cemeteries, 200–201
Chamberlain, Neville, 206–208, 210–211, 224
China
  capitalism and, 21
  economic progress of, 72
Churchill, Winston, 62, 97, 121
Ciano, Galeazzo 24
Claudel, Paul, 91
Clemenceau, Georges, 90
Communism and Nationalism in the Middle East (Laqueur), 122
Communist Manifesto (Marx), 14
Congress Dances, The, 10
Conquest, Robert, 151
Cooper, Robert, 71
Corradini, Enrico, 30
Corruption Perceptions Index, 117
Coudenhove-Kalergi, Richard Niklaus Eijiro von, 60, 90–91
crises, role of, 9
Curiel, Henri, 110–111

Dandieu, Arnaud, 32
D'Annunzio, Gabriele, 37
Danton, Georges, 24
Darwin, Charles, 20
Day of Community, 187–188
de Gaulle, Charles, 97, 121
decadence/decadents, 36–37, 44, 72–73
Degeneration (Nordau), 41
Demuth, Helene, 19
depression
  France and, 11
  rates of, 4
Dernburg, Bernhard, 168
Die Räuber (Schiller), 29
Disraeli, Benjamin, 33, 142

Dmowski, Roman, 220
Doriot, Jacques, 170
Draghi, Mario, 61
Drushiny, 237–238
Duberman, Martin, 38

Eagleton, Terry, 14–15
Ehrich, Max, 195
Ehrlich, Paul, 201
Eichendorff, Joseph von, 46
Eichmann, Adolf, 24
1848, comparison to, 6
Eilon, Amos, 144
Eisenstein, Sergei, 15
Eitel Friedrich, 83
Engels, Friedrich, 20, 86
escapism, 10
Essentuki, 239
Euro-optimism, 53–56
Europe
  future of, 59, 61–67
  Monnet and, 59–60
  See also European Union
European Constitution, 53
European Union
  counterfactual essay on, 90–92
  false optimism and, 8
  future of, 74–78
  mistakes of, 70–71
  overestimation of, 9
  pessimism toward, 64–65
  reactions to, 53–55, 69–70
Evola, Julius, 156
Eyth, Max, 36

Facebook, 99, 105–106, 114–115
fallen heroes, cult of, 155–157
Fanon, Frantz, 42
Fantoffel, Deborah, 234
Farouk (King), 98, 110, 122
Fascism, 30–31, 110, 122, 156
Federzoni, Luigi 30
Feldman, Noah, 7–8
Feuer, Lewis, 30, 33
Fichte, Johann Gottlieb, 31
Filimonov, 235
First World War, 39, 57, 72, 79, 168–169, 175–176
Fischer, Karl, 45
Follen, Karl, 30
Fontamara (Silone), 160

246

Index

Foucault, Michel, 116
Fountainhead (Rand), 14
Fourier, Charles 5
Frank, Semyon, 171
Franz Ferdinand, 80–81
Franz Josef, 81
Frederick II, 95
Freud, Sigmund, 87
Friedman, Milton, 14, 21
Friedrich, Caspar David, 45
Friedrich II, 175
Futurists, 34

Gabriel, Mary, 19–20
Galili, Lily, 127, 131
gender segregation, 46–47
Genet, Jean, 42
Gentile, Giovanni, 31
George, Lloyd, 89
George, Stefan, 174–175
Gini coefficient, 97, 117, 122
global economic crisis (2008), 25, 139
Goebbels, Josef, 24, 84, 172, 186, 188–190, 211
Goering, Hermann, 172
Goldman, Nahum, 143
Gorbachev, Mikhail, 243
Gordon, A. D., 139
Goschen, Edward, 82–83
Gossman, Lionel, 167–178
Grandi, Dino, 24
Grass, Guenter, 149
Gray, Gordon, 7
Great Waltz, The, 10
Green Shirts (Misr al-Fatat), 110
Greenberg, Uri Zvi, 143
Greenmantle (Buchan), 169
Greens, 48
Gresh, Alain, 111
Grey, Edward, 82
Grundrisse (Marx), 16
Gudie, Mohammed, 115
Guevara, Che, 163
gulags, 148–149, 151
Guttentag, Esteban, 160
Guttentag, Werner, 159–165

Ha'am, Ahad, 143
Hadi, Auni Bey Abdul, 144
Hagen, 214
Halevy, Daniel, 170

Hanke, Karl, 217
Hanseatic League, 76
Harbig, Rudolf, 185, 187
Hauptmann, Gerhart, 200, 225
Hayek, Friedrich, 21
Hegel, Georg Wilhelm Friedrich, 31
Heisenberg, Werner, 47
Henlein, Konrad, 187–188
Hermann-Goering Stadium, 186–188
Hero of Our Times, A (Lermontov), 233, 235, 240–241
Herriot, Eduard, 90
Herzl, Theodor, 128, 130, 143
Hess, Rudolf, 24, 185
Hesse, Hermann, 34–35
Heydrich, Reinhard, 24
Himmler, Heinrich, 24, 186–187, 189–190, 217
History of Paris University in the Middle Ages (Thurot), 28
Hitler, Adolf
 age of, 24
 Arabs and, 169
 assassination attempt on, 174
 in Breslau, 223
 Bund Deutscher Osten and, 219
 counterfactual history and, 79–80
 Hanke and, 217
 at Hermann-Goering Stadium, 186, 188–190, 226
 holocaust and, 148, 171
 mentioned, 6
 Oppenheim on, 170
 Second World War and, 57–58
 Snyder on, 147, 169
 Stalin and, 150
 students and, 31, 33
 Sudeten question and, 207, 209
Hizb al Arabi al Dimokrati, 115
Hizb al-Wasat (Center party), 115
Hoffman, Stanley, 54
Hohe Meissner, 46–47
Hohenlohe, Count, 82
Hölderlin, Friedrich, 38, 155
holocaust, 147–152
holodomor, 147, 149
Holzmann, Guenter, 111, 177–178
hospital stay (author's), 206–211
Hotel Terminus (Ophüls), 163
Hugo, Victor, 71–72
Husain, Adel, 111–113, 122

247

Husain, Ahmad, 110, 122
Hussein, Saddam, 117

immigration
  in Europe, 56, 74
  to Israel, 127–130, 137–138
  pre-Second World War, 191–194, 199
  restrictions on, 182
  into Wroclaw, 218
In Defense of Decadent Europe (Aron), 72
indignados movement, 25
Internal Macedonian Revolutionary Organization (IMRO), 80
Iron Guard, 32, 156
Islamism, 112–114, 122, 168
Iwaszkiewicz, Mayor, 226

Jahrhunderthalle, 214, 225, 230
Jasienski, Bruno, 171
Jasmine Revolution, 7
Jastrun, Mieczyslaw, 171
Jerusalem, 141–145
Journal of Contemporary History, 154
Jouvenel, Bertrand de, 170–171
Joyce, James, 15
Judt, Tony, 54
Jugendbewegung, 154

Kalvariski, Moshe, 144
Kamikaze pilots, 157
Kantorowicz, Ernst, 174–175
Karl Marx (McLellan), 19
Karl Marx (Mehring), 18–19
Karolyi, Mihaly, 98
Keniston, Kenneth, 34
Keynes, John Maynard, 21, 70
Khaddafi, Mu'amar, 101
kibbutzim, 135–140
Kipnis, Alexander, 194
Kislovodsk, 239–242
Kissinger, Henry, 159
Kleist, Field Marshal von, 236
Kluge, Alexander, 15
Koch, Richard, 182
Koerner, Theodor, 155
Kohl, Helmuth, 243
Kohn, Hans, 144–145
Kolbenheyer, Erwin Guido, 186
Kolchak, Aleksander Vasilevich, 131
Kolehmainen, Hannes, 84
kolkhoz markets, 233, 236–237

Konwiarz, Richard, 186
Koran, 156–158
Kotzebue, August, 30
Kraepelin, Emil, 82
Kulturpessimismus, 36, 40

Landmann, Edith, 174–175
Langhans the Younger, 223
Lara, Jesus, 163
Lasch, Christopher, 38
Lassalle, Ferdinand, 18–19, 215
Last Days of Europe, The (Laqueur), 55, 69–70
Latin America, as model, 75–76
Lawrence, T. E., 168
Leander, Zarah, 211
Lenin, Vladimir, 17, 20, 24, 35, 86–87, 241
Lermontov, Mikhail, 233, 235, 240–241
Lesman, Boleslaw, 171
Lesman, Wiktor, 171
Lieberman, Avigdor, 131–132
Lisbon earthquake (1755), 9
Lisbon treaty (2009), 75
Litvinov, Emanuel, 129
Logau, Friedrich von, 222
London Marx House/Memorial Library, 18
Longfellow, Henry Wadsworth, 222
L'Ordre Nouveau, 31–32
Louis Philippe I, 116
Love and Capital (Gabriel), 20
Luchaire, Jean, 32

Maastricht treaty (1991), 53
Magic Mountain, The (Mann), 87
Magnes, J. L., 144
Maigret, Jules, 163
mail, 198
Malley, Robert, 7
Mann, Thomas, 37, 87, 91, 156
Marcuse, Herbert, 31
Martov, Yuli, 86
Martynov, 235
martyrs, 156–157
Marx, Eleanor, 17
Marx, Karl, 13–22, 42, 219
Marxism, 110, 112–113, 122
Matwin, 226
McLellan, David, 19
Mehring, Franz, 18–19
Meidner, Hans, 177

248

Index

Meir, Golda, 144
Mensheviks, 86
Menuhin, Yehudi, 149
Merkel, Angela, 64
Metternich, Prince Klemens, 71
Milner, Alfred Viscount, 89–90
Milosz, Czeslaw, 176
Misr al-Fatat (Young Egypt), 110
Molotov-Ribbentrop pact, 150
Monnet, Jean, 9, 59–60
Morales, Evo, 164
Moscow Institute IMEL (Marx-Engels-Lenin), 18
Mosse, George L., 153–158
Mubarak, Hosni, 97–98, 101, 115, 121–122
Muslim Brotherhood, 5–6, 8, 98, 109–110, 112–116, 122–123
Musset, Alfred de, 36
Mussolini, Benito, 24, 30–31, 58

Narzan, 239–241
Nasser, Gamal Abdul, 97–98, 110, 121
Nasserism, 112, 122
Near, Henry, 135
negative bias, 3
Neisser, Albert, 201
Neue Schar, 33–34
Neue Zuercher Zeitung (NZZ), 182–183
Nibelungen, 214
Nicholas II, 85, 239
Nordau, Max, 41–42, 155
Novalis, 46

Obama, Barack, 109
Occident Triumphant (Spengler), 84
occupy movement, 25–26
Olympics, 46, 83–84
Ophüls, Marcel, 163
Oppenheim, Max von, 167–178
Oppenheimer, Franz, 138
optimism
  false, 10
  official, 10
  studies of, 3–4
optimism bias, 3, 8
Optimism Bias (Sharot), 3

Palmerston, Henry John Temple Lord, 19
Pan-Europa project, 90–92
Panglossianism, 8–9
Pan-Islamism, 168

Parvus, Alexander, 86–87
Pasternak, Boris, 171
Pasternak, Leonid, 171
Peck, Gregory, 235
Peres, Shimon, 128, 132
pessimism bias, 3
Pevsner, Nikolaus, 174
Pilsudski, Jozef, 88
Pirates, 23, 25–26, 48
Piscator, Erwin, 29–30
Pope, Alexander, 12
Princip, Gavrilo, 33, 79, 80
privatization, 136, 138
Proudhon, Pierre Joseph, 5
Proust, Marcel, 170
Pulitzer, Joseph, 81
Pushkin, Aleksandr, 235
Putin, Vladimir, 131
Pyatigorsk, 233–243

Qaradawi, Yusuf al-, 109, 114–115

radicalization, of youth, 24–25
Rancière, Jacques, 16
Rand, Ayn, 14
Rashdall, Hastings, 27–28
Rasputin, Grigori, 85
Rath, Ernst von, 211
Rau, Johannes, 47
Reed, John, 88
Reichsbund jüdischer Frontsoldaten (RJF), 175–176, 196
Reinhardt, Django, 149
Remembrance of Things Past (Proust), 81
Richard III, 79
Rilke, Rainer Maria von, 91
Rivera, Jose Primo de, 156
Robespierre, Maximilien de, 24
Rogel, Naqdimon, 144
Roland, Chanson de, 155
Roma, 149
Roosevelt, Franklin D., 10
Rosen, Willy, 195
Rosenbaum, Alexander, 131
Rossi, Tino, 10
Rothfels, Hans, 174
Roubini, Nuriel, 14
Roy, Oliver, 114
Rubinstein, Anton, 171
Ruppin, Artur, 144
Ruskin, John, 36

249

Sadat, Anwar, 98, 110
Saint Just, Louis Antoine, 24
Salafis, 6, 8
Sand, Karl, 30
Sarajevo, 79–81
Schachner, Nathan, 27–28
Scheubner-Richter, Max Erwin von, 57
Schiller, Friedrich 29–30, 151
Schleiermacher, Friedrich, 31
Schmidt, Joseph, 194
Schnitzler, Arthur, 91
Schoeps, Hans Joachim, 174, 176
Scholem, Gershom, 136, 145, 174
Schopenhauer, 9–11
Schubert, 45
Schumpeter, Joseph, 14
Schwarz, Arturo, 111
Schwarze Korps, Das, 191
Schwarzes Faehnlein, 175–176
Schwerin von Krosigk, Lutz Graf, 20
Second World War, 57–58, 61, 72, 147–152, 169, 173, 207–212
Shaltiel, David, 141
Sharanski, Natan, 131–132
Shari'a, 112–113
Sharot, Tali, 3, 9
Shertok-Sharett, 144
Silone, Ignazio, 160
Single Market Act, 63
Sinti, 149
Smilanski, Moshe, 130
Snyder Timothy, 147–152
Social Democrats, 70
social media, xx, 24, 98–99, 105–106, 114–115, 117
Solzhenitsyn, Aleksandr, 112, 151
Soviet Union, predictions regarding, 8–9
Spengler, Oswald, 35, 77, 84, 87
Sperber, Jonathan, 15, 19–20
Spitzweg, Carl, 77
Stalin, Josef, 87, 147, 150, 234, 241
Starace, Achille, 24
Stauffenberg, Claus von, 174
Steed, Wickham, 81
Steffens, Lincoln, 88
Stern, Gavriel, 145
Strauss, Johann, 172
Strauss, Richard, 91

students
 as freedom fighters, 29
 in Middle Ages, 27–29
Students for the Democratic Society (SDS), 27
Sturm und Drang, 29
suicide bombers, 156–157
suicide rates, 4
Susanin, Ivan, 155
Suyuti, Jalal al-Din al-, 156–157

Tagore, Rabindranath, 35
Tahrir, Midan al-, 114, 123
Tailhade, Laurent, 37
Tancred (Disraeli), 142
Tell, Wilhelm, 155
Tevet, Shabtai, 144
Thurot, Charles, 28
Thursday's Child Has Far to Go (Laqueur), 181
Time Machine, The, (Wells), 213
Tolstoy, Lev, 235
tonsillectomy, 206–211
Toynbee, Arnold, 89
Transparency International, 117
Trotsky, Leon, 87, 241
Turnau, Irene, 226
Tuwim, Julian, 171
Twitter, 105, 114, 117

Uhland, Ludwig, 156, 177
unemployment, 24–25, 74, 106–107, 118, 123
universities, 31–32
Universities of Europe in the Middle Ages (Rashdall), 27–28
university, history of, 27–29

Valéry, Paul, 91
Vargas Llosa, Mario, 159
Vishnegradski, 87
Vogelstein, Hermann, 221–222
Volksdeutsche, 190–191
Voltaire, 5, 9
Voyage au Bout de la Nuit (Celine), 213

Wagman, Aizik, 171
Wajda, Andrzey, 148
Wandervogel, 45–49
War of Independence, 136–137

Index

Wazyk, Adam, 171
Weavers, The (Hauptmann), 200
Weber, Eugen, 32
Weber, Max, 142
Weigert, Karl, 201
Weizmann, Haim, 143
Wells, H. G., 88, 213
Weltsch, Robert, 145
Werfel, Franz, 91
Wessel, Horst, 156
Wheen, Francis, 14, 20
White Horse Inn, 10
Why Marx Was Right (Eagleton), 15
Witte, Sergei, 87
Wolf, Theodor, 80–81
Wordsworth, 116
World Wars. *See* First World War; Second World War
Wroclaw. *See* Breslau/Wroclaw
Wyneken, Gustav, 34

Yadin, Yigael, 198
Yerushalayim (Rosenbaum), 131
Yisrael Beiteinu, 131
Young Germany, 45–49
youth, revolt of, 23–26
youth bulge, 106, 118–119
youth movements
 in America, 40–44
 dual character of, 29–30
 in Egypt, 115, 117
 First World War and, 39
 in Germany, 48–49
 motivations of, 32–33, 35–36
 political orientation of, 35
 See also individual groups

Zhdanov, Andrei, 205
Zionism, 112, 143
Zisman, Wiktor, 171
Žižek, Slavoj, 16

For Product Safety Concerns and Information please contact our EU
representative GPSR@taylorandfrancis.com
Taylor & Francis Verlag GmbH, Kaufingerstraße 24, 80331 München, Germany

www.ingramcontent.com/pod-product-compliance
Lightning Source LLC
Chambersburg PA
CBHW062123300426
44115CB00012BA/1785